"No Arm In Trying"

Steven Robinson

To Gill and Gareth
I hope you enjoy
my book.
Steven Robinson

S Rob

Contents

Dedication

I'd like to dedicate this book to my absent friends and family. Those who still remain in my thoughts and will for evermore, they sadly departed this earth way too early, but they lived their lives well and for what might only be a brief moment in time were a part of my life.

Acknowledgement

From the very beginning of this literary journey my family have been behind me all the way, never doubting that I would achieve my goal when in fact I had my doubts. There were times I never thought this work would ever see the light of day. I would like to thank my mum Pauline and sister Tracy for reading and commenting upon the manuscript and having faith in me.

I realise my father may not like the things said about him in this book, but these are my memories and how they have affected my life. They are not intended to cause any upset.

Some names have been changed in this book to protect their privacy.

Several people have been invaluable during this process, my friend Richard McCann who encouraged me to write this book. Guy Dixon and Duncan Farrar for coming up with the title "*No Arm In Trying*".

Taryn Johnston for her professionalism and total re-edit of the manuscript and Davina McCall for extending the hand of friendship and writing such a lovely foreword.

Foreword

Meeting Steven was a revelation. He is the best tonic! His take on life is pretty unique and if we could all look at tricky situations and think "*what would Steven do*?" I bet we would all feel happier! For me, gratitude and purpose are the bedrock of happiness and Steven has loads of both. You've made a huge impact on me Steven

Thank you!

Davina McCall

Note From The Publisher

It's not often that I comment, however, in Steven's case I felt that it was important.

Steven is a Yorkshire man through and through, raised at a time when emotions and feelings were strictly the woman's remit.

It's taken a great deal of time and effort to encourage Steven to write openly about how things affected him, initially the manuscript he sent was focussed on the practical ways he went about life and overcame problems. I have pushed him hard in order to get him to think deeply about his life and to remember some of the things that he would perhaps, have left unwritten and yet these are the areas in which we see the true qualities of the man.

For those who know Steven, he is a generous, warm and incredibly clever man, for whom no challenge is too great. I hope that you will join with me in recognising the strength he has shown throughout his life, even though he'll tell you he doesn't see it that way!

Chapter 1
Do You Know Where You Are?

It was 1982 The Rolling Stones rocked Roundhay Park to a staggering audience of 150,000. I was woken by a deafening noise as the room vibrated from the sound of a Lancaster bomber during a low-level fly past over the city of Leeds. Completely disorientated, I didn't know what was happening or where I was, then a soft voice said to me,

"Hello Steven, do you know where you are? You've been in an accident on your motorbike, you're in hospital, you're in the Leeds General Infirmary and you've lost your right arm!"

"Do you know where you are Steven?" these were the first words I heard. *"You're in hospital!"* *"You've had an accident on your motorbike, and you've lost your right arm."*

"Do you know what's happened Steven? You're in the Leeds general infirmary, you've lost your arm!" *"You know you've lost your right arm don't you Steven?"*

I lay in bed, in a strange room, these words echoing in my head, I didn't understand, and I couldn't remember anything.

Every time a nurse passed my bed she would say, *"do you know where you are Steven?"* And *"do you know you've lost your right arm?"* As far as I was concerned, they were talking rubbish! I could feel my right arm so

5

didn't understand what they were saying. What were they talking about? They must have me mistaken with another patient.

I had been bed bound for a number of weeks, as were all the other patients on ward 16 of the Leeds General Infirmary (LGI). What I didn't know was that I was experiencing *"phantom limb syndrome"* how could I? It's strange the things you realise you don't know about until you have to face them.

I'm often asked if I was overcome with fear, anger and injustice at this point in my life, the answer is no. Strange as it may seem and maybe it was the drugs, but I had a quiet acceptance and a driving need to get out of the hospital as soon as I could. That was what consumed my thoughts. How soon could I get out?

One day I asked my nurse, Janet, to take me to the toilet, I didn't want to use the commode again. Being bed bound meant that all patients on the ward used commodes.

"Please Janet can I use a proper toilet and not the commode?"

Janet said *"yes, OK"* and I was so grateful. It took me twenty minutes to walk half the length of the Victorian style ward with approximately twenty beds either side. She helped me onto the toilet and said

"Give me a shout when you've finished, and I'll come and clean you up."

How degrading, I wasn't even capable of cleaning myself and for a young man of eighteen, I found it hard to ask. I knew deep down it was only a temporary thing, but this was yet another reason I was determined to get up and out of the hospital as soon as I could. *"Janet, Janet, I've finished"* I shouted, and she came to clean me up, then took me to the wash basin to wash my hands.

Janet had forgotten that there was a mirror in the bathroom.

Mirrors weren't allowed on ward 16, so many of the patients had horrendous disfigurements and mutilation and so it was in their interest I suppose that they didn't have to look at themselves, but the toilet Janet took me to was the staff toilets and she had forgotten about the mirror. That's when I saw it for the first time…

But this was not the beginning nor the end, it was just a change of what I thought was, normal. 18 years of *"normal"* but now I was like a caterpillar going through its metamorphosis, would I emerge as a beautiful butterfly or a miss-shaped shell of my former self?

Life, experience and education had not prepared me for what lay ahead. All I knew was where I had come from and not where I was going and in fact my memories of where I came from were somewhat sketchy and seemed more like a story that someone had told me, rather than remembering and reliving those moments where life began. Again, I suppose that this was due to the trauma and the drugs.

Where do you start to tell your life story? At the beginning? At the moment when life is coming to an end? Or at that one (defining) moment in time that shapes your life forever? An event that changes you in ways you never dreamt of.

All good stories need a beginning though, so let me set the scene.

Chapter 2
The Beginning

A shot rang out and the world stopped in disbelief as President Kennedy was assassinated in Dallas, Texas. Beatlemania swept across Britain and the US. The Profumo affair shook the British government at its core. The Russians pulled out of the space race and Martin Luther King was immortalised with his awe inspiring speech, *"I have a dream"* A man speaking about the injustices of racism and discrimination (I never thought, that later in life I would experience discrimination, and feel such an affinity with those persecuted because of their skin colour or physical ability or disability). 1963 was a year that changed the world and was the year of my birth.

As the noise of change was sweeping through the world, the sweetest noise to my mum, was that of her beautiful baby boy born 7lbs 3oz, taking my first breath of air and crying with all the effort I could muster. Mum was delighted, yet surprised as she was expecting a girl and had chosen the name Julie!

All limbs intact and perfect in every way according to my loving mum and free-spirited father, they had worried about me being a Thalidomide baby because Mum had taken the infamous drug for morning sickness while she was carrying me. I was the first boy born into our family. A boy to carry on the male name of *"Robinson"* although I was their second child, Tracy was my sister and older by twenty-one months.

The memories I have of that time are that we were poor, but very happy children. Whilst fleeting now, these are some of the most profound memories I carry and have helped shape my adult life.

The first memory I can recall in vivid colour, is being dangled by my feet over a bridge by my father. I don't know to this day what possessed him to do this, but a fear of heights, lifts and bridges have afflicted me all my life!

Be careful what you inflict on others, you have no idea how you may affect their life.

Chapter 3
Buggy Park

Life began in a suburb of Leeds, along North Street, the one made famous by Barbara Taylor Bradford for her tales of poverty and struggles to escape drudgery. It was an area near Meanwood public baths, and swimming pool, a well-known landmark in Leeds. A place where people would go to take their weekly bath and do their dirty washing, not as in gossip, although much of that went on, but more the washing of dirty clothes! It was an area in Woodhouse, where I was born, known locally as *"Buggy Park"*. Not because it was an area with a lovely green field park as its name suggests, but because it was a slum housing estate. Rows and rows of back to back houses with outside toilets shared between multiple households. The area was infested with bugs, cockroaches, woodlice and a nasty insect called a silverfish, that bred in damp conditions and wreaked havoc on the respiratory system. The smell of human effluence lingered in the air and pity you if you had to follow your neighbour, who had suffered a bout of dodgy tummy! In certain places, walking in the street was like walking over Rice Krispies with bugs crunching under your feet. Harsh as it may sound It seemed OK to us young children, we didn't know any better, but it was probably the worst slum in Leeds during the 1960's.

During the 60's there was a programme of slum clearances and *"Buggy Park"* was raised to the ground, the land was incinerated to eradicate the bug infestation. In fact, the demolition and incinerations were happening whilst we were still living in the area. It became less and less cohesive as houses disappeared street by street, as did neighbours, it became like a ghost town. The song from the Specials, Ghost Town, feels like it was written about this moment in time. Eventually it was our turn to move and we were off to Crossgates, in the East of Leeds.

Chapter 4
Crossgates

Crossgates was an area to the East of Leeds and was historically famous for the Barnbow tragedy of the 5th of December 1916. On that day thirty-five women were killed, and many more female workers mutilated in an explosion in room 42 at the Barnbow munitions factory. They had been working for the war effort of WW1 1914-18. Mr William Parking was awarded an engraved silver watch for his bravery in rescuing injured workers. There are 2 memorials to the Barnbow tragedy at Crossgates, the factory later became Vickers Engineering famous worldwide for the manufacturing of tanks including the Centurion, the Chieftan and the Challenger.

We were moved into one of those white pre-fabricated, concrete houses. Made after the second world war to house all the displaced population. Built of large concrete sections that appeared to be rendered with a bumpy surface and painted in white, I say white, but it was more cream/magnolia in colour. I loved Crossgates, and even today when I return, it feels like I'm going home.

It was the first address I learnt as a young boy, 22 Orchard Grove. One of the great things for me was the big tree in the back garden. It had these strange peas in a pod type seed, at the time I didn't know what type of tree it was, but my mum told me they weren't peas, they were poisonous to little boys! I now know the tree was called a laburnum, when it flowered the smell was beautiful, and if I smell one today, it can take me right back there. I loved that old tree and spent most of my time in it. I was a boy after-all and climbing was my thing.

We were there for only a short period of time, four years in fact but, whilst my memories of Crossgates are sketchy, I remember my first days at school really well. I guess I remember it because I hated it. Perhaps it was being parted from Mum for the first time, nevertheless, I can recall being desperately unhappy to be there, and wanting to leave immediately.

The school I attended was called Crossgates Primary. It had large metal railings all around the school yard and an equally large metal gate that was locked once all the parents had left. I'm not sure if these barriers were to keep us children in, or to keep others out. The large metal railings and gates didn't pose an obstacle to me however, for I was far too good at climbing. For me, they were just an inconvenience! I suppose it was a challenge and they were fun to climb, I looked forward to overcoming it, plus my mum was on the other side of those gates, working in the Arndale Centre at a place called Baby Fair, (the predecessor to Mother Care), I knew how to get there, so I wasn't going to be stopped by anything.

The Arndale Centre is still there today although much changed. Back in those days it was a new building, but typical of a 1960's monolithic structures and of course made from concrete precast sections. The Arndale Centre first opened on the 21st September 1967 and was the first indoor *"American-style"* shopping mall in England, there were around sixty stores in the centre of an L shape construction with each leg being approximately the same length, Mum's shop was halfway down on the left-hand side from the side entrance.

Mum of course had to take me back, which she did with the help of the manager, they drove me back in his car. For a young boy this seemed like a drive of doom, there was nowhere I hated more.

To me school was a prison, although at the time I couldn't explain why, I didn't understand why they wanted to lock me up with lots of other boys and girls I didn't know. I suppose it was an indication of things to come, that for the rest of my school life, my time there would feel like a sentence.

Perhaps my hatred would have lessened had I not been punished every day. At the end of every afternoon, after classes had finished, the teacher would tell us a story. We would all be sat on the floor with crossed legs listening to tales of trams, trains, trucks and tractors. I couldn't contain my excitement and would make the noises of the trains *"chuffa chuff chuff, woo woo"* and *"moo"*, *"baa"* for the animal sounds of the farmyard. I thought I was making the stories come alive with my vivid imagination, I loved story time, and today this may well have been encouraged and nurtured. It wasn't though, it was rewarded with punishment and being made to stand with my face and nose pressed into a corner of the room with my back to the class. It didn't stop me making my impersonations though. Mum would pick me up in the afternoon, only to be told I was a disruptive influence and had to be punished.

I think I must have been a prisoner of war in a previous life, if you believe in that, as I do, because for me, the school became something that needed to be escaped from, and like those plucky soldiers from The Great Escape, I wasn't going to let anything stop me. However, after weeks of attempted break outs I was ultimately threatened by the school and authorities with childcare. If I didn't stop running away from school, they would take me away from my mum and lock me up in a childcare unit.

I didn't really understand the implications, but I knew I loved my mum and didn't want to leave her, after all, that's why I was running away from school to be with her. The threat of care really frightened me and in retrospect it was a cruel thing to say to a young boy of five. However, this was the cruel nature of teaching and education in the 1960's.

I was happy at home with my mum and big sister Tracy, I don't ever remember Dad being present. It was a godsend however, that I didn't remember Dad being there because he was a cruel, vindictive and violent man, who treated Mum as a punch bag. I am truly fortunate that I don't remember seeing Dad being violent, but I remember she cried a lot, which made me desperately sad and cry in support. No child should see their parent desolate, to see my mum so sad hurt me too. I felt her pain as if it was mine. I didn't realise that my mum was a victim of domestic violence. That she was beaten on a daily basis for any amount of ridiculous reasons my father saw fit to bestow upon her. In order to end the violence Mum was experiencing and to protect me and Tracy from becoming victims or growing up to think violence was normal in a relationship, my mum decided the only thing she could do was to leave Dad. She plucked up the courage to get him out of our lives. This was one of the hardest, most selfless things our mum could do for us. Mum was still a young woman with two young children, she would now have to cope on her own to bring us up and overnight we were labelled a single parent family and all the negativity that was associated with that, my mum would have to endure alone.

One particular day I said to her,

"Mum you don't cry anymore."

I didn't realise it was because Dad wasn't there to beat her.

We lived in Crossgates for four years without Dad, I loved it there, spending days with my mate Gary Sorby, playing in the valley, an area behind the school, where a train track ran, it's still there today and is part of the East Coast Line out of Leeds city station. Wybeck Valley was its name, although as a young boy I knew it only as the valley. It was a place where I wasn't allowed to go, but I couldn't resist, it was so exciting. There were trains, deep storm drains and a supposed haunted house, it would have been impossible to keep a young boy away!

I'm not sure if the house really was haunted, but that's what I had been told. Maybe that was just to frighten me so I would stay away, but it just made me more inquisitive. The house was a run-down, old stone building, double fronted with a central wooden door, all weather beaten and torn, with missing planks. A straight, old stone flagged path ran one hundred yards through a garden full of weeds, the whole garden was surrounded by a stone wall, collapsing in places, and a single wooden plank gate which was falling off its hinges.

I wanted to go in the house but only ever made it to the door. It wasn't habitable, certainly not for anyone living anyway, but maybe for a ghost or two.

Life at home was good, and although Mum had left Dad, we saw him from time to time. He never got to know me or

Tracy, occasionally he would want to take us to watch him play football. I hated football and standing watching a grown man trying to play football and losing his temper with the other players was not my idea of fun.

Dad would sometimes take us out, but our days with him were never good, maybe deep down I knew that he was the reason for Mum's upset, or maybe it just registered that he wasn't a good man. Whatever the reason I didn't enjoy my time with him. Dads favourite place to take us was Meanwood park, Dad was from Meanwood and the park was local for him

Dad was a womaniser, and if there was any chance of fun with a woman then he would take it. The last outing that Dad took us on, when I was about five, was to the park and here he met a woman. Dad told us we had to go home by ourselves and left us in the park! Me and Tracy didn't know what to do, we had never been abandoned before. We saw a police man and asked him to help us, it was a lot different back then to how it is now. The Policeman put us on a bus and told the bus driver where we should get off, he then gave us a note that we had to give to the bus driver in the city centre, who would take us back home to Crossgates. Mum was so angry she never let dad take us out again. I didn't miss it. Truth be told I was a Mummy's boy and my grandad was the best surrogate father me and Tracy could ever have wished for. Grandad took us everywhere. He became our male role model as we didn't see much of Dad at all, but that was better for us.

Grandad was there for all of us, he had the patience of a saint and taught me that sometimes it doesn't matter if you don't have all the knowledge, you can learn anything with enough time and patience.

He was always immaculately turned out and I know that he passed that on to me, I would never dream of going out untidy or scruffy and he was the same. I even look like him.

Mum needed the support of *"Gangan"* and Grandad, (Gangan was the name my grandmother liked to be called) and so mum had put her name on the council waiting list for the Scott Hall estate, we moved to be near my mums family, to start our lives away from the past and the upset, our lives would now start over.

Chapter 5
The Scott Hall Estate.

It was 1971 and we had moved into a house on the Scott Hall estate, the government was in turmoil, Edward Heath was fighting with the miner's unions and we, as well as many other families, were without coal and freezing during a hard winter. It was only three years later that the whole country was brought to a standstill by the miners' strike. 1971 saw the sale of the first video recorder for home use, the first readily available VCR (Video Cassette Recorder) cost £600, that was as expensive as a Morris Mini the car of the day and equivalent to over £7000 by today's standards, needless to say, we never had one, it was way out of our budget.

Both me and Tracy were starting a new school, Potternewton primary school.

I remember my first day, I was a little nervous and worried because I didn't know anyone and as you now know, I wasn't a fan of school. I met a boy called Philip Wilson who was to be my first friend, quickly followed by Tony McMaster, we're still close friends today and I know I'm lucky to have had their friendship this long.

Potternewton primary was a good school, although I wasn't a top student. In fact, I was much lower than average and had to take extra reading lessons from the head Mistress, Miss Thomas. She ran extra reading classes for those struggling, they didn't know about dyslexia back then, something that I know I have now. I was a gentle boy who was brought up in an all-female family. I didn't have the guidance of a permanent male figure to teach me how to be a man, we didn't see Grandad all the time; so by the time I reached middle school I had become the boy that people pushed around, the one who didn't fight back.

I remember playing rugby, a lad bigger than me kept getting the ball, but I was small and fast and kept catching him, stopping him from making a try. The third time I stopped him he grabbed me by the throat and said…

"If you don't stop tackling me, I'm gonna kick yer ed in."

He was of West Indian descent and so this was said in a broad Yorkshire accent with a bit of Patwa interwoven. Very intimidating for me and cemented my dislike of sports.

That was the end of school sports for the rest of my school years. I avoided PE with sick notes and excuses. As I write this, I can recall another disturbing memory, which as a young boy, something I didn't even pick up on. Before leaving the sports changing rooms the teacher would insist on looking down the boys shorts to make sure we weren't wearing our underwear. I'm pretty sure that there was no reason not to wear underwear and the more I think about it now the more I realise it was wrong. It's funny how the brain blocks memories, but also frightening at just how naïve children were back in the 70's. Should it happen today, thankfully and rightly there would be a terrific outcry.

However, these and other events like being the last person to be picked for cricket teams were enough to drive the nail into the coffin of sports. No thanks, no sports, not for me, I wasn't a macho boy and didn't want to play boring football, rugby or cricket. Why couldn't we do gymnastics, dance and racket sports or learn a musical instrument? These were the areas I was more interested in. In fact, I did try learning an instrument when I went to Stainbeck High School. I wanted to play the trumpet, but the school only had the one and another student had claimed it, so I was given the tenor horn, but tenor horns weren't cool… not like a trumpet. This became just another weapon that could be used on me by the bullies, not by physically beating me with the instrument, but by more psychological abuse and name calling, *"It takes a big puff to blow that"* it did, but not in the way they were implying. I never really mastered the tenor horn, maybe as I never applied myself. Albeit that was the same with all of my subjects at school, I never wanted to be there in the first place.

The Scott Hall council estate consisted of terrace and semi-detached houses built around 1935. The main road that ran through the estate was Scott Hall Road, the A61. We lived opposite the junction of two fields, Sugar Well Hill and Prince Philip playing fields. It was in 1975 that something truly horrific happened, that shocked the UK, the murder of a local woman called Wilma McCann at the hands of Peter Sutcliffe, known as the Yorkshire Ripper. It wouldn't be known for a while that Peter Sutcliffe was a serial killer and would go on to murder thirteen women, of which Wilma McCann was the first. I could not foresee that the Prince Philip playing fields, where Wilma's body was found, would be the same field where my life would change forever or that I would become friends with Wilma's son Richard, many years later. In fact, it was Richard that encouraged me to write this book. I couldn't know these things but there was a man who could!

Mr McGill was the local *"lollipop man",* a name known to anyone who went to school near a busy road. Mr McGill, however, wasn't your average lollipop man, he was a medium. I don't mean his jacket size, but rather he was a spiritualist and believed in talking to spirits.

One day whilst we were crossing the road, I was only young maybe seven or eight, Mr McGill told mum he had had a bad dream about me. He was really worried and upset and told mum to keep a really close eye on me, because he had seen me in a really bad accident, a life-threatening accident. He thought it was a road collision and wasn't sure I would survive it. Mum thought it was the ravings of a mad man, but I could see she was upset by the encounter, although I didn't understand what he was talking about. It would all become crystal clear in the future, but it was ten years away. How could he have seen into the future? The only way he could have known was if my life had already been planned and I was just living out that plan, one that was unknown to me but not to Mr McGill.

Day to day life did continue but Mr McGill's words were constantly with my mum.

In October 1975, me and Tracy were going on a trip with Mum, she was a member of a women's club called *"Women's Circle"* and we were going to Manchester airport for a day out to watch the aircraft taking off and landing. It doesn't seem like much now but at the time we were happy to just enjoy the atmosphere of the airport. We'd never been to one before and we were all so excited, but also a little upset because it was a very foggy morning and we were disappointed that we wouldn't be able to see the aircraft when we got to Manchester.

Just before we set off there was an unexpected knock at the door, it was really early 7:30 maybe 8am.

It was a policeman, who said that there had been a murder on the field near where we lived. He asked if we had seen anything strange, any unfamiliar men, something out of the ordinary? The weather matched the scenario, it was an eerie, silent type of morning, you know one of those days when you could hear a pin drop? The fog and damp seemed to work like a natural soundproof barrier, perhaps the earth itself wanting to hide that gruesome discovery.

That was the start of a spate of murders by Peter Sutcliff…

I didn't think about the murder back then, I was too young to understand, all I wanted was for the fog to clear. I was excited to be going on a coach, which was new and fun, but when we eventually got to the airport the weather hadn't improved that much. We still had a great day though, sat in those old, plastic moulded, 1960 science fiction type chairs, watching people waiting to fly and imagining where they might be going to. It was a great adventure and was so exciting. Years later the band *"The Motors"* sang their song *"Airport"*, it felt like it had been written about our visit that day and the excitement we were feeling.

Even without the murders the Scott Hall estate felt like a scary place to live, there was a lot of racial tension and after a while, women were told not to walk home alone for fear of an attack at the hands of the serial killer, it was good advice as he struck twice in the estate. Peter Sutcliffe went on to kill thirteen women and attempted to kill seven more before his capture in 1983.

The one thing I loved about where we lived were the fields over the road, I spent hours there with my dog Dandy, he was a little brown and white, short haired mongrel terrier, who had never been trained. He wouldn't go on a lead and he hated water, especially after Dad had thrown him into the beck at Meanwood park. He was a tough little dog, he would always fight bigger dogs than himself and often came off worse, but he had no fear, except water of course. He would follow me everywhere, he was my best mate but then, one day he disappeared, and after searching everywhere we could, we never found him.

Many weeks later a girl down the road from me told me she had seen Dandy run over on the busy A61 road, the dual carriageway outside our house. She said he had laid dead the whole day until the refuse men took him away. Why didn't she come and tell me he was there so that I could have brought him home and buried him in the garden? I was so upset by that experience, I kept thinking he had lain there injured and needing my help and I wasn't there for him when he needed me the most. I was only a young boy, but I wanted to help my dog. He wasn't used to the busy roads of the Scott Hall Estate; he was a dog more at home in the quiet streets of Crossgates. It was winter and there were clumps of snow still on the ground, Dandy must have just looked like another clump of snow at the side of the road and I didn't see him. I didn't realise Scott Hall Road was so treacherous for animals, after all we hadn't been there long. I would soon learn the amount of heartbreak Scott Hall Road would bring us and other families, from losing numerous pets to the high-speed traffic that passed our front door.

Chapter 6
Young Businessman

It was 1973 the same year that VAT was introduced in the UK, initially at 10%, £20,000,000 compensation had just been paid to victims of Thalidomide, after eleven years of court action, and I was a 9 year old watching *"The Generation Game"* on TV with my Mum and Sister. The Generation Game was a family gameshow presented by the brilliant entertainer Bruce Forsyth. Family members from different generations would compete with each other. They would be taught a new skill by an expert and then try to copy that skill. Tasks would range from acting, singing, dancing and craft making.

One particular night, Mum, Tracy and me had sat down in front our black and white TV, cuddled up in front of the crackling coal fire, drinking a hot cup of Oxo. It was my favourite drink on a cold night. We were laughing at the new skills the families were trying to copy when a task came on that suddenly captured my full attention. I was like a rabbit caught in the headlight of an approaching car. I was totally mesmerised. The craft the family members had been tasked with was to make a paper bag. All the contestants struggled with the challenge, but I rushed around to find a piece of paper to see if I could do it. I found an old newspaper and said to Mum and Tracy, I'm going to try.

I folded the paper just as the expert had done. I made

some glue with flour and water and glued the bag together in exactly the same manner as had been demonstrated. I had memorised every movement the expert had made. A couple of minutes later I had a perfect paper bag. It was wintertime and approaching Christmas. Wrapping paper was in every shop and the *"Christmas song"* playing on the radio this year was the new release by Slade *"Merry Xmas Everybody"*. I asked Mum if she would buy me a few sheets of Christmas wrapping paper. She did, and that was when my mini business started. I made Christmas shopping bags. I made them in the same way as the expert had shown the contestants on the generation game. The only difference with mine was I put handles on them. They were great, they looked really professional. You wouldn't have known they had been made by a 9-year-old.

I enjoyed making them so much that I started giving them to my family and friends until one day my Grandma said she had asked her hairdresser if she would like to sell them in her shop. She said yes, 50 pence per bag was their price. They sold like hot cakes. Everyone loved them. As an adult, when I think back, that was my first entrepreneurial adventure, but it certainly wouldn't be my last. That was 48 years ago, and I still remember every fold like it was yesterday.

I had learnt a valuable lesson as a 9-year-old. You don't need a lot of money to be successful. Your most valuable assets are your imagination, creativity and determination.

Chapter 7
School Years

By now you're aware, that from day one, I HATED SCHOOL - I've written it in capitals so that you know I'm shouting. I can't even begin to put into words how much I loathed it. I spent my time gazing out of the windows at the freedom that lay beyond them, wishing I owned a time machine, just so I could fast forward the day to home time. Never have I wanted time to pass so quickly before.

I hated it for a good reason. I was bullied throughout my school life. Coming from a single parent family back in the 1960's and 70's meant something, these days of course it's no big deal. However, back then people treated my mum with contempt, and Tracy and I were labelled as damaged, expected to fail in life. I also received free school meals and that made me different from the other boys and girls, which put a further target on my back for the bullies.

Middle school was just as bad, I just tried to get through it and not be noticed. The thing is when you try not to be noticed the wrong people notice you. The bullying started to increase with more frequency, ferocity and intensity.

In what was still a heavily male dominated time, I didn't like the rough and tumble of sports and furthermore, I enjoyed needle work and cooking. I had a lot of female conditioning in my life, something I'm grateful of these days but at that time, the influence of a man was something

I longed for. Grandad didn't understand and it wasn't really something I could talk to him about; he was from a different generation. I felt a *"father"* would have given me the tools I needed to survive each vicious encounter. It was brought home to me one day, during the summer holidays. It was one of those peaceful days that only holidays can bring, I was playing with my neighbours, 3 girls a couple of years younger than me, in their front garden. I recall the day so clearly; we'd had a water fight with their father, and we made paper cubes by folding old newspaper and filling them with water through an opening on the top. I really enjoyed the day and when I went home, I remember saying to my mum,

"I wish I had a dad Mum".

In hindsight that must have been hard for her to hear. I said it with no intention to hurt Mum, but I was so envious of my neighbours because they had something, me and Tracy had never had, nor would ever have. A decent dad or even one that was present and respected.

I wasn't a gifted student at any subject except art. Tracy and I had both taken after our mum as she had a talent for drawing. Art at school was at best crude and un-inspiring, in the early 70's at least. I was fortunate though that the art teacher recognised I had an eye for it and just let me draw when the other children were doing the boring stuff.

In the centre of our middle school was what they called the *"Quadrangle"*. It was a little piece of nature inside a concrete monstrosity. We had a peacock and peahens; we were never allowed near them, but we could hear them. I used to escape my hatred of school by daydreaming and imagining I was away in the middle of an adventure, surrounded by the animals I could hear.

I've attended four schools, each one of them a time of pure misery, the best of the bunch, if you could call it that, was Scott Hall Middle School.

I recall 1976, the year we had the worst draught in history. I remember well the fields at our school, all the grass was yellow and parched and the ground beneath had cracked from lack of moisture. There was a dry, hot earthy smell in the air, I loved that smell, that hot summery smell of a foreign country. Advertisements were on the TV constantly telling us not to waste water, share a bath or take a shower instead, there were hose pipe bans and people were told not to water their gardens. Standpipes had been introduced to many parts of the country, it was very serious, and we were only a matter of weeks away from having our water supply cut off.

One memory sticks in my mind, the girl in the TV ad was from my school, she was a pretty blonde girl and super popular, with star like qualities and fame. She didn't see me or notice me, unsurprising as I was invisible to everyone except the bullies of course. At the time she was a beacon of something I couldn't reach, yet I don't even remember her name now, but for sure she never knew mine.

When I turned thirteen it was time for high school, something I dreaded. In those days we had to attend schools that were in our catchment area. Of the available schools, there was only one with vacancies, that was the notoriously bad Stainbeck High School. In hindsight they probably had vacancies because no one wanted to be sent to the school that had the worst reputation in Leeds. I remember the year before I went there, 1976, the students had gone on a strike, after a student started a school wide rebellion against the introduction of school uniforms. I knew about that because my sister Tracy was there at the time. She was two years ahead of me and it was a feature in the Yorkshire Evening Post newspaper.

The school lived up to its horrific reputation. I was a small underdeveloped boy, who had just started with acne, this really didn't help my cause and it became another tool in the arsenal of the bullies. I was beaten on a daily basis, the bullies know who they are, so I have no need to mention them here. I imagine they don't even remember, or if they do, put it down to how *"lads"* behaved. If you are reading this, I hope that the next few paragraphs show you what your cruelty wrought and just how wrong you were.

There's a song playing in my mind as I tell this part of my life, to be fair there is always a song playing that reminds me of memories long past, good or bad. The music seems to be my saviour and tells my story sometimes better than I feel I can. Prince Charming by Adam and the Ants is the song. Not because I thought I was a prince, by no means, I was more the pauper, but the lyrics meant a lot to me *"Prince Charming, Prince Charming, ridicule is nothing to be scared of"* were the words, but they were something to be scared of when surrounded by thugs.

Sticks and stones may break my bones
But words can also hurt me
Sticks and stones break only skin
While words are ghosts that haunt me
Pain from words has left its scar
On mind and heart that's tender
Cuts and bruises now have healed
It's words that I remember

There's a memory that sticks firm in my mind, it perhaps encapsulates all of the other acts. I was walking down a corridor with lino tiles on the floor, the smell of disinfectant that had been used to clean them lingering. One of the bullies shouted, *"Robo"* how I hated that name, (to this day I dislike my surname simply because of the memories I associate with it). I turned around and received a sharp, strong, aggressive shove, sending me backwards, where, unbeknownst to me, an accomplice was crouched on all fours behind me. I fell over the crouching bully and winded myself. I was shocked and embarrassed but plucked up courage to stand up, fighting back the tears of shame and humiliation. As I stood up, another boy punched me whilst another spat in my face. The spitting upset me more than anything, I remember the awful smell of someone else's saliva on my face. I couldn't wash that smell away no matter how many times I tried.

I remember thinking on a daily basis *"I wish I could escape this hellhole"*.

The bullies never attacked singularly; they always came at me in groups. The bullying went on throughout high school, it increased with ferocity and frequency. It affected my academic performance, because if I studied and tried hard the bullies would notice and their attacks would increase.

By this time my acne was so bad that I had to go to the doctors to try and get some help. Whilst in the public waiting room people got up and walked out complaining to my mum that she shouldn't have brought an infectious child into a public area, I wasn't infectious, but I did look like I was. In those days there wasn't much help for people suffering with this soul-destroying condition. Can you imagine the outcry if someone said that today? The damage to my already rock bottom self-esteem was incalculable. I did attend a *"guinea pig"* trial at the hospital but their methods felt like medieval torture. I know that looking back now, the problems I've had in relationships and my inability to see myself as worth anything, stems from these early days.

In the movies this would be a time where I would survive and eventually thrive, making the bullies pay. Reality was far, far crueller.

I lived for Friday, and at 3.30pm my weekend began. I could escape school. I longed for the sounds of the school pips, on a Friday afternoon; these were loud audible pips, three in total that signalled the end of each lesson, break times and most importantly, home time. Whilst the weekends gave me comfort and escapism, they also brought the fear and depression of knowing, only too soon I'd have to go back.

The fear and hatred became so bad that, eventually, I only attended two days out of five. I didn't play truant as such, depression, anxiety and fear kept me at home, and I was continually dodging the truant officers, although truant officers in the 70's were few and far between.

On one of my un-official days off I was hanging around with some local lads on Sugarwell Hill, they weren't part of the bully culture and didn't care about my acne. I had a go on one of the lad's motorbike. Wow it was great. I loved it and I wanted it!

The lad said *"You can buy this motorbike if you want Steve. I want £10 for it."*

TEN POUNDS!!! Where was I going to get ten pounds from? I had no money; Mum had no money and I had nothing of any value. I remember I searched the house for anything I could sell. I had nothing of worth, even my shoes had holes in the soles and lovingly crafted insoles created by Mum with some cardboard from a Weetabix box. But I searched and searched the house, then found an instamatic camera that my aunt had given me. I remember the films were so expensive that the camera had been relegated to a cupboard and I'd forgotten it was there. I didn't throw anything away. Poverty made me thrifty and careful of all my possessions, even the ones I had no use for. This has made me a hoarder in my life, all of my possessions are like new, lovingly cared for and protected as if they were the crown jewels.

My friend Mark was from a large family of five, him and four sisters. His dad was a window cleaner and they had all the latest gadgets. They had a colour TV and were one of the only families in the area to have a video recorder. I thought I'd ask Mark to ask one of his sisters to buy my camera. I tried and tried to get £10 for it, that was the price of the motorbike.

"No way!!" said Sandra, Mark's' sister, *"I'll give you £5."*

Wow £5 yes, yes, yes!!! I was halfway there to buying my motorbike.

Now where would I get the rest of the money from? I was elated that I'd got £5 towards the bike but I was also brought crashing back to earth with the fact that I had no way of getting the rest of the money. I wanted that motorbike so badly I would do anything, even the things I hated the most, like washing cars and gardening for people.

I was a typical teenager in the respect that I hated everything, except my family and the motorbike I so desperately desired. I had that bike in my sights. I had tunnel vision, lust and a desire so strong to own it, that it consumed me. Every waking hour I was planning scheming and saving. I washed so many cars and cut the grass in so many gardens I lost count. It seemed to take me forever to save the money I needed. I was worried that the lad would sell the bike to someone else, but I managed to get the money together just in time!

Finally, I had £10 to buy the bike!!!! Yipeee I'd done it, I had the motorbike.

Isn't it amazing how we can pull out all the stops when we really have to? Sometimes in life we have to do the things we don't like, to get the thing we really want, this is a lesson that has served me well all my life.

This was my first ever motorbike a Raleigh Runabout. It wasn't really a motorbike though, it was a pedal and pop as we called them, a scooter but I had ambitions, ambitions to own a real motorbike one day.

Mum was OK about me riding the bike despite the fact that I was only about twelve. I think we all thought that because I was riding off road, I would be far safer than on main roads. Obviously, time was going to prove us wrong on this, but that was how we saw it and she knew that I was sensible and didn't take risks.

I really loved that bike and I was great on it. I remember it well. You pedalled like a bicycle at first and then the engine started. The more I got used to it the faster I wanted to go, so I would pedal like a crazy person, my little legs going around and round as fast as possible. I felt a little bit like a hamster on a wheel! I remember riding it in the rain one day, I was completely drenched, soaked through to the skin as was the motorbike, but it went really fast, I guess that's' because it was temporarily water cooled or that's what I thought, until I realised, I hadn't known to put oil in the petrol, it needed two stroke fuel, which was petrol and oil mixed. The fact it was going really fast was because it was running much hotter than it should have been and the engine was giving out its last burst of life, about to seize up, but being momentarily held at bay by the rain. It did, however, eventually seize up and my fun was over.

I learnt a valuable lesson that day. Know which fuel type your bike needs and look after your toys better.

Chapter 8
Motorbikes

My dream was to have a real motorbike, what I mean by that is I wanted a proper motorbike, with the petrol tank in the traditional position and not hidden away in a down tube or under the seat.

I used to walk to a petrol station on Potternewton Lane, it was next to the Shoulder of Mutton pub, to buy 2 stroke fuel, that was 2-star petrol and oil pre-mixed, this was to ensure I wouldn't seize up another motorbike.

Honda C50's, C70's and C90's were great little motorbikes (or better to call them scooters). I owned one of each, starting with the C50 and eventually working up to the more powerful C90. I was only around thirteen and had started work as a bottle boy at a local social club. I wasn't earning much, but I saved everything I could in my Post Office account, all the money I had went on motorbikes. I was using these bikes as off-road scramble bikes, a word my Grandad used because that's what it was called in his day. I used to strip the bikes of their fairings, lights and even the seat. The fuel tank was under the seat so when it was removed the fuel tank became the new seating area. Stripping all the extra weight off made the bikes go much quicker, this was normal practice with rally and formula one racing cars. I wasn't a racing car driver; I didn't even have a driving licence, but nevertheless I wanted to get as much speed out of my bikes as possible.

On a beautiful hot summer's day, I had a go on a stolen bike, nicked by some lads in the area. I didn't know them, but my friend Mark did. They were riding a beautiful Yamaha DT125. I felt bad for the owner and the theft of his pride and joy, even though I didn't know who he or she was. The bike was being ridden on a part of the fields over the road from my house, we called the *"Plateau"*. It was only accessible by off road motorbikes and by foot. It was a beautiful part of the fields that was isolated and away from public view. There were bramble bushes and beautiful yellow Spanish gorse, whose aroma lingered in the air.

The Yamaha had gears and a clutch, I'd never ridden anything like it before, but I asked if I could have a go. One of the lads told me how to operate the clutch and the gears and told me to give it a try. I stalled it the first time and they said, *"get off if you can't do it"*. I was determined to ride it and knew that they wouldn't give me another chance if I failed again, this was my last chance. I pulled in the lever on my left-hand side, that was the clutch, I had just learnt. Then my left foot clicked a lever, one down, six up the main lad had said. I didn't really know what that meant but Mark said click it down then pull in the clutch and keep clicking up. I held the throttle at a steady rate, pulled in the clutch, clicked the gear lever down one and then let the clutch lever out slowly and steadily. I was off! I did it I was riding a real motorbike, the feeling was amazing, it was exhilarating. I was controlling a machine that had a 125 cubic centimetres capacity (cc) As the bike picked up speed, I pulled the clutch in again and this time I clicked up on the gear lever. Wow! It was great, I was doing it and going faster with every click up; I was riding along dodging the daffodils and boulders which were ever present and carpeted the plateau. This was a major event in my life that would inevitably shape who I was to become. The time went too quickly, that was it, my turn was over, a one and only deal never to be let on the bike again.

I was a small, very shy boy who saw beauty all around, flowers, nature and the ferocious beauty of machines. I wasn't a Neanderthal with zero intellect and a *"if it didn't fit, push it harder"* attitude., so to be fair it was amazing they let me even sit on it!

The next time I heard about the motorbike it had seized up because they hadn't put oil into the petrol. The Yamaha DT125 didn't actually need oil adding to the fuel like my old Raleigh Runabout, it had an ingenious system called an autolube pump. All they had to do was to keep a separate oil tank filled with two stroke oil, the autolube system would do all the mixing automatically. They didn't know any of that and that was the end for the motorbike, it was ruined. What a shame!

To me, it was a beautiful bike, one I would never own. It was out of my reach and it was stolen anyway. Mark told me the lads were trying to repair the bike with the help of a neighbour, I went round to watch the attempt at the repair, it was incredibly interesting, they were being instructed by an older, and wiser neighbour but they were not doing such a great job. They had no finesse, nor intellect but their attempts, nevertheless, were interesting and amusing but also very saddening, a real mix of emotions because I realised they were just compounding the problems. I soon realised that this beautiful machine would never run again, at least, not in the hands of these people.

There was a Chinese boy called Chan in my class, a

friendly boy whose English wasn't great because he hadn't been in the country that long. While we were talking one day (of sorts) at school, he told me his uncle had had his motorbike stolen, but it had just been recovered. It was the same motorbike!

I asked if it was for sale and he said that it might be. I knew where his uncle lived because it was over the road from a friend of mine. I went round, knocked on the door and a Chinese man answered. I told him I was a friend of Chan's and that I'd heard he was selling his motorbike, that I knew it was seized, not running and not complete.

The man said

"Yes, I want £100 for it."

Wow that was too much I thought. So, I said

"I'll give you £10".

He said *"No"* and closed the door in my face, he wasn't impressed! Not a surprise really! But I didn't have any more money. I would have to sell my Raleigh Runaround that I'd managed to un-seize and do extra hours as a bottle boy at the nearby Sheepscar Working Mens Club to buy it. A week later I went round and asked again, again the man said no! I went round every couple of days and asked if the bike was for sale, the man must have thought I was like an irritating itch he couldn't get rid of, always there, ever present and gone for only a little while, I was a boy on a mission. I was trying to convince the owner to my way of thinking, that was of course that the bike wasn't worth any more than what I offered as it didn't work and was incomplete. The frequency of my visits reduced to every week and after going for 3 months the man still wouldn't accept my derisory £10 offer. I forgot about the bike for a few months, I had accepted that the bike would never be mine, then one day I thought I'll go round and ask one final time.

"Hello" I said *"I haven't been for a long time! Will you sell me your bike please?"*

"How much will you give me?" Said the owner

"I'll give you £10, I don't have any more."

"OK" said the man

I couldn't believe he was serious. I didn't waste a moment and I bought it there and then. My first real motorbike!

The one I had wanted for so long was finally mine, but it was in a really bad state and needed intensive surgery if It was ever to be resurrected.

However, I knew that I had to persist, persistence had got me the motorbike of my dreams, hopefully the same determination would get it working somehow.

Also, my first lesson is to never give up and always chase your dreams!

Chapter 9
Grandad

I can hear a song playing in my head as I start this chapter, it's called *"Grandad"* by Clive Dunn. My Grandad *"Bernard Hanshaw"* was a great man, he was no stranger to poverty, loss, hardship and also love. From a poor Irish background, his mother, was an Irish immigrant, Bridget Keeley who left Cork in the late 1800's to escape the potato famine. Most of the Irish immigrants that came to Leeds in the 1800's settled in the Hunslet area and my grandfather's family did just that. Grandad met my grandmother dancing at Mark Altman's ballroom, astonishingly the building is still there today, it's on the corner of Great George Street and Leighton Street, close to Leeds General Infirmary, although not nearly as romantic a place as it once was.

Everyone met their partners dancing in the 1920's/30's. Grandad was a great dancer; he was a semi-professional in ballroom and Latin, women used to queue to dance with him. He must have passed on those genes to me as I too love dancing, I wish I could thank him for that gift, that and many others I have inherited from him. Grandad however, only had eyes for Gladys Hesling, my grandmother; but marrying her would cost Grandad everything he held dear. He was a good catholic man who fell in love with a protestant woman and ultimately paid the price. The price of love was the loss of his family, he was from a large family of 11. He was cut-off and ostracised for marrying out of his faith. My grandad was always a true gent that would let nothing get in the way of love. Only near the end of his life did his family start talking to him. I wish I knew his family, but I don't know any of them nor my Irish ancestors. I'm digressing and that is a story for another time.

Grandad was the best surrogate father me and Tracy could have wished for.

He used to babysit for us when Mum went out with her friends. I used to look forward to spending time with him. He was a gentleman who resembled one of those well-spoken RAF officers, with his good posture, slim physique and he always dressed well, even when he just sat at home. He was saved from national call up during the second world war because he was in a reserved occupation. He was a railway guard, blowing his whistle and waving his flag in the billowing smoke of the steam trains of the 40's.

Grandad would take us for a walk on the nights Mum went out. We would walk to a pub Grandad liked, in Seacroft. It was called The Cricketers, there was a large grass area facing the pub which was used as a cricket pitch; I now look back with affection at this place. Around the pitch there were tree trunks marking the six boundaries. Grandad would go into the pub, bring us out a glass of pop and a packet of crisps, then came our challenge to walk around the pitch along the tops of the tree trunks. We only ever knew the pub by its important name to us small children, that was *"the tree trunks"*. On the way home we would call at the fish and chip shop near our house, fish and chips with the most important picked onion. Exhausted we would eventually get home and go to bed tired, excited and content all thanks to Grandad.

It was only natural that I would go to him for his help to get my new motorbike running again. I had no clue what to do to get it un-seized and running. Grandad had always loved bikes. He had been a scrambler too and told me about the stories of Post Hill, a hill climb challenge that was popular in his youth, near Pudsey in Leeds. It's still there today, but sadly no organised hill climb remains, as, after a tragic death in 1931, the organised hill climbs were cancelled. In its heyday 20,000 spectators would regularly attend. He told me many tales of his mates, yet their names have long since escaped my memory. I do remember the name Tom Langton though, one of his motorbike mates.

I felt sure Grandad would know how to repair my bike, so the day I bought it I pushed it up to his house. Grandad wasn't a mechanic, but he had a lot of knowledge, or so it seemed to me, a very young thirteen-year-old. He took the top of the engine off, he said *"this is called a cylinder head"*, we then removed bits at an alarming rate, despite that, he named all the parts and we made drawings for reference purposes as we went. After the cylinder head was the barrel, then the piston had to be removed, along with something called a gudgeon pin and little end bearing. The engine was still seized, and I remember him saying that it was the crankshaft that had seized, but he didn't want to strip the whole engine down, so he said

"Here's what we're going to do. We'll pour some oil into the area where the crankshaft is."

The crank housing, Grandad said it was called, however we didn't have any oil, so Grandad went into the kitchen and got some of Grandma's cooking oil

"Here" he said, *"this will do."*

43

Grandad poured in the oil and put the bike in gear, we then slowly and gently rocked/pushed the motorbike forwards and backwards. An hour later nothing was happening

"Do you think it will work Grandad?" I asked

"It will work, we just need to keep going and be patient." He replied without hesitation.

Suddenly the crank turned a little, but only a little and I wasn't sure at first if it was my imagination or wishful thinking. Again, it moved about quarter of an inch. We kept going and slowly but surely the crank started to move a little more, then more and more. Eventually the crank moved all the way round. It had taken a whole day, but Grandad had done it. A valuable lesson was learnt that day, or even a few valuable lessons. One was my grandad was great, more than my dad could ever have been. The next lesson was with determination Grandad could do anything, and he never gave up, he kept going so he could help me. He also drew everything so we wouldn't forget where things went. Grandad had the patience of a saint.

The next day we tried the bike again to see if the crank was still free. Overnight it had seized, but Grandad had said he thought it might do that. So, we started again, pushing the bike backwards and forwards while it was in gear, and with a plentiful supply of Grandma's cooking oil, we got it unseized again.

We put all the parts back together from the drawings. My motorbike was complete except for the petrol tank but I knew where the original one was, it was in the back garden of a local kid I didn't get on with. I hated that guy; hate is a strong word I don't like to use, but you get the picture? I disliked him intensely, it's hard to say that now, because he died at a young age, he passed away in his late 30's due to alcoholism. He did however let me have the old petrol tank. I think he wanted money for it, I can't remember if I gave him any, knowing myself as I do, I doubt I gave him any money, I didn't have any to start with.

The motorbike was finally in one piece and unseized, but still it failed to run. It had a decent spark, so the ignition system was working. As a last-ditch effort, we took the bike to a local motor bike shop on Buslinthorpe Lane called *"The Leeds Motor Exchange".* They told us come back in a couple of days to see how they'd got on. Two days later I went back. They'd got it working, and to cut a long, mechanic story short, apparently the piston had been fitted the wrong way round and there had been a fuel starvation problem. They told me a few other things, but the only words I heard were *"its working"!* The repair cost me £10 - ironically the same price as I'd paid for the whole bike. I paid the bill and rode my motor bike home, across the plateau, where I had first ridden it as a stolen bike and the last time I had seen it running.

Now it was running again, it was legal, and it belonged to me. The feeling was amazing, finally I had a real motor bike, I felt alive and euphoric. All mine and Grandad's efforts had led to this triumphant moment.

I wasn't any good at anything else. Mainly because things didn't interest me or stimulate my imagination, but finally there was something I could do. I was brilliant on my bike, I could get up and down the steepest of hills, get over any obstacle and pull the best wheelies.

Over the road from where I lived were fields, beautiful wild and uncultivated fields that rang out with the sound of nature, the wonderful sounds of grasshoppers in the baking sun and the yellowed grass of the fields of Sugar Well Hill.

Sounds of horses neighing and dogs barking. A truly lovely, peaceful sound that was disturbed only by the roar of my motorbike engine. I loved those fields and wanted to own them so they would be protected forever. I find it ironic that I liked nature so much, but I was the one destroying the peace and quiet. I wanted both the adventure and the peaceful beauty of those hills.

I was considerate on my bike though and avoided people, dogs and horses, they were all no-go zones for me. Horses were a no no. *"Stay away from us"*, the riders would say. I didn't really understand why, but I soon realised that horses and motorbikes didn't mix. I had friends that rode horses and would argue that horse riding was better and that horses were faster; they obviously hadn't been on a motorbike! I hadn't been on a horse either, well not unless you count the time I was scared to death on a beach pony on Morecambe beach, during a family holiday! I enjoyed the solitude of me and my bike, it was a time to be free in my mind and spirit from everything else, from all the sorrow and sadness that school created and torment of the bullies.

On one of my days out on my bike I met a young guy called Michael Tighe, he was 12 and at the time and I was 13. Michael was great on his bike too. He had a Girelli Tiger Cross 50cc.

Michael and I used to have great adventures together on our bikes, we went everywhere, challenged ourselves to get up hills that motorbikes didn't normally go up. I'd walk to my usual petrol station on Potternewton Lane, there I would buy 50 pence worth of 2 star fuel that would keep me going all week. Wow those were the days! I enjoyed this part of my life and lived solely for the freedom.

There was another guy who wanted to join us, only thing

was he wasn't a boy like me and Michael, he was a 30-year-old man and couldn't keep up with us. He didn't have the abilities that we had and frankly he was dangerous, so we avoided him like the plague. If we saw him coming, we'd head in the other direction, it wasn't difficult to lose him, he couldn't follow us and go to the places we could. Everybody knew he was reckless.

An important lesson I would come to learn was that you can't avoid things forever!

Chapter 10
College

The time spent riding my bike was pure heaven, it challenged me in a way school never could. It tested me physically, intellectually and mentally because I had to study obstacles, hills and other challenges to assess the risk and the likelihood of succeeding. Motocross, trials riding and enduro took a lot out of me. I needed to be fit and healthy and emotionally stable with a strong character to achieve my dreams. I lived for that bike. It was the only thing I had ever wanted. I wasn't bothered about women at that time, which was good as they weren't interested in me either! No, my life was simply about bikes.

It was, therefore, an obvious choice to become a mechanic.

The year was 1981, Peter Sutcliffe, was finally arrested and charged for the murder of 13 women. The Government had welcomed plans by the Japanese firm Datsun to build cars in Britain and I would be 17 in that December.

I thought I wanted to be a motorbike mechanic, but I also considered becoming a chef, or joining the RAF as an aircraft engineer. In time though, I decided to enrol in Leeds Kitson College of Technology on a motor engineering course. I loved it, I was treated like an adult and as a result I excelled. When it came to motor engineering, I just got it, even when the other students struggled, I simply under-stood. I guess I must have a predisposition to mechanical engineering. I often think it might have been genetic knowledge, (past memory) if you believe in that sort of thing, there was no explaining why or how I understood me-chanical things I'd never seen before.

I would study at the Blenheim annexes in the morning, it was over the road from Leeds university and was pretty shabby and run down, with basic facilities. To be honest it was just a makeshift classroom site made up of portacabins where the theory part of the course was taught.

In the afternoon we'd cross town to the Water Lane site, where all the practical work was carried out. Getting there took half an hour but I really enjoyed the walk and didn't mind it taking up some of my lunch time. We would call into a local café, it's long gone now, but it was an old-style greasy spoon type of place, with the smell of bacon sand-wiches and cooking oil lingering in the air and greasy tables that you slipped off! Even walking in was a risky affair and you had to walk tentatively to avoid slipping! Yes, it was a dump, but it had something that always drew me... A juke-box. I would put my 10p in the coin slot, make a selection and watch the records being selected and played. It was in-triguing to me because of its design, how it resembled a classic American car, but the true beauty was the elegance and precision of the jukebox mechanism.

Just before we got to the workshops on Water Lane, we would pass by the Mill Hill Amusements in Leeds city cen-tre. The year before I'd been introduced to Space Invaders, and I discovered that I had an additional talent in playing video games, my mate Sweeny however, was an ace at the video game *"Defender"*. He was so good we'd be late on occasions to the workshop as he kept getting extra plays. However, the teachers were never angry with us nor did they tell us off. They simply said,

"This isn't school, if you miss the lessons you miss them! It's your education you're missing out on, you are adults now and you are here because you want to be and not because you have to be."

Good attitude! I liked that. I loved working on cars and interesting vehicles, not as much as motor bikes, despite that I enjoyed the challenges I faced and the pace of learning was fast, just how I liked it.

It was a strange revelation, I actually enjoyed learning and especially the practical lessons, although during winter the workshops were crazy cold. We used to be sent home when the temperature dropped below -5. Why do I want to do this job? I thought on many occasions. It was often colder inside the building than outside, but that was the working environment of a motor mechanic, still I loved my time as a first-year student, although the winter of 1981/82 was a hard winter, the frost lit up the workshops like a bright shining light and the floors were scattered with sawdust to stop us from slipping on the fluorescence and spilt oil.

The second year was great because all the first years used to look up to us as knowledgeable and experienced. What a difference this made to my confidence. I was already a completely different boy to the one who'd left Stainbeck High School, and this further built me up. We were then moved from both the Blenheim annexes and Water Lane workshops to a brand-new, custom built college building.

Another lad Terrance Braithewait and I were top of the class, we were the golden boys because we were good at what we did, and we always got the job done. I knew all the lecturers so if there was a good project to be had, they'd give it to us.

The college used to buy all their cars from the Rothwell motor auctions, the crappier the car the cheaper the purchase and more cars could be bought for the students to work on or dismantle, many times they would not be able to re-assemble them.

On one occasion a lecturer asked me and Terrance if we fancied trying to get an old Skoda working. They were notoriously difficult to work on. This one was no different, it was an ex-Soviet Union brand and built like a tank! They were rear wheel drive and were pretty hard to destroy. Although the first years had given it a good try, they had lost lots of parts and had made a bit of a mess of it. To me and Terrance though, it was a great opportunity to show all of our peers, first years and lecturers just how good we were. We accepted the challenge.

We worked on that car most of the day, searching for parts, making some parts and getting new nuts and bolts from the stores man, we needed a chitty for everything and we first had to get the chitty from a lecturer.

The time was 3pm and we connected the exhaust fume extractor to the car exhaust, all the students and lecturers gathered round, I turned the key, err err errr errr errr errr… vrooom. It started! We had successfully repaired what was an incomplete engine that was falling to pieces. All that came with it was a box of spare parts the previous students had forgotten to put back on. The lectures always said if you have any parts left over after a rebuild, you've done it wrong but me and Terrance were good.

After that, I had job opportunities lined up with a

number of the lecturers. One of them had a friend with his own garage, I had a job waiting for me there. Another lecturer had contacts in the formula one circuit pits (Mr Colley, he also held a land speed record on his homebuilt dragster motorbike) and I had a job offer to start with them too, I liked that one, offers from the lecturers were coming in thick and fast.

I had also been looking a few times at the RAF recruitment offices on Wellington Street in Leeds. I liked the idea of being a mechanic or an engineer working with aircraft or helicopters. I went in one day to enquire about signing up. They told me they could have taught me engineering and I hadn't needed to go to college at all, but because I was so near the end of my course, I should finish it and then return to their offices, they would take up training from there.

My name was put on the list, I would return on completion of my two-year full-time City and Guilds motor engineering course.

I was stunned, a boy with no qualifications from school, but top marks and top of my class at college, had been given this amazing opportunity. I would complete my course and then join the RAF as an aircraft technician or take up the opportunity on the formula one race circuit. Had you told me this when I was at school, I would have laughed at you!

One day, one of the lecturers brought in a motorbike he was repairing, he said he had just bought it. I liked it, it was a Yamaha DT250 so much bigger than my own DT125, in fact it was double the capacity. I liked Yamahas and what's more it was my favourite colour, yellow. It was a big beautiful beast of a machine and I wanted it.

I asked him if he was selling it and if so, how much? He wanted £80, which in those days was a lot of money, money that I simply didn't have. That night I told my mum and sister about it, I didn't have £80 but my student grant was due and that was about £90, to last me the whole term.

I made a decision. I told the lecturer that I wanted it and asked if he'd wait until I got my grant money. I was over the moon when he said yes. He delivered the motorbike the next day and told me I could pay him when my grant came through. The first time I rode it I was scared by its power. It had double what I was used to, but it was great, I loved the adrenaline rush, it was fast, I mean really fast. As time went by, I became really good on it and the fear of all that power just disappeared. I paid the lecturer when my grant came in. He was a decent man and never doubted I would pay him, as I never doubted I would.

I was only a teenager and now the owner of two motorbikes. Every day after college and on my time off, I would be out riding. Either alone or meeting up with my mate Michael. The DT250 was super powerful, it had been customised power-wise by my lecturer. Nobody could catch me, not even the police. *"Woop woop, that's the sound of the police"* by KRS-One makes me smile and think of those rebellious days.

I was just too good; my motorbike was like an extension of my body. The engine always sounded tired because it had lots of piston slap, basically the barrel had been either re-bored or worn and the piston was moving around inside making a noticeable noise, but it also seemed to add to the power, it was a phenomenal machine.

The lesson here was that with the right attitude and approach, you can learn how to handle anything.

Chapter 11
The Accident

It was April the 19th 1982, the Falklands war had just begun. I was in the second and final year of my motor mechanic course, it was my first day back of my final term. This term would be dedicated to automatic transmissions and was considered the most difficult subject of all. It comprised of two elements, the first of which was stripping down, rebuilding and understanding how the automatic gearbox worked. The second was fault diagnosis.

I was looking forward to this term because even though I didn't have a driving licence, I wanted an automatic car. I liked automatics because they were associated with high quality cars and were a really smooth drive.

My first day back was Monday and to ease us back into what would be a difficult term we were given half a day off, so I rushed home to go out on my motorbike. The fields always called me out to play, a nagging voice in my head saying, *"Come out to play Steve, Steve come out and play."*

I don't actually recall much about the accident.

Funny, this catastrophic event, that was to change everything about me, both good and bad, is just a blur, I have no memory of it. I presume that it's my mind protecting me, of course without the story of the accident though, the book has, like my body, a missing part.

In preparation for writing this book I asked my friend

Michael, who had been with me that day, what he remembered.

Michael set the scene.

"I called for you and we went out on your motorbike, as mine had run out of petrol. We were having a great time as we always did, I was on the back when I saw my girlfriend, I told you to keep going and ignore her, but that wasn't your way and we stopped. She told us that the dangerous guy we always avoided was out on his bike, I got off and you rode away in an attempt to avoid him but unfortunately for you, headed directly towards him without knowing. You set off down the steep hill towards the Prince Philips Centre, passed the five aside football pitch that had a four-foot wall all around, and high fences erected all around the top of the walls, to stop the footballs from being lost over the steep hills of Sugarwell Hill."

Me and my friend Michael always had a spotter waiting at the top of the hills for us to make sure the area was safe and that there were no dog walkers or animals that we might injure, but on this day our spotters weren't there. As I approached a smaller hill right at the side of the five aside pitch, there was a group of kids that distracted me.

I don't remember the impact.

Michael continues

"The guy we'd tried to avoid had thought he could jump over you, Daredevil style, on his bike whilst you were coming down the hill. The force of the combined speed of the bikes meeting was sufficient to rip your right arm off there and then, it landed a hundred yards away at the feet of that group of kids. Particularly at the feet of a young guy called Brownie. The motorbike of the other guy impacted your chest, he was thrown over a fence and sprained his wrist.

I was frantic and ran as fast as I could to your house to tell your mum and to get an ambulance, but your mum wasn't at home and neither were your neighbours. I was going to run to your grandparent's house, but I realised you simply didn't have that long to survive. I made the decision to run around the corner to Mark's house to tell him. As I ran around the corner, I found a policeman, I can't tell you the relief I felt. I grabbed him and dragged him to the scene of the accident, all the while frantically trying to tell him what had happened. We ran as fast as we could, and he radioed for an ambulance. By the time we got back to you the ambulance was already there."

It was 8 o'clock in the evening, my mum and sister were swimming at Scott Hall Sports Centre, blissfully unaware of what had just happened, when someone ran in to tell them I'd had an accident. I can't imagine what must have gone through their minds as they rushed to be by my side.

One of my neighbours, Bob was a bus driver and a paramedic for the territorial army, he was at the scene by the time an ambulance had arrived and had taken his white shirt off and had stuffed it into the socket from where my arm had been pulled off, he applied pressure in an attempt to stem the arterial blood flow that was leaving my body with incredible force. He also performed mouth to mouth because I had stopped breathing.

The impact had not only resulted in a traumatic amputation, but it had punctured both my lungs, ruptured my liver, my gall bladder, my spleen, fractured my right pelvis and broken my right leg.

People tell me I was still conscious and asked about my arm. Many people claimed they put my arm in their fridge to protect it, I think that is probably not true because of the timings involved.

I know I was lucky that day, a sequence of events and people saved my life. Michael ran for more than his life was worth, Bob stopped me from bleeding to death and the policeman was in the right place at the right time.

Most importantly, I was surrounded by people that cared.

The next thing I remember was opening my eyes and looking up, there was an angel looking down at me. She had long blond hair, the most beautiful face and perfect soft complexion with piercing blue eyes. They looked right into my soul, that angel was call Janet. She was a staff nurse on ward 16 at LGI and she said in a lovely soft and gentle voice

"Hello Steven, you've had an accident on your motorbike, you're in the Leeds General Infirmary and you've lost your right arm"

I was so weak and tired it didn't even register and even if it had I didn't have the energy to speak back. I had been in a coma for two weeks and it would take me a little while longer to fully regain consciousness.

Every time I awoke, someone said I'd lost my right arm. I wasn't interested, I was more concerned that my right arm was aching, it felt like I was laying on it and it was twisted right up my back. I had pipes up my nose and pipes coming out of my body, I couldn't move. I was so weak, there was a plant pot on my stomach and my roller skates were under my right arm that's why my arm was aching, and I was wearing my wellington boots! There was a really strange smell up my nose, it was a mixture of sour milk and disinfectant. I had also been moved to a petrol station on Meanwood Road, then the next day I'd been moved to

Yeadon airport. I knew I was at Yeadon because I could hear the low flying aircraft.

My mind was playing tricks on me, the morphine was making me hallucinate, it was 1982 and the low flying aircraft was a Lancaster Bomber flypast, it had something to do with the Falkland conflict.

I climbed out of bed, it was one of those old Victorian beds that had a cot side to stop you getting out; but I managed to get out by sliding to the bottom and standing up, I wanted to go home I didn't want to be in the petrol station or at the airport.

I stood up and tried to walk, but someone had tied my catheter to the bed and I heard someone say,

"OH NO! Steven's out of bed."

I went down like a tonne of bricks and smashed my head on the floor. I remember there was lots of activity, doctors checking me every five minutes. There was a man at the foot of my bed; a shadowy figure who was unrecognisable, but he stayed with me for a long time.

I now know that this is a phenomenon known as the *"third man",* where a shadowy figure appears to those in their hour of need.

The first mention of the shadowy figure was by the anaesthetist to my mum and sister. One day they had visited me, and I told them the anaesthetist had been to see how I was. There was concern that I might have suffered brain damage from lack of oxygen after my lungs had both collapsed and ruptured; but when my mum spoke to the anaesthetist he told her that I'd be OK and that there was no brain damage because I had recounted a conversation to my mum I had with him. He also told her he knew I would be OK, because he had seen a shadowy figure at the foot of my bed. He'd seen these figures before, he recognised the shadow as the third man, a guardian angel, someone or something that was watching over me.

My injuries were really bad, I didn't realise how bad. Both my lungs had been punctured and collapsed, my liver was ruptured, and three quarters had to be removed. My gall bladder had been ruptured as had my spleen. My right hip was fractured, and my right leg was broken. I died three times on the operating table and had been resuscitated. Maybe during a dying state, I had met the third man and he had come back with me, I guess I really needed his help at that moment in time.

The third man stayed with me for quite a long time, even when I was at home, I woke up in the middle of the night to see a figure stood at the foot of my bed, I put my head under the covers rubbed my eyes and told myself not to be so stupid, yet when I looked again to make sure he had gone, he was still stood there. It freaked me out at first, but I've got to tell you since my experiences I have become more spiritual and I believe more in the unbelievable. The song from Stan Ridgway, *"Camouflage"* would top the charts in 1986, a song all about the third man and a song that touched me deeply.

Everybody on Ward 16, where I was put after intensive care, was bed bound due to loss of limbs, the majority were older gentlemen who had lost legs through diabetes, in fact I was the only young man on that ward. Sewing my arm back on had failed after a nine-hour attempt. After losing me 3 times on the operating table, the surgeons abandoned my arm to reconstruct my shoulder, stabilise me and save my life. The surgeon according to my mum and sister, was a really young man, not much older than me, he was the registrar for Mr Doige the consultant.

When I was eventually allowed visitors other than my immediate next of kin, my mum called the college I was studying at to tell the lecturers I was allowed visitors. The next day, ward 16 struggled to cope with the amount of people that had come to see me. It was a surreal moment that was akin to Noah's Ark where animals were brought in 2 by 2, although in my case it was groups of visitors led in groups of five at a time until they had all seen me.

On the occasion I couldn't go to the toilet because my stomach muscles weren't strong enough, they had been cut from my sternum to just above my pubic bone. I couldn't go to the toilet because I couldn't push down, I had to have suppositories inserted up my back passage, not very pleasant really, especially when it's a young attractive female nurse. The suppositories did the trick, but I didn't like using the commode, so one day I asked the nurse if she would take me to a proper toilet. She said she would and walked me to a toilet at the very bottom of the ward.

My bed was at the top of the ward nearest to the nurses' station so they could keep an eye on me. It took what seemed a lifetime to get to the toilet, on other occasions I'd not been able to get there quick enough. I had no control of my bladder due to being catheterised and had wet myself before I made the toilet, I wouldn't let that happen again, so the nurse would carry a bottle with her in case I got caught short.

I couldn't even clean myself. My neck muscles were damaged I had very little mobility, my head was against my right shoulder and was frozen in position.

Those nurses were wonderful, I fell in love with most of them but Janet the most. They would do all my personal care for me. I was an ugly, shy, self-conscious, spotty boy with very low self-esteem and here were these beautiful, young educated women doing everything for me. I was truly humbled by that experience and my admiration for nurses is beyond words.

"Janet! Janet I've finished" I shouted.

Janet came to clean me up and then she took me to the wash basin to wash my hands. Janet had forgotten there was a mirror in the bathroom, mirrors weren't allowed on ward 16 and they weren't allowed for a good reason because everyone was mutilated and disfigured, but Janet had taken me to the staff toilets and she had forgotten about the mirror, the song from The Beat, Mirror in the Bathroom was ringing in my ears.

I looked in that mirror and couldn't believe my eyes.

All my spots had gone! What's happened? Where are all those blackheads and yellow heads that tormented me? I had a perfect complexion over night or so it seemed. I was absolutely overjoyed.

I looked again in the mirror to see if I could see my right arm, all the time Janet was watching me to see how I reacted. I couldn't move my head to see properly, but it looked like my right arm had gone. I couldn't really tell but it wasn't important anyway because the euphoria that swept over me was pure heaven. The acne that had tormented me for years and had been the ammunition of the bullies had gone! I was the happiest I'd ever been.

Janet said

"Are you OK Steven?"

She was waiting for me to breakdown, but I never did. I didn't realise how mentally strong I had become, maybe the bullying had strengthened my character and was a preparation for what was to come. Isn't it amazing how we can see the good in what at first might seem like a bad situation?

This has to be one of the most important lessons ever learnt. The Chinese call it Ying and Yang. For every bad thing there is an equal and opposite good thing. There is always a positive to a negative, in fact one can't exist without the other. Push and pull, Ying and Yang, good and bad, call it what you will, but I was experiencing it, first hand.

Chapter 12
The Uninvited Visitor

The previously mentioned *"third man"* had been an uninvited visitor, but one that gave me comfort and guided the way to survival. But there was another uninvited visitor, one that definitely didn't comfort me and wasn't there for me at all. You may have heard his name before…

Whilst in the intensive care unit, I was unconscious, semi-conscious, delirious and hallucinating. My mind played tricks on me. I'd been given a lot of drugs to fight off infection and dilate my blood vessels to stop embolisms, one of the side effects of this was a constant erection, which by the way, is how Viagra was discovered. Sildenafil is its clinical name and its purpose was to dilate blood vessels to stop embolisms and increase blood flow for angina patients. On one occasion a man I recognised visited my bed, he let his hands wander under my bed sheets to touch my privates. It was Jimmy Saville at my bed-side.

The whole event felt like a dream, like the plant pot on my stomach and the wellington boots I was wearing. In my rational state and looking back now, I ask myself if it really took place. I don't want to believe that it did, everything was mixed up in my mind. I didn't have the energy to talk let alone fight off wondering hands. Drifting in and out of delirium meant I didn't know reality from dream state. When I told the nurses about my experience, they said I must have been hallucinating, so I accepted the explanation. However, Jimmy left his calling card, a child's get-well card that he signed to say he had visited while I was sleeping

Someone had tied my catheter to the cot side which resulted in damage to my urethra. I can't imagine for a moment that a trained member of staff would do that. All I can assume is that it was done by my unwanted visitor, so as not to draw attention to my erect appendage. I can't prove any of this, but knowing now what I know about Jimmy Saville, I feel that it is much more likely that it was an actual event that took place, one when I was incapable of responding and stopping his disgusting sexual advance.

I met Jimmy Saville after my accident, he acted strange towards me, not wanting to talk and not acknowledging that he had even visited me, yet I had his signed card. It was odd that he didn't want to chat to see how I was, especially if he was in fact the genuine, caring person as his ward visits implied. Or were we all just easy victims, too ill to do or say anything?

The irony of all of this is that I applied for Jim'll Fix It in 1984, only two years after our encounter. I wrote and told the TV that I'd been visited by Jimmy whilst in hospital and asked if they could arrange for me to breakdance with the Rock Steady Crew to their song *"Hey You"*.

In hindsight, maybe my request was thrown away when I said I'd been visited by Jimmy in Leeds General Infirmary, especially in light of what we now believe, that the BBC were aware of what he was up to.

After it all came out, I contacted Slater Gordon's, the solicitors handling Jimmy Saville cases, to make a claim. I was told that I didn't have any evidence, that the signature on the card wasn't his. A simple Google search proved the handwriting to be his. They then argued that I was a young adult of 18 at the time and so it wasn't an assault of a minor which was what they were investigating. Once again, the man seemed to get away with despicable acts simply because of who he was. I wasn't jumping on any bandwagon, nor did I really want compensation, I suppose I just wanted someone to hear about what he'd done, for it to be acknowledged and to give me answers as to how he was allowed to carry on, unfettered for all that time.

I'll leave you to make up your minds about this. I know what I believe and whilst it has no bearing on the man I am today; it was a cruel and despicable act to abuse someone as injured and vulnerable as I was at that time.

The lesson I learnt was people aren't always what they seem to be and that people in power are often held unaccountable.

Chapter 13
Born Again

Losing an arm seemed easy, when I say that, what I really mean is that it took no effort on my part. I was just in the wrong place at the wrong time. Or maybe I was in the right place at the right time, because I'm not sure I would be the person I am today, without that experience. However, I wasn't thinking that when I was laid in bed contemplating my future with one arm.

I'd never thought about being disabled, inclusivity wasn't a *"thing"* when I was growing up and we had never been taught that at school; so, it was something I wasn't prepared for, physically or emotionally. The initial ripping off of my right arm had left my body contorted. I couldn't move my neck and my head seemed fused to my right shoulder. Frustration hadn't hit me yet. I was way too ill to do more than simply recover.

Prior to my accident I had weighed 12 stone, after my accident I'd gone down to 6 stone, I was so weak. I looked like a skeleton in a skin bag. I shouldn't have left hospital so quickly, but I wanted to be at home with my mum and sister and Sheba my lovely big German Shepherd dog. So, I jumped through all the hurdles the doctors and occupational therapists had set, determined to get home.

Later in life, jumping through other peoples' imposed hurdles would become a regular thing. I had to prove I could walk the distance of the ward and back, it was a long Victorian style ward that had 20 or so beds down either side and a nurses station strategically placed at the top, so all the patients could be seen and attended to if needed. What a great idea, why did we ever do away with these wards?

The occupational therapist said I had to be able to dress myself without any help before she would let me go home. So, I practiced and practised dressing myself and walking the corridors of the LGI. I love the LGI, it was my saviour and my soul still walks the old fashioned and beautiful corridors. I'd walk up and down, back and forth singing, the acoustics were amazing.

One day a nurse stopped me and said she had heard an angel singing and had I heard it? I said no, but I said I had been singing, she asked what song I was singing, when I told her she didn't believe me, I was the angel she had heard! I was singing *"Gaudete"* by Steeleye Span, it's a beautiful tune that reminds me of a Gregorian chant that echoed through the Victorian corridors, like a medieval monastery.

Walking was difficult and painful. My hip had been fractured and I lost all my strength and suppleness. The pain in my right hip was excruciating, but the morphine I was on was doing the trick and numbing my pain receptors. Even when I did feel the pain, I just continued, such was my determination to walk and get out of hospital, every step felt like a nail was being driven through my hip.

Getting dressed without one arm was frustrating to say the least. I knew of course how to dress myself with two arms and I kept trying to use my right arm. I'd put my right arm out to grab something or even to stop myself from falling; but my right arm wasn't there, it just felt like it was, to be honest, I still wasn't one hundred percent convinced it wasn't there. I say that, but I guess I knew deep down it had gone. If I was in denial, when would it hit me?

While I waited for the full emotional impact to hit me, I tried putting my socks on. It was so frustrating, I couldn't just put them on like I was used to, I had to think about how I would do it. I sat for twenty minutes, thinking about it, coming up with a method in my mind before I actually tried. The idea I thought of was to put the fingers of my left hand inside the opening of my sock, expand my fingers enough to get my toes inside and then pull my socks up. To my surprise it worked first time. I had a process that I would now use, I still use that process today.

A week later when the occupational therapist visited me, I demonstrated how I could dress myself and walk the length of the ward and back. Whilst she was happy that I had managed to do her tasks so quickly, she said I still wasn't ready to go home; but a deal was a deal and I had fulfilled my side of the bargain.

No one ever taught me what to do, I guess they didn't know either. It was up to me to struggle and find out for myself what would work and what wouldn't. My mum and sister were told not to help me, they were told to let me struggle. If I was ever to be independent, the doctors had said it was important that my family allow me to do things for myself, no matter how frustrating it may appear. Every aspect of my life had changed overnight, it didn't help that I couldn't stand straight, physiotherapists would help with that over the next six months.

What the doctors didn't know, was that I wasn't suffering from *"woe is me"* or any real depression. My mum was told to keep an eye on me as it was likely to hit me hard and

68

that she should be prepared. It didn't. I'm still waiting for the *"realisation"* to kick in that I only have one arm and for the melt-down. That's just not how I'm made though. I never had any counselling, it wasn't available in those days, it was a case of "get on with it".

People used to ask me really personal questions like how do you masturbate now? Left-handed was my standard reply. *"Does it feel like someone else is doing it for you?"* was the strange question I was asked on numerous occasions. I always replied yes it does, but I'm practicing a lot! I was a healthy young man, so it did get more practice than other things! I enjoyed these strange questions because they felt like a light-hearted way of people asking me real questions, they were intrigued to know the answers to.

People asked me what it was like having one arm. I feel quite privileged to have experienced life as a two-armed person and as a one-armed person. It's like I've lived two lives in one lifetime. The strange thing is I feel no different, I just look different to others! I could still feel my right-arm, I can still feel it now. I didn't know about phantom limb syndrome back then and I can only describe it as still being able to feel the missing appendage, despite its absence. I now know it is common amongst those who have lost a limb and as weird as it may feel, it was nothing to worry about.

The more I thought about that though, I realised I knew a lot of people that were suffering from something very similar. Phantom barriers, barriers that were stopping them doing the things they wanted to do, barriers that were stopping people achieving the things they really wanted to achieve in life, barriers that feel real, but just like my right arm, aren't really there! I decided I wouldn't let phantom barriers stop me ever again. Another important lesson learnt, but at such an expense, the cost of an arm.

People often say *"I'd give my right arm for that"* I've never said that or used that expression, but I guess I did give my right arm for the life I have now, a life I wouldn't change at any cost.

The science behind phantom limb is quite interesting. The nerves that supplied my right arm are still there and so, my brain thinks my arm is still there. There are times I'm in the shower and if my right shoulder touches the cold tiles it feels like cold water is running down my missing arm and dripping off of my fingers. I quite like the sensation.

I told a friend just the other day about the science behind phantom limb and he replied

"No Steve that's not why you can feel your right arm!"

Intrigued I said, *"Well what is it then?"* thinking he must have a lot of medical knowledge.

He replied

"It's because your soul is still intact!"

I liked that.

What a lovely thing to say, for some reason it gave me inner peace knowing that my soul is still whole. The answer I give to the question of what's it like to have one arm was simple.

I'd say, *"put your right arm up your back as far as you possibly can, then lay or sit back and put your weight on it. Leave it there until it goes numb, then bring your arm back to the front of you. That moment between pins and needles and not being able to fully feel your arm is what I'm feeling on a daily basis".*

It's not a bad feeling, it's just different to what I was used to; but change is inevitable, it will come to us all, so why not embrace that change? I read something that made me reflect inwards, it was - Everybody at some point in their lives will be disabled, whether it be through birth, accident or age. I realised I would just be better prepared than most.

Just four weeks after my life changing accident I was released from hospital and could return home. I was so happy to be home. I can remember the first time I walked with Mum to my grandma and grandad's house, I was so exhausted I had to go to bed, I didn't wake up for 4 hours. I was shattered, it wasn't far to walk, only a few hundred yards, but it felt like a marathon. Mum came to collect me when I had woken up. We walked back home and again I needed to go to bed with exhaustion, another 4 hours later and I awoke.

I enjoyed my regular visits to the LGI physiotherapy unit, although not all of the treatment was pleasurable. Heat pads would be placed on my right shoulder and neck for twenty minutes to half an hour. The physiotherapist would then put one hand on my head and another on my shoulder and try to force them apart, hoping to get my shoulder into its normal position and to try and straighten my head and neck. It was excruciatingly painful, but I knew the physios were doing their best for me, it was working slowly; but it was working. I had to try and turn my head and look over my left shoulder and then my right. That had to be one of the hardest exercises I had to do. I couldn't do it really, I had no movement or flexibility at all, and to this day I still have no neck mobility. It was as if my whole body had been placed in a splint or plaster cast that was restricting my movement, and I was simply fighting that restriction. If I was to survive though, I would have to learn to fight the things that would try and hold me back. I would have to become a Survivor, ironically there was a song playing on the radio one day, as I was getting my physio treatment, the band was called Survivor and their iconic song was called *"Eye of The Tiger."*

I was still trying to walk on a daily basis even though, often the pain got the better of me; but what option did I have? I could either give in or fight on.

I struggled at first to do most things, even the little thing that we all take for granted. Eating my breakfast, it was only Weetabix, but I kept missing my mouth with the spoon, I had no hand eye co-ordination with my left hand, after all I was right-handed. Cutting my food didn't work either, I couldn't use a knife, when I tried, it would simply push the food around the plate. I even tried one of those forks with a serrated knife-edge, but it was designed for a right-handed person so that was very tricky to use.

Another area that gave me problems was personal hygiene, this was so difficult, using toilet paper was almost impossible, fortunately that's one task you have to learn very quickly!

I spent so much time sleeping and recuperating it felt like an eternity. I was always OK about losing an arm and the nurses and doctors were shocked at my attitude. They expected me to break down at any point in realisation that I had lost an arm. I knew that I had and wasn't sure how the medical people wanted me to behave or react.

I'm often asked if I got frustrated or lashed out. The answer is no! That's not my style. Yes, of course I got frustrated, but it was the kind of frustration you get when you can't see the answer to a puzzle. I don't shout or bang about, I bide my time and figure out a solution.

In fact, there were only two times I cried.

The first was when I saw my motorbike and how badly

it had been damaged. That somehow seemed so much worse than the injury to me, perhaps because I had such low self-esteem, I didn't value my body, but I valued that bike more than anything, it had been my escape and a training ground for new skills.

The second time I cried was over a girl. I'd been chasing a local girl, she was beautiful, she looked like Daryl Hannah from the film Splash, long blond/ginger crimped hair, I never told her and to this day she probably doesn't realise how much I liked her, but she didn't seem interested back then and true to my nature I lost interest. After my accident however, she seemed interested, maybe because my accident was so well known about and I had become a local legend overnight, but it was too late I'd moved on and my life had changed.

She came to my house to visit one day and she brought me flowers, I was so touched and happy to receive them, whoever said flowers are just for girls or women are totally wrong. They were truly beautiful, a kaleidoscope of colours and smells, including my favourite bright yellow daffodils, yellow also being my favourite colour, she had either re-searched what I liked, or she had just gotten lucky, but they were wonderful. I loved receiving flowers, but unfortu-nately, I had lost interest in the beautiful young ginger haired beauty that had brought them.

My close friend Mark came to visit shortly after, I told him the story of the beautiful princess I'd dreamt about but no longer wanted, he said I should make her my girlfriend because no other woman would want me, now I only had one arm!

When Mark left, I broke down in tears, I'm sure he

didn't mean it, but his words hit home and made me contemplate a life of singledom. I hoped his words were wrong but only time would tell. I was OK the next day, yet that statement made me stronger, I wouldn't settle for someone just in case I couldn't get anyone else, that would be the wrong basis of any relationship.

Women would of course discriminate against me but so would employers. I was unsure how to deal with those two facts. People, children and attractive women would look at me, well it would be more accurate to say stare. Children would say cruel things to their parents.

The first time I heard a child say *"errr mummy mummy that man hasn't got an arm, look look, ha hah ha."* That was so upsetting, the only way I could deal with this was to ignore the world around me. If I ignored everyone I wouldn't be upset by the cruel remarks and the staring.

Tony my lifelong friend used to get upset and shout at people, *"What you staring at?"* The downside of ignoring everyone was I wouldn't see the signs of interest from women, I wouldn't see friends. I walked through life looking inwards and never outwards at the world around me. This was the only way I could deal with the stares.

Employers were not interested in me. I went to two interviews and was turned down point blank on the basis that I had one arm and would not be able to do any job. I was unable to change that, no matter how much I tried, I could not grow my arm back or change their negative perception of disabilities.

I decided never to go to an interview again. It was a great pity that I was no longer wanted by employers, but I would show everyone what a one arm man can do! So, I decided that I would employ myself, create my own destiny and forge my own future.

It might have been easier to give in but that wasn't in my nature and no amount of pain or problems would hold me back. Although at times I must admit, things were really difficult, and I needed to think a lot about how I would tackle them. I had to think outside the box. The things I had taken for granted when I had two arms were now taking me a long time to do and had now become a problem-solving exercise.

Sometimes we look inwards to avoid looking out at the world around us but what opportunities might we miss? I know I missed a lot, but I won't ever miss them again.

Chapter 14
The Mechanic

I had trained as a mechanic, so it seemed the natural job for me to do once I was fit enough and able to work. It was 1983 and petrol cost £1.67 a gallon, that's 36.7 pence a litre. I started by servicing friends' cars. I'd spend hours working on them, doing body repairs, replacing brakes or complete major engine and gearbox rebuilds. I was really good but very slow in comparison to others.

Losing my arm hadn't cost me my skill, just my speed and this was a problem when customers were paying by the hour. As you can imagine, they preferred a quick worker! The other downside was that friends wanted to pay me with thanks and not cash.

I once spent the whole day repairing a carburettor on Paul's Vespa, my neighbour's boyfriend. I got it working for him and he said he would pay me later rather than when he collected his bike. That evening, I was at the Sheepscar Working Men's Club with my grandad and Uncle Dennis, when Paul's father asked if Paul had paid me for the work I'd done.

I told him not yet, but he had said he was going to pay me later. Five minutes later Paul came over and gave me £1. I was so upset. Did he really value all those hours at £1? A pint of Coke would have been less insulting. I hadn't wanted to do the job in the first place and only did it because he was the boyfriend of my next-door neighbour. I didn't say anything at the time, but I was really upset and bothered by the lack of value he placed on my work. He just didn't appreciate all the effort, skill and time I'd put into the repair. Not even to mention the years of college education I'd had to go through to give me the necessary skills.

On another occasion a local guy came to the house and asked if I could put his motorbike gearbox and crank cases back together. He had striped the engine and couldn't rebuild it.

I saw a plastic washing up basin full of engine parts, I took a good look asked if all the bits were there. He told me that they were, he also said he had spent days trying to put it back together. I told him to bring it to the house and I'd sort it for him. The bike engine owner was also called Steven. He brought the engine to my house and I started rebuilding it.

Dave Clark Five sang a song called *"Bits And Pieces"* and that was an accurate description of his motorbike engine and gearbox.

A few hours later I went down to Steve's, he looked worried.

"What's wrong," he asked, *"is it too bad?"*

"No" I said, *"it's done."*

"It can't be done" he replied.

I smiled *"Come up and see, it's done."*

Whilst I didn't get paid again for my time, this was different, he was genuinely grateful so that was payment enough. To be honest, I'd enjoyed doing it, it was slightly challenging, and I enjoyed fixing it and making it whole again.

In the end I stopped working on other people's cars and

motorbikes because they just wouldn't pay. I decided to work for myself by rebuilding motorbikes. It was a personal passion of mine. Despite the accident, I never lost my love for them. I rebuilt everything from trail bikes to high powered road legal racing bikes. I could never road test them though, so a friend of mine would take them out on the road when they were finished.

I rebuilt a lovely Suzuki TS100. I'd spent hours restoring it. It truly was beautiful. I used to keep track of all expenses in an A5 diary, I checked my records when it eventually sold, and I'd made a miserly £20 profit! To be fair the most profit I ever made on a motorbike was the sale of a Yamaha RD350LC. Again, hours of my time had been spent on totally rebuilding that beautiful road rocket. It was a masterpiece of engineering and in the 80's one of the most desirable road racing motorbikes and worth a small fortune today. My profit was £50. It just wasn't worth all the effort I was putting in. I used to buy stock from the Bradford Motorcycle Auctions but the stock from there was very difficult to make a profit on.

I also started making my own tools. As you can imagine, it's quite fiddly working on engines with only one arm. This meant that I needed to get ingenious and make or adapt my own equipment. I could probably write an entire book detailing the inventions and the way I crafted tools. That was all part of the thrill though, it added to the problem solving, that I enjoyed so much.

I finally came to the realisation that motorbikes and cars were never going to make me any money. Whilst I loved what I did and knew that I was good at it, this wasn't making me a living. On top of that my hand would be constantly dirty because washing it one handed was really difficult, in fact near on impossible, I could never get it clean enough. My fingernails were always dirty, and it made me look like a tramp. What woman would want that dirty hand touching her or holding her? I certainly wouldn't!

Letting go of motorbikes must have been one of the most painful things I ever experienced, they were my life after all and had been my salvation during the years of horrendous bullying. It would prove more difficult than I thought though, the realisation that I would never ride again was too much to handle.

My whole life had changed and the one thing that kept me going, through the hardest times of my life, had now been taken away from me. How would I keep going? I could never replace my motorbike or that's what it felt like. Not only had my first love been taken from me, but so had all of my job opportunities and dreams I had of work. The great jobs I had lined up and the bright future that lay ahead of me.

All the expectations of a teenager had been cruelly taken from me. It was obvious for others to see I had lost an arm, but it was not so easy for them to see I had lost much more. I had lost my independence, my future and my dreams. How could I continue without visions and desires? Without them I was an empty shell, and now I was an unemployable empty shell. I was so worried about my future, what would I do now for work?

One thing was for certain I had to change my way of thinking and how I would approach every aspect of my life. Nothing could be taken for granted ever again. The tasks that lay ahead were momentous.

Simple tasks to others would feel impossible to me. I missed what I had previously taken for granted, things that

I loved doing would be forever lost. One day I went to the local fish and chip shop with my mate. I'd bought my fish and chips and soon realised I couldn't walk home and eat my lovely hot supper. I hadn't even realised I couldn't feed myself while holding my fish and chips. How stupid I felt, my mate was eating his meal and said why aren't you eating Steve, to which I replied I can't. I didn't have a spare hand or arm to pick my food up with. I needed to find somewhere to sit down, but there was nowhere. I eventually found a wall to sit on, but by then my meal had gone cold. Still, I was determined to eat my meal outdoors. I rested my newspaper wrapped meal on my lap and ate my fish and chips. However, it wasn't the same as walking home and eating at the same time, also my lap was now soaked with a mixture of cooking oil, salt and vinegar. I smelt like a fish and chip shop and looked like I'd wet myself. I would never enjoy a walk home with my fish and chips again.

My workshop in the back garden was a home-made shed, it was a frame I had made draped in transparent plastic sheeting to keep the rain out but let the light in. I spent hours and hours in there prior to my accident.

But whilst great for the projects I liked doing, it hadn't really been ideal for my ever-increasing business ideas. I'd needed something bigger and better. This eventually arrived, it was a twelve foot by eight foot wooden shed my mum's chap had built for me, it was perfect and I'd spent my life in there, it was full, from floor to ceiling with motorbikes and spares, and so many tools I'd acquired over the years. However, with the decision made that being a mechanic wasn't the money maker I had hoped. I rang a motorbike spares shop that was in Holbeck, Leeds, to ask if they would consider buying my complete stock of spares.

They were of course very interested and snapped up everything for a pitiful £100, but I wanted the space for my new interest… Jukeboxes, slot machines and video games.

I didn't want to change my life, but it didn't matter what I wanted because my life had been changed regardless! Change is seldom expected but it's how we deal with that change that will define us.

One thing was for certain, I would need to find another passion and try and achieve new goals, whether I would ever be able to reach them or not. The main thing was to have something to aim for, I would set my goals really high and push myself more than was necessary, it would take a lot of time to master any new skills, but all I had was time. I had no skill with my left arm, I had no skills at all really. I had always worked with both of my arms and I was right-handed. Mentally I still am.

Having said all this I wasn't depressed, I was happy. Happy to be alive and given a second chance. Throughout the post-accident journey, I had an overwhelming feeling of gratitude, thanks for being given a second chance at life, albeit now, with one arm but I was so happy to still be alive, that I would not waste the opportunity I had been given. Yes, things were going to be difficult, but in a strange way I was looking forward to having to learn new skills and the challenges that lay ahead intrigued me.

I realised I needed to become a problem solver and I had to become one quickly. I didn't have the luxury of waiting for my right arm to mend, the same way as a broken arm would. My right arm would never mend, it would never grow back that would be science fiction, all I could do was try my best and not worry about failure. This after all was inevitable, but I would never perceive it as failure, it was just another lesson in life.

I realised later in life that failure does not exist, just different degrees of success.

Chapter 15
Learning To Drive

I'd taken my first driving lesson at the age of 18 in my mum's chap's manual Vauxhall Viva, at Tockwith disused airfield. It was an 'N' registration that was a 1974-year suffix. This was the year the Soviet car maker Lada began selling cars in the UK, the 19th Eurovision Song Contest was held at the Brighton Dome, Jon Pertwee left the TV show Dr Who after his final episode *"Planet of the Spiders"* and I'd been trying to drive Brian's Vauxhall, and not doing a great job with it at first. I'd stalled a few times but eventually got the knack of it. I enjoyed driving his car although I remember distinctly thinking that I'd love an automatic, because it would be much easier plus they were associated with high quality/luxurious cars, the car I dreamt of owning was a Daimler Sovereign or the Jaguar XJ6. But I was a million miles away from owning one of those cars. I was just trying to survive the challenge of clutch control.

Brian had paid for an hours use of Tockwith's driver training grounds on the old airfield and I'd learnt to stop, start, circumvent cones and generally handle the car. It was over really quickly and I'd enjoyed the experience, I was waiting excitedly for my next lesson with Brian. That next lesson never came though, because the accident that changed my life, put a stop to it.

I didn't give up on my dream to drive it was just put on

the shelf, on hold until I was well enough and confident enough to give it another go, albeit now with only one arm. I would now have to drive an automatic, the strange thing was, I now didn't want an automatic or maybe I should say I only wanted to drive a manual, because I thought I had to drive an automatic. When options are taken away from us, it's amazing how hard we fight to get those options back.

I wasn't really sure how to approach the whole task of getting driving lessons. Driving instructors with automatic cars were almost non-existent, but I found a guy in Wakefield, the lessons were aimed predominantly at female drivers or that was what I was told when he answered the phone the day I called to enquire. I wasn't really convinced the time was right to start my lessons, but the instructor offered me a free trial to see if I liked it and if I could do it.

I loved it, so, I started my driving lessons with him. The only issue was that he was Wakefield based so my lessons were always taken there. I'd drive there from Leeds, do all my training in the area, before picking up the next learner who would then bring me back to Leeds as part of their lesson. When it came time for my test, I knew the streets of Wakefield better than the streets of Leeds, so, it was logical to take my driving test there.

I was quite worried about taking my test. The indicator lever on the car I drove was on the wrong side for a left-handed person, which I was now forced to be. The instructor had fabricated a piece of metal bent it around the steering column so I could operate it from the left side, he had attached it as an extension to the indicator lever on the right with Gaffer Tape. It was a crude device to say the least. It worked intermittently at best so the only way I could confidently operate the indicator was to put my hand between the spaces in the steering wheel and directly operate the right-hand indicator lever. The problem was, the instructor wasn't sure the examiner would accept that and I could fail before I even started. The uncertainty was driving me crazy and adding to the tension that was building inside me like a volcano ready to erupt. The instructor said try it, if you fail, we'll rethink the indicator issue.

The day of the examination arrived. Wakefield waiting time was shorter than Leeds and I really didn't want to take my test in Leeds anyway. The one occasion I had taken a lesson in Leeds, a friend had seen me and shouted *"Steve, Steve, go on Steve"* he was encouraging me, bless him, but it totally put me off so I didn't want to risk that during my test.

I sat in the driver training centre waiting for the examiner for what felt like an eternity, it was only 10 minutes but it certainly felt longer, my instructor had pre-warned the examiner I only had one arm so that he wouldn't be shocked when he met me. He was a stern looking character who told me not to speak to him unless to answer his questions. There would be no friendly banter that I was used to with my instructor and there was an air of tension.

The words of my instructor echoed in my head *"watch your speed"* as did the words of The Madness song, *"Driving in My Car"*. The exam started well until the examiner said I'd like you to reverse around this corner. I was reversing doing all the correct checks when all of a sudden, I felt something strange.

A light thud and the back of the car shuddered slightly. Oh no I thought, what have I done? Have I hit the curb or dropped down a gutter? Totally devastated and convinced I'd hit the curd and just failed my exam, I stopped the car, rolled the car forwards slightly then continued my reversing manoeuvre. The rest of the exam was a doddle because I had totally relaxed, believing I'd already failed in the first 10 minutes of the exam. When we returned to the testing station, the examiner got his book of highway code signs and question out and proceeded to ask me to identify signs and answers questions on breaking distances, which I'd memorised. At the end expecting him to say I'm sorry Steven you've failed because of the curb issue or because of my indicating method, he said *"I'm very pleased to tell you, you've passed Steven"* That was my very first victory as a one armed man. I was 19, it was 1983, the same year that wearing a seatbelt in the front seat became mandatory and I had a grin from ear to ear while telling my instructor I'd passed.

"Brilliant" he said, *"I thought you would. You drive us back."* he said.

Strange, I can't remember my instructors name, he gave me so much. He gave me my independence and he gave me my first ever victory.

When I announced to my friends I had passed, they said
"Were you given special treatment? Did they go easy on you?"

They thought I'd had an easier test or somehow, I had been given favours by the examiner. I guess they couldn't believe I'd passed first time when it had taken them multiple attempts and I'd done it with one arm. They didn't however, want to get in the car with me when I drove, I guess they were worried or a little scared but didn't want to admit it.

The lesson I learnt was when everything seems to have gone wrong, keep calm and keep going. Treat every perceived setback as character building and remember the show must go on.

Chapter 16
The Wheel Came Off

I'd just passed my driving test and wanted to buy a car. The only problem was I didn't have much money and the only car that was within my reach was a cheap, second hand Mini 1000. I went along to look at the Mini that had been advertised in the local paper *"The Yorkshire Evening Post"* It looked great, but I made a big mistake, I went to view it when it was raining. The golden rule of thumb is never buy a car you view in the rain. Why? you might ask. It's because they look their best in the rain, all lovely and shiny. But I didn't know this at the time and I bought the car.

When I got it home and started to properly inspect it, I soon became aware that I'd bought the wrong one. All the floor pan and outer sills were rotten and had been stuck together with roofing felt and tar. There was no way this car would go through its MOT. It drove well though and the engine and gearbox were flawless, excuse the pun! There was no other option but to look for another Mini 1000 that had a good body shell and a bad engine. After looking for a short time I found one in the local scrap yard. It was complete with sound bodywork but a damaged non running engine. It was perfect, just what I had been looking for. I bought it there and then.

I was about to embark on a mammoth job, well, a mammoth job at least for a one armed teenager. Surprisingly I wasn't at all phased or daunted by the task that lay ahead. I was more excited at the prospect of the major car surgery I was about to perform. I was going to be a like a surgeon doing a heart and lung transplant, except I would be transplanting an engine, automatic gearbox and all the ancillary connectors and controls.

I hired an engine hoist from my local tool hire shop and the major surgery began. It was a long operation, possibly longer than normal because I was overcoming obstacles on an hourly basis. How could I hold a nut while trying to loosen the bolt? The nut simply spun and I didn't have another arm or hand to stop it. This is where I had to get my inventive juices flowing. Aha! I thought, what I need is a right hand or something that can do the same. In fact, the solution was much simpler than I thought. A pair of molegrips held the nut, I would then lodge the molegrips against a fixed object and that would resolve the problem. It did but I had to come up with so many other devices that the job took a whole week, when it should have only taken a couple of days.

This was the golden age of inspiration and innovation for me, having only just lost my arm, everything needed to be adapted or I had to create a tool for a specific job. This was the point where my creativity in engineering was really put to the test and I was able to begin building my own specific toolbox.

When it was finished it worked like a dream. I'd done it. I'd built my own car! There was only one thing left to do, take it for a test drive to make sure everything was working correctly. It drove like a dream. It moved up and down it's gears as it should, the kick down worked, brakes and accelerator worked correctly, steering functioned perfectly. I was happy and returning home, driving up a steepish hill in Leeds called Potternewton Lane, as I operated the kick down to drop into a lower gear, my nearside front wheel came off. My car hit the ground hard and my wheel went hurtling down the road or should I say *"up"* the remaining part of the hill at 40 miles per hour. It was like a Keystone Cop moment. I jumped out of my car and ran after the wheel. I eventually caught up with it and carried it back to my car and refit it. I had done major surgery to my car, but I had forgotten to tighten the left side front wheel nuts sufficiently.

I leant a very important lesson that day, one I would never forget. The Devil is in the detail. Be a perfectionist every time, double and triple check everything and... Always check your nuts!

Chapter 17
Jukeboxes

As a young boy I had spent hours trying to design a mechanism for a jukebox or what at least I thought would be a jukebox. A mechanism that would auto change records at the press of a button. CDs and digital music didn't exist, well to be more accurate CDs did exist because they were invented in 1965 by an American inventor called James Russell, but they wouldn't become popular until the 80's.

The history of the jukebox dates back to 1890, yet the jukebox as we know it today didn't become popular until the 1930's in the midst of the American great depression. Everyone knows the name Wurlitzer, but there were in fact four major jukebox manufacturers all competing with each other.

The three manufacturers that are less well known to the none jukebox enthusiast are: Rock-ola, Ami and Seeburg, I had a dream to own the best of every model. An aspiration that I didn't even realise had been implanted in my mind from the moment I saw the old jukebox in the greasy café, but an aspiration I would pursue. My life now had become one of dreams, but would I ever bring them to fruition? Only time would tell.

I didn't know a great deal about jukeboxes if anything, but like my time in the old cafe, I was drawn to them. I had asked my mate Mark to look out for one for me because he worked buying and selling antique furniture and reclaimed timber and was likely to come across one in the course of his work.

One particular day Mark was stripping out the timber from an old mill in Halifax, prior to demolition. He rang me to say, he'd found an old jukebox in the mill. He'd asked the owner of the mill if the jukebox was for sale and had been told that he wanted £100 for it. I went to look the next day, Mark took me over as I couldn't yet drive.

When we got to the filthy run-down old mill, Mark told me to be careful where I walked and to follow him. It was a dangerous place; one false step and you could fall through the holes in the floor where the demolition team had removed the floor boards. In a dusty corner was a tarpaulin with a big rectangular shaped object beneath it. I felt like a kid at Christmas, it was so exciting and maybe the first step towards something new. I didn't know what model it was anyway, but I would know if I liked the look of it. I can remember that moment so clearly, the air was full of dust, there were creaks of structural weakness all around and the sound of men shouting over the noise of heavy machinery. The moment is etched in my mind forever.

When the tarpaulin was removed, there was an old chrome jukebox underneath, it resembled the one from that old café, it was as though I'd been primed for it. I told Mark without thinking, I'd have it.

I felt that it was meant to be. I had saved the £100 that I'd received from the sale of my motorbike parts and I gave it to Mark, he said he would bring the jukebox over to my house later that week.

As promised, he brought it over and I was ecstatic, but realised suddenly I didn't know a thing about jukeboxes and couldn't get it to work. There was a large amusement machine company in Leeds, called Dransfields. I rang them and spoke to a jukebox engineer called Norman. He was a Seeburg specialist who had been trained by the Seeburg factory in Michigan, Illinois, and was recognised as an industry expert.

Norman came to my house to repair the jukebox. He replaced a valve and got it working, he knew exactly what to do, it cost me £5 to repair. Norman said it was a good model, a Seeburg KD200, but he also told me a major part of the jukebox was missing.

This unknown to me at the time was the start of a lifelong friendship with Norman who became my mentor, teacher, technical advisor and friend. His knowledge was vast, he knew so much about jukeboxes, he was an encyclopaedia of all things jukebox. Sadly, many years later he died taking all that knowledge with him. It seems such a shame that his knowledge could not have been recorded in some way for future generations.

I was upset that it wasn't complete and frustrated that I didn't know how to fix it. This showed me that if I wanted to make a career out of repairing and rebuilding these machines, then I had a lot to learn…

I rang a company in London called the London Jukebox Company, Ironically the first record I played on that jukebox was *"London's Calling"* by The Clash, although London didn't call me, I called them. The owner said he had the missing parts to make the jukebox complete, he wasn't selling the parts, but he would give me £200 for the jukebox. Wow! I thought that was a quick £95 profit, so I said yes to his offer. A delivery guy came to collect it and bounced it down the 3 steps from my back door. I was amazed that the delivery guy took no care whatsoever. When I told him to be careful, as I wanted it to work when it got to London, the delivery guy said it wasn't important, the London Jukebox Company would sort everything out or use it for spares. I suppose it shouldn't have mattered to me because it was the quickest £95 I'd ever made, it still rankled though as I don't like to see any machine poorly treated, let alone one I've invested time, energy and money in!

What a difference though in comparison to my time working on cars and bikes. Having only ever made £50 after hours and hours of work, I knew then that I could better use my skills elsewhere. I was going to be a jukebox engineer instead.

The lesson I learnt was some people will gladly share their knowledge and experience if you ask and be happy to see you succeed, Norman was one of those men for me.

Chapter 18
Grandma To The Rescue

It was 1984, Arthur Scargill was leading a year-long miner's strike that was crippling the country, the Apple Macintosh computer had just been released on the market and I was celebrating the success of my first jukebox purchase and sale. I was hungry for more, I wanted more of everything, more jukeboxes, more knowledge and more money. The next jukebox I found was a Rock-ola model 453. The seller also had a fruit machine that looked fantastic, I just had to have them both. The two machines cost me everything I had, plus a bit more, £280 for the pair and I asked a mate of mine to collect them for me.

I can recall a real sense of excitement when I got them home. I turned the fruit machine on and immediately, there was a bang and a puff of smoke! Had I made a mistake? I was starting to think so when I realised later that the juke-box was only playing A sides and wouldn't play B sides. I knew that I needed help again.

This time I needed both a fruit machine and a jukebox engineer. I only knew one person and that was Norman, so I rang him. He said I needed a Rock-ola jukebox specialist and gave me the telephone number of Terry a specialist Rock-ola jukebox engineer who also worked at Dransfields.

Terry came round and I watched very carefully as he stripped the jukebox and cleaned a circuit board with

Brasso. He made a long-winded affair of what seemed to be a simple task. One that cost me £40, but Terry did solve the none playing B side issue, he also said he'd take the fruit machine circuit board into his work for a colleague to look at, that repair cost me another £15. The fruit machine engineer was called Paul Lockwood, little did I know he was to become another life-long friend and fellow jukebox enthusiast.

I was now seriously broke, but my two machines were working fully. The fruit machine had short circuited because when we transported it, we had laid it down on its back in the van and some of the tokens had come loose and had become trapped behind the circuit board, it was my own fault and I couldn't blame the seller. These are lessons that you learn along the way, never to be repeated.

I knew that I needed to learn to repair these jukeboxes to make it more cost effective but how would I learn? There were no classes that taught jukebox repairs and technology, fortunately I had a good understanding of mechanical equipment due to my mechanics course. I was looking for an opportunity when I saw a jukebox for sale in The Autotrader, they used to allow non-vehicle related adverts back in the 80's. The advert was for a Seeburg Mustang jukebox, it said *"not working"* but it was cheap, the guy had four for sale at £50 each.

I thought that this was my chance to learn how to repair them. The only problem was, I now had no money. I wanted to buy one of them to see if I could repair it but couldn't afford it. I would have asked Mum, but she had no money and was struggling to look after me now that I was unemployable. I felt awful and at that time as though I was a burden on her. I know she never felt this way, never blamed me for making things harder at home, after all it had been a silly accident. I do wish Mr McGill had been a little clearer with his warning though, or even if he had, would I want to change it?

Although I was doing my best to create a living for myself, it still bothered me that I couldn't get a job and employers would unashamedly discriminate. It was prior to the disability discrimination act of 1995 and I couldn't claim benefits because I hadn't paid into the system. Many people thought I had received compensation for the accident, but I didn't receive a penny. I remember thinking I wish I had lost my arm for a purpose like fighting for my country, it was the time of the Falklands war after all.

Don't get me wrong, I didn't want to go to war, it just seemed a waste to have lost an arm for no good reason, just playing around on my motorbike. I did think for a brief moment that I may have been able to get compensation from something called the Motor Insurers Bureau, which basically covered uninsured accidents on public highways.

My solicitor at the time said we'll get you £50,000 which would be a lot more by today's standards (2021) approximately £175,000. I was scared and didn't want it, I thought it would change me and my life. I told Mum that I would no longer know if my friends were true or just fairweather friends due to my sudden wealth.

Mum said not to be daft, if I had a chance of £50,000, I should take it. The option to accept however, never came to fruition because the land I was on, when I had my accident, was the Prince Philips playing fields and it was classed as common land not a public highway.

All I was left with was suing the guy who had caused the accident. I wasn't too keen on that idea. It was an accident after all and not intentional. Saying that, I had to consider the option, the drawback was the other rider didn't have motor insurance even though he was using his bike on the roads, so I couldn't make a claim on his insurance, he was also unemployed, so the chances of getting any money from him was looking remote. Even if I won a court case, how would he pay me - 50p a week for the rest of his or my life? It just wasn't worth it.

Better to forgive and move on with my life. I imagine you may think that it's hindsight speaking there, but that's exactly how I felt at the time. Would holding on to the past bring my arm back or make people give me a job? No!

It was to be a life of adventure and learning, but I wasn't yet to know that, and my imminent challenge was to get £50.

This meant that the only person I knew that had money was my father who wasn't part of my life, but he was reasonably successful, as a roofing contractor. I rang him and as usual got his answering machine. I eventually got in touch with him and asked if I could borrow £50. I got the standard reply which was always *"no"!*

I know that I shouldn't have been so upset or disappointed, but I always was. His harsh reply to my request to borrow £50 was,

"You need to earn the money yourself to appreciate it, besides jukeboxes are a waste of money and won't earn you anything."

I can smile now at how wrong that statement would become.

How could I earn £50 and quickly? The jukebox wouldn't be available for long. I had no option but to ask my Grandma. She didn't have much money and was struggling to survive just like me, Mum and Tracy. The Flying Lizards sang the song *"Money, That's What I Want"* it lyrically shouted at me and reminded me that all I wanted to fulfil my dream was just £50.

Grandma worked for a market trader who sold leather shopping bags. She was a home machinist, working from a little outhouse built on the side of her council house, it was an outbuilding come porch with an industrial sewing machine, it was always cold and damp. Grandma came to my rescue without hesitation, the only proviso was, she would need the money back before her electricity bill was due as she had lent me her electricity money. Every week Grandma would put some money aside from her hard earned wages to pay for her utility bills. I was under pressure because it was really important that I fixed the jukebox and sold it to repay my *"Gangan"*

I went with my mate Danny to look at the jukeboxes and as soon as I saw them, I thought, *"I'm having one"*. I paid the £50 pounds and we loaded the jukebox into Danny's van. I was the proud owner of a jukebox that didn't work, but it wouldn't stay that way for long, I was pretty confident I could get it going.

I tinkered and tinkered, lubricated, checked connections were good and re-seated all the plugs, relays and valves. I cleaned all the wiper blade contacts and memory bank brass contacts with Brasso as I learnt from watching Terry. To my surprise, I got it working quicker than I could have imagined. I'm not sure whether it was just luck or my engineering skill, but it didn't matter, I'd got it working.

I advertised it two days later in the Yorkshire Evening Post and sold it the same week for £150. I went to

Grandma's and paid the £50 back. She was so pleased I'd earned some money and done as I said that we threw the money in the air while making silly yelping, yippying and yahoo noises. I was so grateful to her, and I know how lucky I am that my Grandparents were such amazing people.

When I look back, I realise that I should have treated her to something nice. She never would have expected it, but when I think of what she did for me and how without her help I wouldn't be where I am today, I feel a twinge inside and know that I could have shown her how much I appreciated her help but I suspect and very much hope that she knew.

The guy who had the jukebox had another three, originally, he had four all the same model. I rang him as soon as I'd sold the first one to tell him I'd have the others if he still had them, he only had two left, so I bought them both for £100 the profit I'd just made.

None of them worked when I got them but that wasn't to be for long. I did the same thing to the other two jukeboxes, one at a time and I got them working, repairing them started to become easier and I began recognising patterns in the problem-solving process.

I loved problem solving it taxed my brain and made me think outside of the box. I spent hours in my shed, come winter or summer, morning or night I would just keep working until I solved all the problems and got them going. I loved the smell of old things, that old musky smell mixed with an unmistakable smell of years of exposure to tobacco, spilt beer and greasy hands. More often than not people had scratched their names on the glass screens. I guess the girls had been testing their rings to make sure they were diamonds, I think that because there was no other way of scratching names on glass!

I advertised them in the Yorkshire evening post for sale at £150 each. It wasn't long before they sold. I took the money up to Grandma's house and we threw the money in the air again, it had become a bit of a ritual. I loved it, we were showered in money, my money, but all thanks to Gangan.

This began my love affair. On top of the satisfaction I got (and still get) from restoring these beautiful machines, I challenged myself to make new tools, design a robotic CNC router and recently I've designed parts on my 3-D printer. Without jukeboxes I would never have achieved my dreams to fly, to ride horses, to own property and to travel.

It only takes one person to believe in you to give you the confidence to believe in yourself.

Chapter 19
New Kid On The Block

It was the beginning of my love affair with all things mechanical. One arm bandits and other old slot machines were a love of mine too, anything old and interesting and I felt compelled to get it working and restore it to its former glory. I suppose that having lost my arm, I had to become good at problem solving, especially if I wanted to put my socks on, brush my teeth and cut my food. What I hadn't realised is that I was good at it, and I really enjoyed it so now it seemed I was searching out problems to solve, hence my addiction to old mechanical things that didn't work.

I wanted to get into the world of vintage jukeboxes, but it was a very niche market and to be successful I would need to be in the know and know the others and competition in the same field.

My bedroom was a small box room, but it was my small box room and I loved it. It was about ten by fifteen feet with a double window on the narrow side, on the other side was a door to the landing and a box about four feet by four feet and three feet high, it was part of the stairwell that provided head room when walking down the stairs, but on top I had a built in wardrobe or junk cupboard really. On the side that was near the door I had my little office and notice board.

I had a red wall phone with all the telephone numbers of other jukebox dealers and the collectors I had spoken to on the phone. If I met anyone, I would always ask them if they knew any other dealers or collectors. I would then call them and have a chat. I was building up my contact database, before databases existed.

A lot of the time I wouldn't be taken seriously by the dealers because I was so young, I was still only 19, and when they found out I only had one arm they wrote me off all together. However, I wouldn't give in and I would still call them until they took me seriously. Eventually, when I started spending cash or selling and doing deals with them, they started to realise I was serious and started to treat me differently, but it took a long time to gain any respect as a serious jukebox collector / dealer.

Jukeboxes are my passion and have been so for the majority of my life, I still deal and restore in jukeboxes today at the age of 56. They are the one constant that have kept me sane and given me purpose. I've met some incredible people, those I've admired and even wished had been my father due to their drive, attitude to life and success but, not everyone in the jukebox world was nice.

I met a jukebox company owner who was someone I had on my contacts list, his shop wasn't very big and when I walked through the front door there was a main showroom. It wasn't a flashy place, interesting, but not a high-quality joint, more like a pub tap room. The strong smell of WD-40 lingered in the air. There was a back room that was a kitchen come workshop, where I saw a guy working on some jukeboxes. I introduced myself *"I've come to buy a stand that I'd called about earlier"* I said.

In his main showroom he had a jukebox that was the same as one I had just bought, only half an hour previously. I asked how much he was selling his for, but he was very shady and wouldn't tell me. I told him I'd just bought one of the same model and he asked how much I had paid for it, in retrospect I should have been shady back with him but I was friendly, innocent and a very open guy, so I told him I'd paid £35 for it.

He was suddenly very interested, asking a lot of questions like what condition it was in. I told him it was in very good condition but not fully working. He asked where the jukebox was, and I replied it was in the back of the van. He asked to look at it, I thought nothing about it and said he could. I could tell by the expression on his face he liked it.

He said, *"I'll give you £500 for it."*

I really didn't want to sell my new purchase, I wanted to get it going and enjoy for a while, so I told him it wasn't for sale. He wasn't happy with my reply and said I'd be making a good profit without having to do any work, but I was adamant that I didn't want to sell it. This is where it started to get weird, he proceeded to lecture me about restoring jukeboxes, telling me it would take more than spaying WD-40 on it, strange really as his workshop smelt very strongly of WD-40! Incidentally WD-40 was invented in 1953 around the same time my newly purchased jukebox was made. WD-40 was created by the fledgling Rocket Chemical Company and its name stands for Water Displacement 40th formula.

I was very firm despite his attitude. I didn't want to sell, but I was still very polite. I was shocked by his next remark; I really didn't expect what he said next.

"Can you do me a favour?" he said

"Yes, what?"

"Fuck-off and never come to my shop again"

I was so upset by what he said, it affected me all day it

ruined what had been a great day of adventure, meeting people and buying. That was the start and the end of any potential association with him and the passing years would prove what a strange person he was. It was certain we would never be friends nor colleagues despite working in the same industry.

Over the years he would constantly complain to the other dealers that I was responsible for him not selling his jukeboxes and that I was damaging his business. He had been the only Yorkshire based dealer and that had given him the edge, but that had changed now I was on the scene. I was Leeds based while he was in Sheffield, so our customer base was different, he was also established while I was just the new kid on the block. He had no need to see me as a threat, he did though, which I guess in a way was a compliment.

"Two Tribes" by Frankie goes to Hollywood was in the charts at the time and came to describe our hostile relationship to a T.

The lesson I learnt on that day was compliments come in all shapes and sizes and aren't always obvious.

Chapter 20
Ireland

I'd only just started my new business, when I met a big dealer from down south who used to travel the country buying old slot machines and one arm bandits. His name was Jim Collins. His main business was buying vintage American one arm bandits in the UK and Ireland and selling them back to the US.

Incidentally, One Arm Bandit is the nickname given to the old-style mechanical slot machines, with one arm on the side and a left arm at that, just like me. For many years these slots were found in almost every corner of the world, relieving unwary victims of their money! Hence the name.

The first one arm bandit was invented by Charles Fey a German immigrant living in San Francisco 1895, 87 years later people would be nicknaming me the one arm bandit.

Prior to meeting Jim, I had made a great contact with a guy called Joe Stringer. I instantly got on with Joe, he was a lovely man who knew a lot about jukeboxes and old one arm bandits. He owned an electrical store in Wickersley, near Worksop, Stringers of Wickensley, it was a fantastic electrical shop and showroom in the town centre that was akin to the modern-day Curry's. I spent some wonderful, magical days with Joe both at his store, his house and travelling to some slot machine auctions. Joe treated me like a son which I often wished I had been. I respected and admired him for all the amazing things he had achieved. His drive and ambition were unstoppable. He built his own house, dug out lakes with his own digger and dumper truck and stocked them with fish. He bought an old water mill that was adjacent to his land, it came with acres of forest land that could be seen for miles and miles. Every time I visited Joe; I would look in the distance at the hills until I saw Joe's private forest. I'd always approach from Worksop to Lindrick Dale, the name of the sleepy hollow where Joe lived with his wife Jean. He had also bought a stately home that had four wings which created a courtyard that had an arched entrance to the front wing. Joe was rebuilding the property while running all his other interests. What an impressive man he was.

One day I got a call from Jim, he had found a stash of vintage jukeboxes in Ireland that were up for sale as a lot, but being the new kid on the block with no financial backing, it was out of my league, but the stash was too good to be missed. I knew who would be interested though and I spoke to Joe about them and put the two in touch with each other.

Joe bought many of the machines, and along with a friend of his we travelled to Ireland to a place called Bellcara, in county Mayo, where we met up with Jim. What an amazing place! It was an old amusement arcade smelling of damp and decay, with plaster falling off the walls and slot machines and jukeboxes from the 1950's were everywhere, covered in dust. It was an historic treasure trove from years gone by, it looked like someone had closed the doors to the business and simply forgot about the treasures that lay inside.

I did many trips to Ireland with Jim; he would cover all the cost of travel because he wanted the company. I was constantly advertising for jukeboxes and also 'one arm bandits wanted'. Jim wasn't interested in jukeboxes just one arm bandits and those I couldn't afford, I would pass onto Jim. He of course would make the profit and I would get to travel free. It worked out really well for both of us and I got to spend time in that lovely country. During the 80's Ireland was quiet and tranquil, although, Northern Ireland was a scary place to be. Our route would always be from Stranraer in Scotland then by ferry to Larne. Jim said we need to by-pass Belfast, then get straight onto the M1 direct to Dublin as we sang the unofficial Irish national anthem on the way. In Dublin's Fair city where the girls are so pretty, I first set my eyes on sweet Molly Malone.

We travelled to Ireland seven times in one year, buying slot machines. On one occasion we went to a fairground Travellers' site, Jim went into an old timber-built building to view some old slot machines. From the outside Planks were rotten and falling off in places, there were holes everywhere, vines were intertwined with timber, and in fact the vines seemed to be holding the whole structure together; the roof had buckled under the weight of the moss that had collected over the years; it was a miracle the building was still standing, but it was and Jim walked in with a grey haired Traveller who also looked like he had seen better days.

They were gone for quite a while and I was sat in the car waiting, it was an old Volvo Estate, the preferred choice of the antique dealer because it gave comfort and had the advantage of converting to a spacious vehicle akin to a commercial transit van. After around 40 minutes, Jim emerged and I could tell he was excited, he got in the car and said

"It's a gold mine in there, lots of great one arm bandits including some Mills War Eagles, Jennings Governors, and a rare Cailee!"

He was over the moon and had arranged to collect them at a later date. We continued our journey with increased enthusiasm, this time towards Cork. A place I had always wanted to visit because my great grandma was originally from there, her name was Bridget Keeley. The Irish welcomed us with open arms, I'd never experienced such hospitality and such a warm and friendly nation, they couldn't do enough for us.

Jim was a big guy who liked his food, I'd say he was over 6 feet tall and over 20 stone in weight, with shortish dark hair and a full beard that was slightly greyed. He'd been a schoolteacher for many years before becoming self-employed. He had an advertisement that ran on a weekly basis in the World's Fair magazine, a weekly magazine dedicated to the amusement machine and fairground industry, the advert was paid for by an American associate of Jim's. Jim would buy up all the vintage slot machines he could find and ship them back to the states where they had originated from. Because he needed a mobile phone so he could conduct his business while on the road Jim had a state-of-the-art Motorola car phone system that was also portable, when I say portable you certainly needed a strong arm to carry it any distance! He enjoyed showing it off as it was something new that not many people had.

I can recall one time we were eating our food in a Chinese restaurant, whilst on one of our trips. Jim decided he wanted a beer, but with no members of staff to catch the eye of, Jim decided to call the restaurant, their number was on their menu. Jim rang them to order a beer, we were laughing during the phone call as we ordered a beer not for takeaway but for table number 8. Luckily the staff found it funny too as that had never happened to them before! Jim was a bit of a show-off, but I liked that about him, he was an imposing figure with confidence and likeability.

I was making friends and contacts within the amusement industry, but still struggled outside of those within my circle. Dealers and collectors wouldn't take me seriously because I was just a kid to them, one who had no money and perceived as a threat or a young upstart by others. Nevertheless, I carried on, I was determined these machines would earn me some money and if not, I would enjoy repairing them, getting them going and restoring them to their former glory.

I learnt the hard way that I would only ever succeed if I persevered and a handful of good people is all you need to help you through.

Chapter 21
The Walls Came Tumbling Down

I continued my search for vintage machines by placing advertisements in the Yorkshire Evening Post and the Bradford Telegraph and Argos, I would buy anything interesting. Like many people starting a new interest, I experienced a lot of beginner's luck, and made some very good purchases.

One day I rang the Yorkshire Evening Post to place an ad for, *"Old jukebox wanted, any condition, good price paid"*. The girl who took my call said her boyfriend had an old jukebox in their cellar and she wanted it gone, was I interested in it? I asked her all of the standard questions that would indicate to me whether the jukebox was from the 1940's, 50's or 60's. She replied she wasn't sure, but she would get her boyfriend to call me.

That same evening her boyfriend called, it was a visual display type of jukebox, meaning you could see the records playing when it was working, it was in the cellar just as the girl on the phone had said. He wasn't sure if it worked, but he wanted £80 for it. I arranged to go and take a look.

When my friend and I got there, it was a monster of a machine, when I say monster it was the biggest jukebox I'd ever seen, but it was beautiful. It was dirty and rusty, with paint flaking off and broken parts, but the potential was obvious. I didn't know then it was an Ami J200 from 1957, made in the same year that the Soviet Union (USSR) launched Sputnik 1. I wanted it nevertheless and told the chap I'd have it.

However, the couple had just spent a lot of money on doing up their cellar and had built a partition wall near the only exit they had, and the jukebox simply wouldn't fit through the doorway. I thought that's the end of that, there's no way I'll be able to get it out.

I was stunned when the guy said to me

"It's got to go, my girlfriend hates it"

and with that picked up a crowbar and broke down the new partition wall! He pulled and tore at it until the jukebox would eventually fit through the opening.

I wasn't even going to barter with the guy, how could I? The wall he had damaged surely must have cost more than the £80 he wanted for the jukebox!

We eventually got it out into the back yard and lifted it up a flight of 4 or 5 stairs to get it into my mate's van. What a job!

I looked back down the steps and into the cellar to see the devastation left behind us. 'The Walls Came Tumbling Down' by the Style Council came to mind as I visualised the words of that song and gazed on the chaos we had caused. The partition wall was completely damaged, there was dust in the air and an enormous hole in the plasterboard wall. Incredibly the guy was very happy to have gotten rid of the jukebox and I was super happy to have acquired my new project. I did wonder if his girlfriend was happy when she saw what we'd done.

I set about restoring it, the chrome wasn't too bad and after I used my fine wire wool on all the brightwork, it gleamed as if it had been cared for and carefully looked after. The body however was a different matter, the jukebox looked like someone had hand painted the cabinet at night wearing sunglasses! The paint was everywhere it shouldn't have been, but after I stripped all the metal work off and prepped the wood, I repainted it and it looked wonderful. It looked as though I had spent £1000 on restoring it, but in fact it had only cost me the price of the wire wool and the paint, but it had taken its toll in hours. I didn't have a compressor or spraying equipment, so I had to use a mini-roller, but it did a great job.

I had painted the cabinet in a satin black, the jukebox looked really classy, but it was all *"fur coat and no knickers"*. It looked great but it didn't work. I spent hours on trying to get it working but it had a really strange problem. I'd managed to get it almost working, it sounded fabulous when I manually made it play a record, but it would not select through the normal process. Every time I made a selection it made a tommy-gun action and selected twenty or so selections one after another, ding, ding, ding, went the hammer that banged in a selection pin. Got to mention here that ding ding ding, clang clang clang reminds me of the *"Trolley"* song by Judy Garland. I was pulling my hair out trying to find out why it was banging so many selection pins in, it should only have banged one in.

Ironically pulling my hair out wasn't far from the problem. I was so frustrated I got my magnifying glass out looking for anything out of the ordinary. Right at the last moment, just before I was going to give in for the day, I saw something. A really fine dog hair that was bridging two electrical contacts, the hair had been there a while and I'd sprayed some contact cleaner over those electrical contact only a few days before. Unknown to me the contact spray

113

was helping conduct electricity across the dog hair. I thought to myself this can't be the problem it's too minor an issue to cause such a big problem,

I got a fine piece of cardboard and used it to clear away the dog hair and re-tried the normal selection of a record. Hurray it worked! I couldn't believe it; a hair had caused all that.

The jukebox was amazing, it sounded like it had just come off of the production line and looked as though it had too. I really wanted to keep this jukebox, however, that would have made me a bad businessman, so it had to go up for sale. It had cost me £80 plus a maximum of £20 for the wire wool, paint, a few extra bits, the dog hair was free and courtesy of my lovely Alsatian dog Sheba. I sold the jukebox through an ad in the paper for £700.

The Yorkshire Evening Post was where I found it and where I sold it. This was the first jukebox I had sold for a decent amount and the start of my vintage jukebox business.

Another valuable lesson learnt was that persistence and perseverance pays off in the end and every problem has a solution.

Chapter 22
Showing My Stuff

I bought run down vintage jukeboxes and one arm bandits (not a pun!!) and restored them to their former glory. They started off as rusty old wrecks that hadn't worked for years. It was such a buzz and a sense of achievement to get them working and looking like new again. These jukeboxes and slot machines had been sat around idle for years broken-down and unused, most of them had been relegated to cellars, damp garages and outbuildings and some even left outdoors, open to the elements.

I never really earned much money; I was more of a collector than a dealer. If I had dealer status, I was a bad dealer because I didn't want to sell anything. I had spent way too much time and effort restoring these machines to ever make a profit from my time and energy, but I realised that these jukeboxes were getting heavier or maybe it was me just getting older and weaker, I was thirty-four by now and not getting any younger. It's weird looking back to realise that jukeboxes have been an integral part of my life from the age of 19 and still are today. I was looking for a new challenge and university was going to be it – this meant I needed more time for studying.

I had the intention of leaving jukeboxes behind me. However, I had built up a great collection of vintage juke-boxes and decided I would attend the annual jukebox show at Copthorne in the South of England, in an attempt to sell them before my studies really started.

At the Copthorne show I met a friendly chap called Roger. He'd seen one of my jukeboxes and was interested in it, although he was concerned it wasn't loud enough, but this was due to the background noise of the show, I explained to him. I offered to demonstrate it in his own house on my way home (it was actually out of my way but I didn't mind) when I installed it in his house, the first thing he said when I made a selection was, *"Oooh turn it down!"*, it was too loud, we played a song by Gene Pitney, '24 hours from Tulsa', although we were only 6 hours from Leeds. He bought it there and then, it covered my costs for the show, but more importantly it was the start of a friendship that continues to this day. Roger was another impressive businessman I was lucky enough to meet. He was the owner of a successful garden centre and plant nursery in Staines.

I only just covered my outgoings at the Copthorne event, having only sold the one jukebox. On reflection, I decided that I would have to change the way I thought and my sales tactics, I would try a jukebox show one more time. I just hoped I was right in my thinking. I decided I would attend the annual Jukebox Madness show, held at Ascot racecourse. I'd finished restoring another jukebox, so I still had a full complement of nine jukeboxes to take with me. My new attitude and sales tactic would be to display the price I ideally wanted then with some nice graphics shaped like a cloud I'd have the words *"If you like me but don't like my price, Make me an offer. You never know, I might accept"* My new idea was if the offer represented a profit, I would sell.

I learnt a lot at these shows, in particular the art of bartering and setting a realistic price. They were lessons that would serve me well for the rest of my life.

Men were better at bartering than women, sometimes women would talk me down by £10 or £50 but men would talk me down by £1000 and sometimes more. My idea was working, people were making offers and my stock was going quickly. I'm sure it helped that all my jukeboxes came with a three-month warranty.

By the end of the second day, I had sold all nine jukeboxes and bought one. The majority of people had paid cash, some had left deposits and wanted to pay the balance in a cheque, I had told them the only cheques I would accept would be building society cheques and I would have to be present to watch them get the cheque from their building society, it sounded a bit strange, but there had been a spate of fraudulent building society cheques passed in Leeds and people had lost some high value items, I certainly didn't want to join them.

I'd never seen so much money in my whole life. I had a cloth cash bag with £17,000 in and £2,000 worth of building society cheques. That one change of *"mindset"*, I don't like that word because it's what all those marketing gurus and professional speakers use but in layman's terms, I had just changed my way of thinking and of selling.

The downside was I didn't own a van and no company would rent to me, the fact I had one arm precluded me from their hire companies insurance, plus they didn't have automatics for which my driver's licence only allowed me to drive, so I had to rely on my dad . The show cost approximately £1500 in expenses, van hire, and my dad's fees.

Despite all the downsides, Ascot was a massive success,

one I would repeat the next three years in a row. I was studying hard, but at the same time restoring jukeboxes for the annual Jukebox Madness Show. My friend Roger would come and help out at the Ascot show, with his granddaughter. They were there as my guests and received complimentary entrance tickets, in return Roger would get stuck in and help me with un-loading and loading of the van and organising our delivery route, after all he was a Southerner and knew the places the jukeboxes were being delivered to.

I am really upset that my dad would never help me for free or to help me succeed like my mum has done all her life, still does to this day, but Dad wanted paying; plus expenses for his hotel, food and his bar bill but I put my foot down with the latter! I needed someone to help with the driving and with no one else available, he was my only choice. The fuel for the trip plus the indemnity and accidental damage insurance pushed my costs up.

Every show was the same, the arguments would start before we had even set off, he was in a rush to load the van and didn't use the ratchet straps correctly, he preferred to tie the ratchet straps instead of using them as designed. This stressed me out immensely and ultimately resulted in damaged jukeboxes. As soon as we were on the road, he wanted to stop at the first services on the M1 so he could have a big cooked breakfast. The expenses started almost immediately, and he always complained about the food I had just paid for. This took the shine off what was a successful time of my life.

There are a few incidents that are etched in my mind forever, but there is one that I have trouble in forgetting and that heralded the end of my attending of the jukebox shows.

I was taking an order for one of my jukeboxes and the buyer wanted to put a £500 deposit down to secure it, she handed me a wad of cash. Counting money was difficult and time consuming one handed, so I asked Dad to count it for me. After a little while counting he asked me, how much should there be? I told him £500, he confirmed that it was right. I thanked the buyer and told her there was £500 and the amount was correct.

After the buyer had gone Dad told me that there was more than £500, I asked how much more was there? He told me that there was £800 in total.

I said give me the £300 over payment, he said. *"No, it's not yours"*

I told him, *"It's not yours either, it belongs to the buyer, give me it so I can return it."*

He wouldn't, he thought it was a case of finders-keepers, he later said he had made a mistake and it was his money that he'd forgotten he had made from the sale of a slot machine over the weekend. I accepted his explanation although I was suspicious.

We delivered the jukebox and when the buyer paid the remaining balance, she gave me an odd look. As we drove away from their house, I asked Dad again if he was sure the buyer hadn't made an overpayment. He said he had definitely made a mistake and the money was his all along. I felt sorry for him and guilty I had made the accusation and so I gave him the extra £300 he thought he had.

A few days later, he was feeling guilty and wanted to confess that the buyer had in fact paid £300 over. I told him to give me the money.

That wasn't part of his plan, he just wanted to confess.

At that moment he had lost all credibility in my eyes and

I'll never know the true figure that was overpaid.

I felt so bad for the buyer that I returned £300 with my apology for the mistake. I wanted her to know I was an honest jukebox dealer so she could tell all her friends they could buy from me with confidence. My reputation as a jukebox dealer was at stake and really important to me. I never heard back from the buyer, I guess the damage had already been done and perhaps the amount returned was still less than their over payment.

I'd accepted a discounted price from the start on the sale of that one jukebox, but the extra costs had swallowed all my profit and in fact I had made a substantial loss.

More than that I was distraught by the deception. My reputation had been threatened. As far as I was concerned Dad had burned his bridges and he would never work with me again. I bought a cash counting machine so this sort of problem would never be repeated and to ensure my customers knew exactly how much they were paying and how much I was receiving. An important lesson learnt that day was never let someone else do what you can do yourself.

Although there were one or two moments that left their scars, most of my experiences at the jukebox shows were positive.

On one occasion our final drop-off on our journey home was to deliver a beautifully restored Seeburg KD200, (incidentally it was the first model that got me into vintage jukeboxes at the age of 19), the new owner was a really interesting chap. He owned a couple of other jukeboxes he had the most incredible workshop full of second world war radios and communication devices and there was a really big antenna on top of his workshop roof. He told me he used to work for the ministry of defence's propaganda network during the second world war. Wow, what a life he had lived! I couldn't help but compare the memories and secret stories this man had to share with those my jukeboxes had seen, how many partners had danced together, had forbidden love affairs or had seen lovers torn apart?

You see, I am a sentimentalist at heart and was captivated by the thoughts and dreams of those who had gone before.

I learnt two important lessons during this chapter of my life, one was the art of bartering and setting realistic prices. The other was never let someone else do what you can do for yourself.

If something isn't working for you, change your mindset and try a different approach.

Image Set A

1 - Tracy two years old, I'm three months old. 1963 taken at Clayfield Street, Buggy Park.

2 - Me climbing the Laburnum tree in my back garden at Crossgates, age 5 1969.

3 - In the valley, Crossgates with Dandy age 4 or 5.

4 - Family pic in the living room at 22 Orchard Grove, Crossgates.

5 - Tracy age 4 at Buggy Park with her friend.

6 - Front door at 22 Orchard Grove, Crossgates.

7 - Gangan, Grandad at their home in Scott Hall with Sheba, my lovely dog.

8 - Me and Tracy in our Cub and Brownie uniforms with Dandy in Gangan and Grandad's from garden age 7 and Tracy age 9.

9 - Cheeky me at home in Crossgates.

10 - Me and Tracy in the front garden at our house in the Scott Hall estate, age 9 or 10. I loved that bike, the best Christmas present I ever received. It cost £41 from Halfords that was on Vicar Lane in Leeds. Mum paid £1 a week to buy if for me :)

11 - My first real motorbike. The one my Grandad helped me rebuild. I was 13.

12 - The same motorbike, my Yamaha DT125. I loved that bike.

13 - The last photo that was taken before my acne got really bad. I'm 13.

14 - At college during my first year at Kitson College train to be a motor mechanic. I was 16. My right arm is in the air because I was brushing my hair with my hand when the photo was taken. How strange that it's my right arm and so prominently on display.

15 - I was working as a self-employed motor mechanic rebuilding motorbikes. This was a Suzuki ER100 I had built from parts, age 18 or 19.

16 - My first ever jukebox I bought from the demolition site. Now working and pictured with me and Tracy, age 19.

17 - Breakdance practice at my local sports centre. Age 20 or 21.

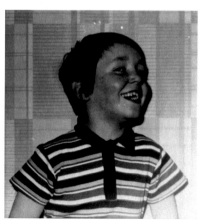

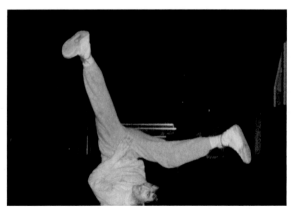

130

Chapter 23
Dancing

Dancing was something, like most boys, I was uncomfortable with, yet it brought me closer to a girl, which at that time was something unexpected. My very first dance with her was a smooch at a school disco at the Seven Sisters Social Club. I was 13 and I danced with a girl from my class. I can't even remember her name, but I loved that dance. I had shared a moment with her that I still remember today, at the age of fifty-six. The song was *"When Will I See You Again?"* by The Three Degrees. It was the first time I'd ever even held a girl's hand and I remember that her skin was really soft. I didn't know it then, but this would leave a lasting impression on me and I remember the dance as clear today as I did age 13.

Ironically, it would take losing an arm, to gain the confidence to get up on the dancefloor and truly enjoy dancing and not feel self-conscious and uncomfortable.

Before my accident I would go with my mates to a local disco called the Cherry Tree in Leeds. It had a really bad reputation for being a violent place. To be fair the reputation was well earned. It was a seedy place, the type where you wiped your feet when you left! On entering you were hit with the smell of stale booze, tab ends and old ashtrays. The carpets resembled sticky-back paper rather than plush floor covering. Needless to say, I didn't like it and I was

131

incredibly bored every time I went.

I'd tag along with my mates, pay the entry fee of thirty pence but then, only stay ten minutes. I couldn't get into drinking, dancing or women, none of those things interested me. I was still very self-conscious about my acne and over-all appearance. I had no confidence, no charm and zero chat-up tactics, it all seemed empty to me.

My motorbike was my real love and I wanted to tinker with it all the time. I would be in my workshop all hours only stopping when Mum would call me in *"Steven it's midnight, how long are you going to be?"* It was my man cave. How could booze, discos and women compete with that? In reality, to me they couldn't.

After my accident things were very hard, but one thing was for certain, I would also have to find new hobbies and pastimes I could enjoy and fill the void now left by my mo-torbikes.

I had decided I would make more of an effort to stay with my friends when I went on a night out. They were all super protective of me so I felt safe, after all I could no longer defend myself in a fight, my left arm didn't know how to punch, it had had 18 years of relative under use, that would certainly have to change now. They were a good crowd even if they did laugh at the stupid things I did. We were on a bus once and one of them nudged me as we went around the bend, I fell off the seat and immediately put my right arm out to catch myself but ended up flat on my face! My mate said

"Why didn't you grab the bar with your left hand?"

I told him *"I didn't even think about it, it was a gut re-action to put my right arm out."*

We all had a good laugh, it was like a slapstick comedy

sketch and I was the clown, but it was good natured, and I liked being with them.

On that same bus ride after my fall, I decided to sit on the other side of the bus to avoid my mates nudging me again and so I could hold on with my left arm. I got talking to a young woman who sympathised with the situation and she asked how I'd lost my right arm. I often used to think of interesting things to say to answer that question, because losing my arm on a motorbike seemed like a waste. I responded to her by saying I'd lost it during the Falklands war. She asked what I now did for work. I told her I had been unemployable ever since. She then told me she was a recruitment consultant and gave me her details insisting I call her, and that she would get me a job.

How I wish I hadn't told such a stupid lie, how could I now let her help me, even though I so desperately wanted her help. I had lied and how could I explain why, I was trying to glorify my situation when in fact to me there had been no glory in the truth. I never rang her out of embarrassment.

Surprisingly, I started to enjoy the Cherry Tree and in fact it became my favourite place for a night out. I do wonder if part of this had to do with my, somewhat strange, new increased self-esteem and self-confidence now that my acne had completely cleared.

It was here that I discovered I could dance; and more than that, I was good at it.

Dancing filled the void left by my motorbikes. When I danced it was like a wild animal had been released into the wilderness, I felt free from the shackles of disability and my mind cleared to a crystal clarity. All my stress, worries and anxiety melted away, like winter snow as spring approached. The season of birth and renewal, I felt like I was in love, you know that warm fuzzy feeling when you are embraced in the arms of someone you love. That was the feeling that engulfed me. My passion was free to be let loose on the dance floor, I was allowed to express my feelings in public and also in private when I danced around the house to the beautiful dulcet tones of my vintage jukeboxes.

My mind seemed to clear when I danced, I'm not sure how or why it cleared but it did. I seemed to be at ease and at peace, an inner peace that had previously alluded me and that I could never find, my daily struggles would always be present, and I accepted they would be present forever with just the brief interlude when I danced.

It was the 1980's, body-popping and break dancing was all the rage. I practiced for hours and hours at home to be a body-popper. I also spent weeks and weeks trying to teach my self how to *"moonwalk"*. It wasn't called the moonwalk back then though, it was called the backwards walk and it wasn't Michael Jackson that created the move, it was originally done by Jeffrey Daniels of Shalimar.

Michael Jackson would copy it many years later and name it the Moonwalk. One day while practicing I accidentally did it, I struggled to repeat it at first but then I did it again and this time I realised how I had done it. That was it, no going back from there! I would practice and practice until I had it to perfection. I had also learnt a few good moves with my body-popping so that when I went to the Cherry Tree, I could show off my skills. To my surprise, people would stop and watch me, I would create big circles of spectators and would be invited on stage to dance.

Can you imagine that? This shy lad, suddenly on stage in front of everyone, putting myself out there. Had you told me this two years before, I'd have laughed at you!

I was also a break-dancer and would practice on a daily basis at my local sports centre, they would let my friends and I practice our routines there. I lived for dancing, I didn't get the same buzz as I did from my motorbikes, it was a different type of feeling, but I loved it none the less.

Surprisingly, even though I was doing all the moves with one arm, I could do them and at the same time I was building up strength in my left arm. A doctor told me that after losing an arm, my remaining arm would compensate and would have the strength of two arms, I didn't believe him at the time, I do now!

Me and my friends had become so popular from our dancing that a local DJ had approached us and asked us if we would perform in demonstrations, in and around the Yorkshire area, he even said that he would pay us! We called ourselves *"Chain Reaction"* after the Diana Ross song, it seemed a good name because when we did a ripple move through the whole team, it was like a chain reaction. We bought matching navy blue track suits and had our jackets emblazoned with our team name. We looked great, or at least I thought so!

I loved performing and realised I had become an extrovert, the complete opposite to what I was with two arms. I didn't know then that dancing would be my life-long love. I thought I would be a break-dancer forever, but things change as does fashion and eventually break-dancing and body-popping would die out, it would later be revived, but not at a time when I could still do it and look cool!

I was 19 and still a virgin and would get a lot of stick from my mates, they would tease me, telling all the girls we met, *"don't bother with him, he's a virgin."* It didn't upset me, after all they were my mates. I enjoyed the digs and banter and it made me laugh, I wasn't as sensitive as I used to be. It was embarrassing at times however, but when the girls asked, I would simply say, *"Yes, I am a virgin, I haven't found anyone I like enough to lose my virginity with."*

You'd be surprised at the offers I used to get! I think that the girls saw it as a challenge!

"I'll help you" said yet another girl one night, *"but how do you do a press-up with one arm?"*

"I didn't do press ups with two arms," I replied. *"I'm not going to start now!"*

"So how do you do it with one arm?" she said again, to which I replied

"I might not be an expert but I'm pretty sure you don't use your arm."

This kind of chat certainly didn't impress me and just because she was willing, didn't mean she would be the one. I wasn't ready to have sex with a woman just because she was available. My mates had already lost their virginity to someone they didn't care about, just so they could say they weren't virgins anymore. I never did things because it's what others were doing, I always did what was right for me, I'm an individual and I follow my own path.

When my mates were drinking, I would just have soft drinks, give the lad a Coke my mate Mark would say, thinking I would be pressured into a beer. The truth was, I hated the taste of beers and lagers and I still do. My taste was more feminine, perhaps because of the female influence growing up, I liked Babychams, Cocktails and Snowballs, all drinks not associated with *"real men"*. I certainly wasn't going to be asking for one of those in the club, can you imagine the stick I'd get? It's different now, men drinking flavoured gin and tonics and of course, cocktails are easier to come by, but back in the 80's it wasn't the *"done"* thing for a young lad about town.

Eventually, I did meet a girl at the Cherry tree, I was 19 and she was 18. She was gorgeous, with luscious dark hair and a petite slim figure, she looked like a Mediterranean beauty and I soon realised this was the look I liked.

Later I found out she was from a notorious gypsy family from Micklefield, not quite the exotic climes I initially thought. Micklefield is a mining village on the outskirts of Leeds that had a bad reputation. I loved how she looked; I really like brunettes with olive skin.

I don't know how it happened because I don't see signs of interest. She was my first sexual encounter. In her mum's house behind the sofa, in a maisonette on Beckett Street Leeds. Not exactly romantic!

My persuasion techniques were non-existent, she was my first, but I was a cheeky chappy, kissing and cuddling round the back of the sofa I said,

"Let's do it!"

That was it, my first sexual encounter, I was hooked.

When we met, I was dancing, and she knew I went out a lot with my mate Mark. We would practice our break-dancing at Tiffany's night club in the Leeds, Merrion Centre. Debra was my girlfriends name and she would come with me from time to time. On one particular occasion Mark had gone away working. It was Thursday night and she rang me as she normally did, I told her Mark was away and asked if she wanted to come to Tiffany's with me? I guess she thought she had control over my entertainment that night and so she said *"no"*, I was surprised as she was often on at me to let her come, but this time she didn't want to go and to be honest I wasn't really pleased.

Debra always kicked up a fuss that I spent a lot of time with Mark, but he was my best mate and I wanted to spend time with him and also with her, I was a 19 year old young man wanting to have fun, but fun dancing, nothing that Debra had to worry about.

We had a bit of an argument on the phone. I was upset and I felt she was being difficult, and the call ended on a bad note.

Later that day Mark rang, he'd got back early from work and hadn't had to stay in Scotland where he had been working, so I rang Debra to say don't worry about tonight, you don't have to come.

"He's back" she shrieked, *"isn't he?"*

Well, I couldn't contain my laughter, she was so annoyed, her power had been removed, she couldn't make my evening difficult nor make me beg for her company. Funny really, she was furious and said,

"You think more about him than me, are you sleeping with him?"

She was very different to me, I'm not sure if I was in love, or more in lust, but after 18 months she dumped me for her ex-boyfriend. I was heartbroken, not because I was in love, but because I had been dumped. I wish I hadn't wasted my virginity on her. It had been fun, and it had opened my eyes to women. If it hadn't of been for Debra, I wouldn't have known what I was missing and wouldn't have wanted what I hadn't experienced.

Women would come and go yet dancing would remain a constant. I didn't realise how much dancing would change my life for the better.

It was 1985, the year of the Bradford City stadium fire that killed fifty-six people, the year the first mobile phone call was made and a mere three years after my accident. I was performing with my breakdance team in pubs and clubs around the Yorkshire region. They weren't the best venues, some rough joints where people were smoking actual joints. Dirty, smelly places that stank of ashtrays and stale beer, but to be honest, most pubs smelt like that back in the 80's. The crowds weren't the easiest either, but we managed to entertain them and got paid for the pleasure.

One thing I wanted though was to dance with a partner, something I'd wished for years I could do. I envied those confident men that knew how to dance with women, how to make them look elegant on the dance floor whilst still looking so cool and in command of the dance. I didn't know about leading and following, I only knew I liked what I saw and wanted to be one of those confident men.

My grandad had been a semi-professional ballroom dancer but as a young man, I thought like most young people, that the type of dance my grandad did was for older people and not for me. I was a child of the 80's when it came to music and thought it was uncool to like *"old timer"* music. I wish I had let my grandad teach me to dance, but it would be years after his death before I realised I wanted to learn. It would have been wonderful to know what he knew about dancing!

Sadly, Grandad passed away of a heart attack at the age of 77 in January 1990, when I was 26 years old. I'd been playing pool in my local pub the Hilltop, Grandad had introduced me to that place when it had been a social club and was known as the Seven Sisters Social Club because there were seven trees planted on a hill that represented the resting place of seven sisters. I received a phone call at the Hilltop from my mum on the day of his death to tell me he had been rushed to hospital and mum thought he was dead.

I was the one who identified his body in a private room at Saint James's hospital, in Leeds. I walked into the room, he looked so peaceful, as though he was sleeping and, in that moment, I wanted to touch him and wake him, but I felt helpless and couldn't bring him back to life; not having that power, I simply stood in shock. I left the room containing my emotions until I had to confirm to Mum that he was dead... Grandad had gone, so had my emotional self-control. I truly wish I'd had the chance to tell him what he meant to me, how he inspired me.

Eventually the Cherry Tree closed down, its troubled past eventually caught up with it and its closure was inevitable, it was the end of an era, it would never re-open as a dance venue, ironically it is now a mosque. Ironic, because once a venue for alcohol, late nights of flirtatious banter and fighting on a scale I've never witnessed before or since, is now a calm and serene place of worship!

Over the years I would take dance lessons to improve my dancing repertoire, meet new people and make new friends. I never expected to meet that special person and fall in love on the dance floor and I never did, my main goal was to learn to be a better dancer so I could experience more freedom and that warm fuzzy loved up feeling I so desperately desired.

Taking classes, having to concentrate on what the teacher taught us would occupy my mind. I've always been the type of person who wants to put one hundred percent into everything I do. I did the same with my dance classes. However, none of the teachers had one arm so they couldn't really teach me how to do the two-handed moves, but with one arm only. It would be up to me to work out an equivalent move but the one-armed version. Sometimes that would take me a long time to work out, sometimes I simply couldn't do some of the moves which meant I would have to step out of the class. That was always a cause of a lot of embarrassment, but I learnt to cope, it was the only way to continue with dance classes.

I've been embarrassed, humiliated and rejected many times on the dance floor by prospective dance partners and by insensitive teachers. I've asked women to dance only to be told, after looking me up and down, no! Not a pleasant *"no"* but one of disgust, some going so far as to turn their backs on me, others have simply ignored me. It is so demoralising, upsetting to say the least. I felt on many occasions that I wanted the ground to open up and swallow me.

I've danced with women that don't want to touch me on my right shoulder. I've placed their hand on my shoulder in case they were concerned about hurting me, but it becomes obvious that isn't the case when they remove their hand immediately. I really hate that when it happens, it makes me feel like I'm dirty, and untouchable. Why would they dance one handed with me? I'm not choosing to dance one handed, I would much rather dance two handed with all of them and embrace them with both arms, but that will never happen no matter how much I wish it would.

I'm often asked why I don't wear a prosthetic limb when dancing and it's a good question. If I did wear a prosthetic, I know that I would have no control over the arm and it concerns me that I might accidentally brush against a woman inappropriately and not realise, plus would they be more freaked out about touching the shoulder cap or prosthetic arm than they are me? It took me a long time to realise that false limbs are more for comfort of others, rather than my own. They're horrible and uncomfortable to wear and so when it comes to dancing, I'm better off being me, instead of trying to look how people expect me to look.

Be honest, be yourself and do what makes you feel comfortable and not what makes others feel comfortable was another hard lesson learnt.

Chapter 24
Swimming In Circles

It was 1986, the year of the Chernobyl disaster and the very first computer virus was released on the world, it was called 'Brain', but I was worrying about other things, not world events but a personal challenge. The main thing that worried me before going to Spain on holiday with the lads was swimming. I'd never swam with one arm before. When I had two arms, I wasn't a great swimmer. I had my 25 and 50 metre certificates from Potternewton Primary School. But I was now 22 and hadn't been swimming in years.

There was only one thing I could do. I had to go swimming. I didn't like the idea really because I knew everyone would stare at my damaged and scarred body and children would make cruel remarks as they always did, but how would I enjoy swimming in Spain, in the hotel pool, or in the sea if I wasn't sure I could swim?

I joked to my friends that I would swim in circles, but would I? I wasn't sure, I had no technique for swimming with one arm, I simply had no idea. I must admit it worried me. Would I sink? Would I in fact go around in circles? Would I panic? I'd had to go and try.

In the 80's Belinda Carlisle sang a song called *"Circles In The Sand"* and I was thinking about circles a lot. I wouldn't be doing them in the sand but there was a strong possibility I may do them in the sea and the pools of the Spanish Costas.

My mates and I decided we'd go to Richard Dunn's sport centre at Odsal Top, in Bradford, so I could try swimming.

We arrived at the sports centre and I remember thinking *"how am I going to do this?"*

My head was full of questions and doubts. We went into the centre. It had some water slides that we had to pay extra for on top of the entry fee. I asked at the payment kiosk if I could have a disabled person's ticket. The lady behind the counter asked me if I had brought proof of my disability with me. She was expecting me to produce a piece of paper or some doctors signed document. It seemed ridiculous to me. I replied to her,

"Oh no, I'm sorry I don't have any paper proof, but I brought my disability with me if that would be acceptable?"

The lady said,

"I'm not sure that's allowed, what's your disability?"

I replied, *"I only have one arm".*

At which point I pulled my jacket off of my right shoulder to reveal an empty sleeve so she could see for herself.

"You'll use as much of the pool as anyone else, won't you?" she said.

She didn't want to let me in at the disabled rate, but I replied with.

"No, I won't be using the same amount of pool, I'll be swimming in circles"

"Oh of course" she said as she smiled and let me in for the disabled price of 50 pence while my mates paid £5 each.

We changed into our swimming trunks in the male communal changing area with the unmistakable smell of chlorine lingering in the air, and the noise of shouting and laughter from children that would surely make me feel uncomfortable and make me feel like leaving as soon as I got in.

I was feeling very anxious; I just didn't know what to expect.

It wasn't until I was in the pool that I felt a little more at ease because I could lower my body into the water to the level on my neck and no one would be able to see I only had one arm. But, my nervousness about taking the plunge and actually trying to swim was building to a crescendo. I thought to myself, if I start to try and swim normally, surely I'd sink, but if I started under the water I could only float to the top and not sink.

I had a plan and I would try it. My mates were all around me in case I got into difficulty as I said

"I'm going to do it now."

With that I took a deep breath and did a shallow dive under the water, I did breaststroke of a sort, it was more like a side stroke and a scissor kick, as I kicked and pulled the water towards me with my one and only arm I floated to the surface as planned. Wow, I was swimming and not in circles either!

The water slides were great fun and we had a fabulous day out and not only that, but I was now ready for my Spanish holiday. That was the first time in many years that I'd been swimming and the first time as a disabled man. I never thought it would be as easy as that.

I learnt one of my most valuable lessons on that day, the struggle was in my head, but isn't that where most of our struggles are?

Chapter 25
The Spanish Speaker

It was 1986, The UK and France announced plans to construct the channel tunnel, journalist John McCarthy was kidnapped in Beirut, the Australian TV soap Neighbours was launched on BBC1 and the world's first heart, lung and liver transplant was carried out at Papworth Hospital, in Cambridge. I was a 22-year-old embarking on my first foreign holiday to Benidorm with the lads. There were five of us, Mark, Danny, Barry, Alan and me.

It was the first time I'd ever been abroad if you didn't count Ireland. We flew from Leeds/Bradford Airport, known back then as Yeadon Airport, to Alicante and then transferred to our hotel on the fringes of the new and old town of Benidorm to a hotel called hotel Easo. The owner of the hotel was from the Leeds suburb of Chapeltown. He told us with pride where he was from. It had been a very posh area of Leeds when he had left, but to us young lads, we knew it only as the troubled ghetto it had become. It had more than its fair share of racial tension and was now pre-dominantly populated by West Indian families. It had a notorious reputation and was well known for its drug and prostitution problems.

I had taken the precaution of having a few sunbed sessions prior to getting away, just to make sure I wouldn't burn quickly or suffer prickly heat. I loved sunbathing and drinking piña coladas and sangrias by the pool side.

I loved the Spanish music that played in the nightclubs of Benidorm, it transported me to a whole new world; a world of a new mysterious language, culture and fun. The popular song that played everywhere was *"Solo Se Vive Una Vez"* by Azucar Moreno, I obviously had to buy that record along with the best of the Gypsy Kings.

My introduction to the Spanish language happened by accident really. My friends and I had found a little bar near our hotel that did cheap but nice breakfasts. The owner was English, and his wife was Spanish. I realised from our nights out that I was incredibly attracted to the Spanish women and fell in love with their look. Their olive skin and black hair was my type, but I couldn't speak to them, so I asked the owners wife to teach me some Spanish phrases. She did, she would write them down for me on a piece of paper and I would try them out that same night. I loved it, I felt like I could speak a little bit of Spanish, but I needed to know more. I would get a new phrase to learn every day. In my second week I would get two or three phrases a day. I was getting quite good and picking up the language really quickly.

Although my Spanish was getting better, it wasn't good enough to get my friend Danny out of a lot of trouble one night. We spent a lot of time in a bar that was called *"Black Sabads"* where we had become good friends with the owner Pepe.

We drank there every night before moving on to some other party places in the area, on one of the nights we had been drinking there we had moved on to a bar around the corner. We hadn't been there long when Danny rested his arm on a table. In an instant the tabletop slipped off under

Danny's weight, it must not have been fixed in place. The drinks went flying in the air and crashed to the floor along with the tabletop.

Suddenly there were loads of muscle-bound Spanish bouncers pushing Danny around in a threatening manner. We didn't know what to do, so I ran around the corner to Black Sabads to ask Pepe to help. Pepe did help but it cost Danny the equivalent of £100. It was either that or he would be beaten up or the municipal police would be called, and Danny would have spent the night in jail, despite not doing anything wrong. However, that couldn't be proved, the broken glasses on the floor implied otherwise.

Danny and I decided we would forget that one bad night and we would set ourselves a new challenge to take our minds off the broken table event. We would swim across Benidorm. We went into as many hotels as possible and swam a length of their pool, we would do this until we had visited a vast amount of pools and we were either across town or thrown out of the hotels.

I returned home from that holiday with a great suntan and a new language ability. I decided I would continue to learn Spanish as I'd enjoyed the challenge so much and didn't want to lose what little I had learnt. I'd already asked Mum on the phone if she'd look in the local paper for a Spanish language teacher. By the time I got home Mum had found a teacher for me who was advertising in the Yorkshire Evening Post. Paco was the tutors name and we started lessons on a twice a week basis. That was it, I was hooked, it was my new challenge and I wasn't prepared to be beaten. I would keep going until I had a good, or at least, a working knowledge of that wonderful Latin language.

My hunger for language knowledge was insatiable, I

couldn't get enough. I enrolled on one night school course after another, I attended the Instituto Cervantes, the Spanish state-run language schools around the world dedicated to educating the globe with the Spanish language and culture. The school I attended was in Leeds, near to the university. In that school they had a notice board, where people advertised for something called an 'intercambio', it was basically a language exchange between two willing participants, each willing to teach their native language for free in exchange for being taught the others native language. In my case it was an exchange of Spanish for English. I met some great people and made some life-long friends while improving my Spanish, at the same time I was still studying there and still getting lessons from Paco.

I finished most of the Spanish course I'd enrolled on and Paco went back home to Spain. I knew the Leeds University also had a notice board in their Spanish and Portuguese department. I put an advertisement there that read. *"Me llamo Steve, me gustaria hacer un intercambio y salir para tomar unas copas"* That meant, *"My name is Steve, I'd like to do an intercambio and go out for drinks".*

A week later a Spanish woman called to say she was studying at Leeds Uni and had seen my ad. She had a friend coming to stay with her in a few weeks' time to work as an au pair and would be staying with her for 5 months, she would get her to call me when she arrived. She did call but I was on holiday in Greece so my mum took the call and told the Spanish girl I would call her when I returned, Mum took her number, she was called Inma.

I called Inma on my return, little did I know that would be the start of a life-long friendship with a young Spanish woman of 22 from Badajoz, a place I'd never even heard of, I was 27 only a 5 year difference between us, but it felt like a big difference at the time. It was 1991, the year Tim Berners-Lee, a British scientist working at CERN, introduced the world to his invention of the *"World Wide Web"*. Helen Sharman became the first British person to go to space with the Soyuz TM-12 mission and I was sat in the front room of a house in Armley, Leeds, talking in broken Spanish and English during my first meeting with Inma. I instantly liked her, she was so friendly with a really happy personality and amazing smile.

We went out so much together during her 5 months in Leeds. I took her to karaoke bars and restaurants to sample Indian food and other cuisines. We went to discos and I even took her to my local bar that had a strip night, I think that opened her eyes a little.

I took her to Batley Frontier, a really big nightclub in Batley. I introduced her to my friends. For 5 months she became my best friend. I was never romantically involved; I liked her friendship too much and didn't want to risk that. Although we had started out with an intercambio, a language exchange we spoke English all the time, it seemed only fair she should speak as much English as she possibly could during her short stay in Leeds. She would be returning home to do Las Posiciones, they were exams she would have to pass if she wanted to work as a schoolteacher for the Spanish Government, a goal she had set herself, little did she know she would be returning with a Yorkshire accent!

She did eventually return to Spain in November of that year and passed all her exams. I visited her for the first time in February of 1992, I had planned to go to Spain with some friends and it was my intention to leave them for a few days and visit Inma in Badajoz. But that plan almost didn't happen.

I was in Benidorm with two of my friends but they didn't want me to go. One of my friends had come with next to no money and they wanted me to stay to help out financially, plus they needed my Spanish language ability. I agreed to stay with my friends and called Inma to tell her I couldn't make it. She was upset I wouldn't be visiting, as I had said I would be. I felt like kicking myself, I had just turned down an opportunity to visit my friend during the 'Carnaval de Badajoz', where the streets fill with over 80,000 people and is considered one of the top three carnavals of Spain. But something would happen that night that would change everything.

It was the night before I would have been going to visit Inma and I was going to bed. Being on a lads holiday was always a bit risky, they would always try and pull some sort of stunt, but I really didn't like the one that was about to be pulled on me.

I was sharing a room with Jason, for a bit of fun he had found a cockroach and had put it in my bed. As I was getting into bed it was on my pillow, but I didn't see it until I was laid down staring into its eyes. I jumped out of bed startled and shocked to see my mates laughing.

At that moment I thought, what am I doing staying here with these two idiots when I could have been enjoying myself with Inma, at the best carnival I'd probably ever see? I slept in the living area that night, not wanting to return to my cockroach bed partner. I lay awake most of the night thinking about how I wanted to leave and visit my Spanish friend, I thought and thought, how can I tell my friends I'm leaving in the morning and how can I tell Inma I would be visiting after all?

I'd decided, and when I've made my mind up it's made up and nothing will persuade me otherwise. I set my alarm clock and it rang out at 5am. I got up, got my things together and told my mates I was going for a few days and I'd see them when I got back. Fortunately, there were no mobile phones so I couldn't be contacted. They were both half asleep so muttered *"OK"*. That was it, I set off to Inma's and she didn't have a clue I was coming. I got to the train station, bought my ticket that would take me first to Madrid and then another train to Badajoz. All trains seemed to go via the capital city even though it would have been much closer to go direct. I rang Inma from the train station in Alicante to tell her I was coming after all. Her mum answered, Inma was in bed after partying hard all night but her mum said great! I'm glad you're coming, she will be so happy to see you and she'll be waiting for you at the train station in Badajoz.

That was the best decision I'd ever made, the time spent with Inma and all her friends was magical, I loved it. I dressed up in fancy dress as little red riding hood with stockings *"Capa Rucita Roja Puta"* and a noble man in Christian crusader clothing. The time passed so quickly, dancing, singing, drinking and blowing whistles in the packed streets and numerous bars of Badajoz, the rhythm of the music that was ever present reverberated through the whole city. It was an assault on the senses, smells of street food, sounds of laughter that could be heard even though there was loud music coming from every bar. There were street vendors selling carnaval merchandise, whole generations of families partying. There were numerous city squares that had thousands of people in, they were dancing to mobile music systems that had been setup. The music of course was all Spanish there was absolutely nothing English about it except for me. My favourite drinks became rum and coke or calimocho, red wine with CocaCola. It sounds dreadful but it was a really nice drink. I didn't get drunk, but I maintained a tipsy state throughout the nights.

Love at first sight was with a beautiful Spanish woman dressed as a cowgirl. I can't remember the name of the bar. I was tipsy after all. Our eyes met as I walked into the bar and that was it, I was in love. I was dressed as little red riding hood and Inma and her friends had gone to town on my makeup. I had big rosy red cheeks of lipstick, lots of foundation and lips that could sink a battleship. I looked a real sight and didn't have the courage to approach her and that was the end of that, a missed opportunity. I would never see her again nor experience love at first sight.

I returned back to my friends in Benidorm three days later with stories to tell of my nights out in Badajoz, I say nights out, they were more like complete days, we left Inma's mum and dad's house at 10pm and returned home at 10am, 12 hours of partying. We went for breakfast on our way home and before going to bed. I slept almost all day, until at least 4pm then it was time to start over again, three days of that was amazing.

That was the only time I've been to the Carnavals of Badajoz, but I intend to go again one day. Benidorm with my friends paled into insignificance when compared with the Carnavals of Badajoz and my time spent with my friend Inma, all her friends and family. I have a fantastic photo taken in Inma's friend, Choni's house, in which I'm sat on the sofa surrounded by 7 or 8 beautiful Spanish women, what a great moment for the shy man I was back then.

I went to visit Inma quite often. I went one time to meet her new boyfriend Chema. We all met up for a night-time picnic come barbecue, in the middle of the countryside. What a fabulous night spent under the stars with some truly wonderful people. Chema was a great guy, I really liked him plus he wasn't jealous of my friendship with Inma, we were only friends and he had nothing to be jealous of, but that's not how all men would feel. Chema is a really brilliant guy who is also a life-long friend.

I've made so many great friends through Inma and Chema, I love to visit as often as I can and particularly for special occasions. Thanks to Inma I speak fluent Spanish, although with a Badajoz accent.

I went to Inma and Chema's wedding. That was over 25 years ago. In fact, in June 2019 I went to their 25th wedding anniversary, where they took their vows all over again in the little chapel they were married in 25 years earlier. The chapel was in the school where Chema works. This is the same school I did my motivational talk for in 2018, delivered in Spanish. Chema was the school counsellor, helping students with their psychological learning issues and helping teachers know how to best support those students. It was a very highly respected job and the chapel was in his place of work, El Colegio de San José, in Villafranca de los Barros, a small town that feels like home to me all thanks to my dear friends.

When I think back, I almost didn't go to see Inma for the Carnavals of Badajoz because my friends didn't want me to go, I'm so glad I went through with it.

I learnt a valuable lesson that day, never let others hold you back.

Chapter 26
Cathy

After the ending of my first disastrous relationship, I wasn't upset for too long because I met Cathy; I was to spend the next nine turbulent years with her. It was a great relationship at times, I was nineteen and she was only sixteen, Craig Douglas sang a beautiful song called *"Only Sixteen"*, I felt like he was singing about our forbidden love, it wasn't forbidden though, it just felt as if it was due to our young age. At the time the age gap concerned me, I was only three years older than her, a three-year difference seems like nothing now but back then it felt like a big gap.

The turbulence in our relationship came from our differing ideas, especially that, she wanted children from a young age, and I didn't. Not because I didn't ever want them, but I wanted to make my mark in the world, earn some money and be a man of means before I could think about bringing a new life into this world. My father had been absent in my life, and I wanted to make sure I wouldn't be the same, that I would always be there for my children.

In my desire to be prepared so as to be a good dad, I was overly careful and super conscious of the mistakes that could happen, even though she was taking the pill. I think that the male pill would be the emancipation of men. I can only speak from my own point of view and I'm sure not all men will even care, but I did. I guess all my growing up sexually and emotionally was with Cathy.

We had some great times together; I've never laughed so much. We often played piggyback and neck shoulders; I loved those stupid playful moments and I miss those innocent times even today.

My girlfriend's family was 'big' and had a bit of a reputation in Meanwood, Leeds. She had four brothers and one sister. When I started dating her everyone would tell me, *"her brothers will get you"*. Although I'd heard lots of bad things, I really liked them, and I counted them all as friends. These days I only see her at funerals, two of which have been her brothers. I can't tell you how sad I was to be there.

Her eldest brother, Paul was a great guy who sadly lost his life along with his friend on a motorbike, on their way home from Otley. They came off on a tight corner and hit the chevron signs head on. Every time without fail when I pass that corner and see the sign that's still there today, I think about them and how sad it was for their lives to be cut so short.

Many years later, Cathy's second brother died of a brain tumour. I went to his funeral too and at the reception afterwards it was great to see Cathy, but it was very emotional, and I couldn't contain my sorrow. I was reminiscing on the days when we were all together, enjoying ourselves at the local pub, playing pool and laughing. I was in the pool team, but Cathy was a great pool player too and would regularly kick my arse and the arses of many a confident male player. I loved the fact she could beat me.

However, it was soon to be the end of mine and Cathy's love.

We had an off and on-again relationship. All my so-called mates were like predators, when we split up, they would declare their desire for her and would pursue her. That made me think I wanted her back. Maybe I was going back for the wrong reasons. I was confused. I wanted her, but I also wanted to experience more of life and some part of me also wanted her to have more life experience.

After one break-up I dated a West Indian girl for two weeks. I didn't want to be single and didn't want a casual sexual relationship and I thought I had found someone new to love. However, a week into my new relationship I ended up getting back with Cathy, without finishing it with the other girl.

I'm going to be brutally honest, I liked them both and it meant I was getting loads of sex. It felt like a win-win, when one had had enough, I'd go to the other. I'm not proud of this part of my life but I was young and young men, and women, do foolish things that on looking back, can seem heartless. It wasn't my intention to be cruel, I was merely thinking with my hormones and so, whilst not proud, I'm not consumed by shame either. It was a one week overlap and I was torn by my emotions.

Incidentally, in 1983 the same year I started dating Cathy an American man, Giovanni Viglotto, was imprisoned for fraud and polygamy after marrying 105 women. Sort of puts my one-week indiscretion into perspective...

However, it all came to an end as Cathy found out I hadn't finished it with the other girl. Ironically, Cathy was related to the father of my new girlfriends' child. She told me I had to end it with her by phone and she wanted to be present when I made the call! It felt like a horrible way to end a relationship, but I did it because I wanted to be with Cathy more.

In hindsight, I think the 'affair' came about because I

was searching for something that was missing with Cathy. I'm not sure what is was, maybe I was a male nymphomaniac, or maybe I don't handle break ups well! I'm not sure either way, but I was certainly looking for a deeper connection than the one I was getting.

Was this the result of being from a broken home and the abandonment issues I had felt? I don't know, all I can say is thank God for ageing! Getting older has mellowed me and I'm much more grounded than I ever was before.

On the penultimate occasion when Cathy and I had split up, there was one of my so-called friends that wanted her. I'd gone back into a relationship with her before, just to stop him getting her, but this time I thought it wasn't for me to try to stop her, if that's what she really wanted.

Not long after she told me she was pregnant. I was devastated. The guy was one of those typical men who just wanted sex and no responsibility, just the type of guy I didn't want to be. He made a sharp exit when he found out she was pregnant.

I thought a lot about Cathy, and I battled a lot of demons. I tried to support her through a difficult time. We got back together again after she'd had her daughter, I loved spending time with her and speaking to her daughter in Spanish, hoping I could help to make her bi-lingual, oh how I wished she'd been my child. My eyes are welling up as I write that, but I truly wished she was mine to care for and protect. I was devastated that our relationship was, in the end just not meant to be. In the end I couldn't handle the fact that she was another man's child and such a waste of a man that would leave a girl in such a desperate and difficult situation. I realised that I would have to end the relationship and stop my visits. That was unfair on Cathy, but I truly wanted her to find someone to love and who could love her back, more than I felt I could.

It was time to move on and so I did but with a heavy heart. I think about her all the time. When we meet by chance, I love our meetings and conversations. She lights up my day, but also makes me think what could have been. She always asks, *"do you ever think about me Steve?"* The truth is, I think about her a lot. I miss her and I miss what we had together.

Despite everything I may have written in this chapter, I wasn't a womaniser and didn't particularly want to be. I realised I really wanted a steady, monogamous relationship.

I had other girlfriends, what my friend Mark said about not being able to get a girlfriend with only one arm, simply wasn't true.

Those words that Mark said have haunted me all my life, but this was just another phantom barrier waiting to be overcome.

Don't allow other people's words to impact you all your life. Erase them from your memory and move on.

Chapter 27
Disc Jockey

One of the most frustrating things about losing my arm, in the early days, was having to rely on other people to take me places. I hadn't yet passed my driving test, nor did I own a car, so friends would pick me up and take me out. One of the bars we'd go to was called 'The Richmond', it was on Richmond Hill estate on South Accommodation Road in Leeds. It was the busiest club in the popular area of East End Park, and I would go there with my mate Danny, he had a works van and gave me lifts.

However, Danny was less than reliable! More often than not I would be all dressed ready and waiting for him, he was generally late, but more times than not he would call. The format of the call was always the same, bad news Steve! I can't make it. That was my night over before it had even begun. When he did come for me, we would start our night out in the popular Fisherman's Hut pub, I loved it there, at the weekend there'd be a singer on and some disco music. It was a great night! We would then do a pub crawl that eventually ended up at the main disco venue 'The Richmond'.

Danny met a girl at the Fisherman's Hut, I was happy for him, it was nice that he now had a girlfriend; but he became even more unreliable, which surprised me as I didn't think that possible! I had become friends with the DJ at The

Richmond, he was a great guy, often DJs get a bad rep for having a superior attitude, but he wasn't like that, he would even play the records we'd brought back from our lads holiday in Spain. I of course was the only person who danced to those records, but I had almost a need to dance. Alan Joy was the name of the DJ, he encouraged me to dance, even on my own. It was ok, I had rhythm and the moves, all the training I'd done body popping and break dancing had taught me how to dance.

One night, after I hadn't been to the club in several weeks, Alan asked where I'd been, I told him about Danny and his girlfriend, I explained that I wasn't able to get to the club without a lift and didn't fancy spending the night there without my friend. He said

"Why don't you come down tomorrow and be my warmup man? I'll teach you to be a DJ, you won't have to pay in, and your drinks will be free. Come down tomorrow at 8" he said.

The following night Danny let me down, so I couldn't go, in fact I didn't go again that week, but the following week when I walked in Alan said,

"What happened to you?"

"I thought you were kidding" I said.

"Right, I'm not messing around, get yourself down tomorrow for 8pm."

That night I decided not to wait for the phone call from Danny telling me *"bad news Steve"*. I lived about 5 miles from the Richmond, so at 7:15 I set off walking, I got there for 7:55.

"Great! You're here," said Alan *"I'm glad you came."*

I was going to be a DJ, not the first. In 1947 Jimmy Saville became the worlds first DJ, a name that seems to follow and haunt me and possibly the reason for my initial apprehension.

I didn't realise then what a gift Alan was giving me, he is a friend I owe so much to today. He taught me how to be a DJ, how to choose music. Which songs would make people dance and which ones would clear a dancefloor. He taught me to talk on a microphone, although I must admit that took years to master. He taught me to be more confident and less shy. I worked at the Richmond for about 5 years, all without pay, but I was learning for free and enjoying my nights out. Danny and his girlfriend, soon to be wife would come in now and then and it was always great to see them.

As time went on, we worked well together, Alan didn't like the wedding gigs so I would do those, Alan also didn't always want to do Wednesday nights, which were band nights, so I would cover those for him. It was a different approach, I had to learn how to introduce the band and liaise with them so I knew which record I would play prior to their entrance, the chosen song prepared the band and I would introduce them with a big welcome, they would let me know which song would be their last and if they were going to play an encore and what their closing song would be. It was great I met some wonderful bands and some fantastic people.

One night I was doing my normal warm up session when Alan came and told me that the resident DJ at the Derby Bar, another bar owned by the same owners had walked out in a fit of anger, taken all his records and left the club without a DJ and no music. I had to go and cover.

I was panic stricken; my microphone skills were poor, and I was worried because I was only a trainee. Alan said to me,

"Steve, nobody knows you there, they don't know if you are a DJ or not, just go and act as if you are, play all your best music and put on a silly or DJ type voice if it helps."

Pretend you're a DJ.

Scared and worried I did what Alan told me. It was a massive success and at the end of the night I got cheers and clapping from the whole place, a standing ovation. My fate was sealed I became the resident DJ, working 3 nights a week from 10pm until 2am.

A DJ saved my life, his name was Alan Joy, Indeep sang the song *"Last night a DJ saved my life"* and that was the song of my opening set.

I worked there for 3 years. I loved it, it helped develop me as a person. I was so shy and really slow at coming forwards when Alan met me, but he has made me a stronger, more extroverted person. I owe so much to him and although we are still in touch today, I don't tell him as often as I should, just how much he helped me become the man I am today.

Sometimes people come into your life for a reason, never push them away!

Chapter 28
Karaoke Presenter

After a while, I got involved with Karaoke and enjoyed it more than being a DJ. I did karaoke for a while at the Richmond and at the Derby Bar, but I eventually left and setup my own karaoke system, with the help of Mark, my lifelong friend and school buddy. Together we bought a Pioneer karaoke system.

Karaoke in Japanese means *"Empty Orchestra"* and was invented in 1971 by a Japanese inventor and musician *"Daisuke Inoue"*

Back in the 90's the Pioneer system was the Rolls Royce of karaoke and it came with a Rolls Royce price tag. Second hand it still cost £3000, it was complete though with a full set of discs, around 20 in total. We upgraded the speakers and bought a radio mic, a video camera and taping equipment, we were all setup and ready to go. I was the karaoke presenter; Mark was the designated driver and moved the equipment. The problem was, he liked a drink, especially on Sundays which was our biggest night of the week at the Wybeck Valley Arms.

We started at 8pm so needed to be all packed and on our way at 7pm. Mark would generally ring at 5 or 6pm blind drunk saying he couldn't drive, and we would have to find a driver and pay him out of our nights takings. I would point out that I had a driver, him, and if he was incapable of driving it was his problem and a problem he should remedy at his cost. Which to be fair he always did but this became too frequent.

It wasn't all bad, I loved my karaoke days with Mark we had such a good time together and laughed so much, not only that, but I was now single again after nine years and although there were many opportunities being a DJ, I never acted on them. Mostly because at the time I didn't recognise them as potential opportunities.

There was a girl who used to come in to the Wybeck Valley Arms. I really didn't pick up on signs of interest from the opposite sex, a fault I believe of my coping mechanism, that avoided me being hurt by people staring at me.

This girl was educated and had a good job as a school-teacher. That impressed me. She was friendly and always came to say hello and buy me a drink. I liked that, but always thought she was just being friendly.

On one particular Sunday, my mum, sister Tracy and my mum's friend came to the Wybeck for a night out. They all said to me, that girl is interested in you.

I said that she was just being friendly, but they insisted that she was interested and that I should offer her a lift home at the end of the night. So, I did. To my great surprise they were right, she was interested. That night the drive back to her home detoured via the car park of Temple Newsan House, a stately home in the eastern part of Leeds. We shared a few kisses; I couldn't take her directly home because she had a live-in boyfriend. She told me they were no longer in love and they didn't share a bed anymore. I didn't really believe that story, it may have been true, but I didn't believe it. Her name was Kathryn.

After we had been together a few weeks, Kathryn told me she was asking her boyfriend to leave. She was taking over the mortgage and would be single so we could be a couple. I quite liked that idea, but I made it clear to her that I would not be replacing him as the live-in boyfriend. I told her to only make the decision if she was fine with that. I don't think that's what she really wanted to hear.

I continued to see her, and things were going well. I loved that she was clever, holding a Degree in French and History. Although, at the same time as loving her for her achievements, it also made me feel a little inadequate. I had always wanted to go to university and my lack of formal education made me feel somehow less.

In a short time, her live in partner had gone and I was able to stay over, which was great. Occasionally she tried a bit of subtle emotional blackmail by calling and saying she was lonely living by herself. I sympathised, but reminded her what I'd said about not taking her ex-partners place, or at least not immediately anyway. Once she realised I didn't want to rush into cohabiting, things went well for a long time. As a teacher Kathryn could never take time off of work for holidays so I went for week's holiday to Benidorm with the lads. My intention was to find Pepe who we knew from our first visit.

Me and Mark went to Black Sabads looking for Pepe, but he had moved to another bar. We spent the next few hours going from bar to bar asking if Pepe worked there. We eventually found him. He was now working in his own bar called the Pink Elephant. It was on the fringes of the old and new town. I loved the old part of Benidorm and spent most of my time there, it gave me the opportunity to mix with Spanish people and practice speaking Spanish. I was never interested in spending time in the British or foreign tourist part of Spain. Having been on holiday to Spain a few times with the lads, I really felt that I could enjoy working there.

On a night out in the Pink Elephant I asked Pepe if Mark and I could come and do a season with our Karaoke system. He thought it would be a great idea, we wouldn't receive much of a wage and would be working for basically nothing, but our food, drink and accommodation would be free, also we would only have to work 3 or 4 night a week and he suggested other bars we could work in to increase our weekly income. He would even get some of the other bar owners to come and see us work. We accepted there and then and arranged to return with all our equipment at the start of the summer season.

A week before the season began and we were due to set off to Benidorm, Mark and I packed the van. It was his van and was an ex-British Telecom van painted in bright yellow and governed to not exceed 50 mph. Bearing in mind how old it was, we sensibly took out AA cover!

We were still working in the local pubs in Leeds and decided we would have our farewell party at the Cavalier Inn, in East End Park Leeds. The farewell party was great, everyone we had met came to our big send-off night. We had a real party, the place was buzzing with an electric atmosphere, laughter, song and plenty of inebriated people.

The Cavalier Inn was a bit of a dump really, the typical pub of the 90's. Prior to the 2007 smoking ban in public places pubs often smelt of tobacco and stale beer, the Cavalier was another such venue that was frequented by some real characters. Nevertheless, the night was fantastic, although quite emotional at the end. What a great send off, spending the night with a group of friends I had come to know just through the love of singing at public bars. If you think about it, it was as far away from my school days as I could get. I was genuinely happy with life.

The day came when we set off for Spain. We packed all the equipment, our suitcases and our bicycles. Bikes would be our main form of transport or so we thought. We had planned the entire route in advance, the European part would take in Cherbourg, Le Mans, the Pyrenees, coming into Salou, Spain, the scene of the Salmonella outbreak in the 90's, then down to Valencia. Finally, we ventured onto *"Blackpool of the Costa Blanca"* Benidorm. It didn't then and I still don't think it deserves that name now, it's a great place but so was Blackpool in its heyday.

The journey started in Leeds full of adventure and eager of spirit, at least that was how I was, I'm not sure what Mark was feeling. I wasn't too confident about Mark's intentions from the beginning, mainly because he had only brought two weeks' worth of underwear with him, no iron nor any self-sufficiency tools. I had the impression that when he had run out of clean clothing, he would want to return home to his girlfriend Susan! I suppose it should have been obvious that he wasn't really up for the entire season.

Mark wasn't the easiest of people to get along with, he liked to drink and fight, neither of which I enjoyed, but we had grown up together and along with Tony and Michael, he was my best mate.

The drive to the ferry in Poole, Dorset was uneventful really, it took a lot longer than I thought it would with us only being able to drive at 50mph, secretly I wondered how we would ever get across France and Spain at that speed!

Cherbourg was a bit of a shock; we were lost as soon as

we arrived. I was the map reader/navigator, but the map wasn't much good when we were stuck on a roundabout not knowing which exit to take. Every sign said *"toutes routes"*, or *"sorte"*.

Neither of us spoke French, I spoke Spanish which was next to useless in a French speaking country whose natives didn't know or wouldn't speak to us in English. I remember saying to Mark

"We can't get away from "toutes routes" so let's go that way and see where it takes us." I didn't know it meant *"all routes"*.

The journey was fraught and full of tension, but Mark wanted to keep driving and we had decided to avoid the motorways and toll roads. The scenery was truly beautiful, there were chateaux's everywhere. I never realised France was so picturesque.

After a while Mark became tired so I took over the driving while he slept, only thing was I, didn't have a driving license for a manual vehicle, just an automatic. Nevertheless, I drove the van 100 miles or so.

We thought it best to stop so Mark could sleep for a few hours. While he was sleeping, I decided to get my bicycle out of the back of the van and go for a ride. Wow! It was beautiful, no traffic, no people, just me and nature. The silence and solitude were amazing, but also intimidating for a young man from a big city. The silence was deafening, I felt uncomfortable and vulnerable in such a wide-open space by myself, with only the birds and trees to comfort me. It's strange how you get used to noise without actually realising it.

I eventually arrived in a small hamlet of two or 3 houses. Some local children were amused at the site of a man with one arm riding a bicycle and were shouting and laughing at me. It was a little uncomfortable, so I did a U-turn and returned to the van. When I think back to events like that, I realise that I missed a lot of opportunities because of my insecurity. Today I would enjoy the change of scenery and ignore the comments, but I was still very young then. With my bike safely in the van, Mark awoke, and we went to a local cafe for drinks. The people were very welcoming and collected bank notes from all around the world. We gave them a £1 note which they added to their bank note collection.

We continued on our journey to Benidorm, but the drive was so long and frustrating that tensions escalated and on our final push down the coast road to Benidorm, I thought we wouldn't be speaking by the time we arrived, but we made it in one piece. He kept saying,

"We're going the wrong way! We're going the wrong way!"

I have to admit we argued a lot on that last push and although it didn't quite come to blows, I threw the map at him and said read the fucking map yourself. It felt as though I was on *"The Road to Hell"* and Chris Rea was singing in my ear as we reached our destination.

We were put up in a lovely apartment on a temporary two-week basis until more long-term accommodation could be sorted out. The apartment was above The Pink Elephant, so it wasn't far to walk to work.

The working day started at 8pm and continued until around 4am. It was a long night, but really good fun. I was the DJ and Karaoke presenter; I attracted a big crowd because I was good at what I did, and I spoke both English and Spanish.

During the day we would try to enjoy ourselves by sunbathing in the local hotel's swimming pool area. I say try because we were so tired from the previous night's work, we would generally fall asleep.

The money wasn't good, but our food, accommodation and drinks were free plus we received a little wage. It wasn't about the money though, it was about the experience, at least it was for me! I needed Mark to help move the equipment around from venue to venue, however, he wasn't keen to do that. The money we earnt and split between us wasn't enough to cover Mark's phone calls home every night to his girlfriend, I on the other hand had told Kathryn I'd only call a couple of times a week, invariably she would call me back at her expense.

Mark was homesick and missed Susan his girlfriend, now his wife. We'd been in the apartment only two weeks when Pepe the owner had found us more long-term lodgings, but Mark didn't want to go. He said he had decided not to stay and was going home. He wasn't interested in staying for the season, he had just been there for a two-week holiday. He suggested leaving me there with the equipment and my bike, but how would I get the equipment back home after the season ended or move it from venue to venue? I didn't have the means to move all of the karaoke equipment single handed.

There was only one thing to do if I couldn't convince Mark to stay, I would have to return with him and let Pepe the owner know we didn't intend to stay for the season and in fact we would be leaving in a couple of days. As you can probably guess Pepe wasn't best pleased, but then, neither was I.

This was our one and only opportunity to work a season

in Spain and it was over before we had even given it a chance. After this Pepe would never speak to us again, on the odd occasion we saw him on our holidays in Benidorm, he didn't want to know us and blanked us! Not only had we lost a great opportunity, but we had also lost a good friend.

We said our goodbyes and set off home. On the way back the van broke down, we were only half way through the journey in the middle of France. Good thing we'd taken out the AA cover. We were towed 750 miles back home. It was a fitting ending to the lacklustre adventure, but it taught me to choose who I would work with in the future.

Of course, when you're young everything seems more of a drama and lost chances cut deep. I was gutted, I still love Spain now and spend a lot of time over there when I can, in fact whilst writing this I have just come back from an English teaching holiday, so it wasn't the end of the Spanish love affair for me.

Early 90's being back from Spain meant working the Leeds circuit again, I was really popular and was working 6 nights a week, but it was incredibly tiring, Mark couldn't present and most of the time just sat around with our friends, which wasn't a bad thing, sometimes he would help with passing microphones, but I felt I had the bad end of the deal. All the hours were taking their toll on me. People don't realise the amount of energy that goes into presenting. Even now when I'm on stage speaking, it takes an enormous amount of effort to help lift everyone in the room and keep it energised. Even though I was young and having fun, I was burning out and falling out of love with presenting karaoke. I knew that I had to get out.

I knew I had to end the Karaoke adventure, I asked around, but couldn't find anyone willing to buy out the equipment, by now it was worth in excess of £4000.

I had a chat with Alan, my DJ mentor, he was interested, but didn't know how to operate the system and wanted me onboard with him. Alan said he would buy out Mark, although it came with some conditions. I would work the system and he would assist me. The deal was made, and Mark was bought out. I expected to get my exit shortly after, once I had proved how good the system was and after showing Alan how to operate it. However, Alan never bought my half out, instead we worked it together.

Unfortunately for me, Alan was a very busy and popular DJ and had other work commitments, so I would be assisted by Dave the friendly giant. Dave was a huge, intimidating looking guy, but the friendliest man you could ever wish to meet. I really enjoyed working with him. He was the muscle and the driver. I had basically swapped Mark for Dave. Dave didn't let me down by drinking though and would do all the heavy lifting, leaving all the presenting work for me. Only problem was, I needed someone who would be more hands on with the presenting, that's why I had agreed to work with Alan.

I realised I was in a worse or at least equally as bad situation as I was with Mark. I needed out, so once again I was looking for a buyer for the complete karaoke system, I got in touch with a few people and after a couple of weeks I got a call from a chap called Terry who was interested in buying.

Alan and I set up the system for a demonstration in Alan's garage, Terry and his business partner Jim loved it so much that they said there and then they would buy it, with one condition. They owned a bar in the South of France on a camp site called Camp du Pylon their condition was simple, they would buy it if I would spend a couple of weeks at the camp site setting up and operating the system for them. This was my only get out, so the decision was easy, I had to do whatever it needed, and I thought that it could be a great opportunity. I said I would, the deal was done, we shook hands and £4000 was handed over. I would travel in a week or so and could bring my girlfriend for a two week all-expenses paid working holiday.

We were given a lovely static caravan and made to feel really welcome and special. We arrived on Saturday, but were told to relax, enjoy ourselves and I could set up the karaoke system on Monday. The campsite was quite nice and the local tourist spots were wonderful.

I really enjoyed my time there with Kathryn, we had some great adventures along with some silly arguments, we were both stubborn and pig headed. In hindsight I should have just said *"I'm sorry, let's put it behind us"* and told her I loved her, but in all the time we were together I never said those three little words. There is probably a reason for this, but I don't know what that is, those words mean so much to us and yet they are so hard to say.

I completed my two-week obligation and showed the other members of staff how to be karaoke presenters, but they couldn't do it. I was asked to return to do the summer season and I agreed, but Kathryn would have to stay back in Leeds as she worked as a schoolteacher and couldn't commit herself to spending the whole season with me.

I had wrongly assumed I would be staying in a similar caravan on my return, how wrong was I?

I was given a seedy little room attached to the back of the kitchen. A kitchen that unbeknownst to me had a cock-roach problem. I came into my room one day to find a corner of my room was infested with them, as I spotted the cockroaches something ran across the wall at lightning speed. Like a mouse, but it couldn't have been a mouse on the wall! Was it a mouse with spider man like abilities? No, it was a gecko lizard. It scared the life out of me and really made me jump.

As I jumped in the air I screamed like a little girl and landed in the middle of the cockroach infestation! Oh, what a horror. I complained to the management, but they found it really funny.

Terry tried to calm down the situation by telling me not to worry about the gecko it wouldn't come anywhere near me and I wouldn't have any fly or spider problems because that's what geckos like to eat.

"Great" I said, *"will it eat the cockroaches too?"*

"No" was the answer, geckos don't like cockroaches!

Cockroaches are notoriously difficult to kill, they are one of the only species that are capable of surviving a nuclear war, they are not susceptible to radiation! Not that I had a nuclear weapon to drop on them but how was I supposed to eradicate them? It took me back to my early years when I was born into 'buggy park'. I don't believe in going backwards in relationships or life in general, but this was out of my control.

There were a couple of perks. As entertainment's manager I had to trial all the new trips that were being offered to the camp site guests. If the excursions weren't good enough, I would give constructive feedback on how to improve the experience before I would promote it during the evening's entertainment.

Whilst I enjoyed my time there, it was short lived, three

weeks in total. I just couldn't cope with the cockroach infestation.

I had to make the decision to abandon ship. That was the advice given to me by a new friend I had made whilst there, he was a ships skipper/captain who sailed private yachts and motor cruisers around the world for wealthy customers, hence his nautical theme of abandon ship! I took his advice and I was home on the next available coach.

I'm a good-natured person and I like helping people, particularly, when it includes something that I'm passionate about. Over the years this attitude has seen me taken advantage of time and time again. Just when I think I've learnt a lesson I go and set myself up again for another fall.

Don't get me wrong, I take responsibility for my own actions and accept that these lost opportunities aren't the fault of others, they were just mistakes, mistakes I had to make, that I alone would have to live with and regret.

For me though this was the end of DJing and Karaoke. I needed to do something else with my life and needed to push myself harder.

Although we don't always get the results we'd really like, the lesson I learnt was there is no such thing as failure, just different degrees of success.

Image Set B

1 - My Honda CR250 ATC, three-wheeler, I'm 19 just a year after losing my right arm.

2 - In my wooden shed that my mum's chap built. Surrounded by my motorbikes and parts before selling to the motorbike shop in Hollbeck. Age 18/19.

3 - My first ever car. I had to swap out the engine and gearbox to make it an automatic. I'm 19, I passed my driving test age 19.

4 - Age 25, this was my DJ promotional photo. I wanted to work abroad and thought I needed a promo pic.

5 - My collection of jukeboxes at one of the jukebox event I attended about 27 years ago, age 35.

6 - The Rockola jukebox I bought that the Sheffield dealer wanted to buy. I'm about 21 at the time. My shed was now a jukebox, slot machine and video game shed.

7 - My Wurlitzer 750 jukebox. This is actually a recent photo taken in 2019 and still awaiting restoration.

8 - Fancy dress at Inma's house. During the canavals of Badajoz.

9 - Fancy dress at Inma's house, photo is with Choni. During the canavals of Badajoz.

10 - In Choni's house with all the Spanish girl friends of Inma.

11 - Working on my DIY CNC router. Age 45. I think.

12 - My graduation photo taken in 2002 at Leeds Metropolitan University.

13 - Group graduation photo 2002.

14 - My creation, a robotic CNC router.

15 - My busy and super exciting workshop as it is today. Taken in 2019.

16 - Posing with my trumpet, I still play the very same instrument. Taken around 2016.

17 - Salsa dancing with Kate at the Engine Shed in Weatherby, taken around 2018.

182

184

185

Chapter 29
Catalyst For Change

The death of my grandma was the Catalyst for change in my life, Grandma died at the age of 87 in St Gemmas Hospice on December the 18th 1996, from secondary stomach cancer, she'd had undiagnosed breast cancer. It was such a traumatic and painful death, that left us all devastated.

When Grandma died it was a mixed blessing, I didn't want her to die, but I didn't want her to continue with her suffering either.

After the death of my grandma I ended my relationship with Kathryn.

I suspected she had been seeing someone else, I had no proof, but my gut instinct and her increasing emotional distance led me to believe she was. That and the fact she didn't want to go to our weekly night out to the local pub quiz.

One day she told me she was doing teacher training at a local hotel, but would be staying overnight, I suggested that I came over later in the evening to have dinner with her and her reaction was not what I had expected. She definitely didn't want me there, apparently it wasn't a good idea. It seemed illogical to me to stay at a hotel that was only five miles from where she lived. I suspected she was staying with another man.

To be fair, her previous history in seeing me whilst she

was living with another man, put doubt in my mind and made me question the credibility of her story.

Despite my suspicions about Kathryn's infidelity, I expected her to reach out to me with some emotional support during this hard time. My Grandma was dying of stomach cancer and I mistakenly thought Kathryn might still be there to support me. I didn't feel that and when someone so close to you dies, it makes you realise just how short and precious life is, that was my catalyst for change and so, I ended the relationship. After the breakups with both Cathy and Kathryn the song *"Cathy's Clown"* by The Every Brothers, haunted and taunted me.

Even though I had ended the relationship, I had hoped Kathryn would have contacted me to try and make things ok. I guess I was hoping that she might just say *"sorry I haven't been there for you"* and convince me that she wasn't seeing someone else, or just an attempt at a makeup to let me know she really cared. That didn't happen and I was truly devastated. I thought about her constantly and drove past her house reminiscing what used to be, but I was way too proud to back down.

Two years after we broke up, I met her brother by chance in an Italian restaurant when I was with some Spanish friends. It was good to see him, I asked after his sister and asked him to pass on my regards.

A few days later I received a letter from her. It was a beautiful letter that brought tears to my eyes.

Like a love story, it told of loss and longing, reminiscing on all the great moments in our relationship, it was a masterpiece. Oh, how I'd wished it hadn't taken two years to send. The letter ended with, *"if you are still single and would like to get back together please contact me, but if not please ignore this letter."*

I can't tell you how much I loved that the letter came from her heart. If only she had shown such emotion earlier. I threw the letter away about two years ago after holding on to it for such a long time. I knew I finally had to move forward, but even now; I wish I hadn't thrown it away. If only to remember how much she must have cared for me, but never actually put it into words before.

At the same time as feeling happy that she had finally contacted me, I had a moment of realisation that released me from my inner turmoil, I realised I was ok, and in fact I was over her, but I owed her at least a reply.

I contacted her not really knowing what I was going to say or do. I still remembered her telephone number and instead of writing, I called her.

"Hello Kathryn, it's Steven."

We talked for a while and agreed to go out for a drink to an Irish bar called the Regent, that used to be on Regent Street in Leeds. I liked going there and enjoyed listening to the Gaelic music.

We had a lovely night that ended with us back at her house doing what couples do. It felt like a mistake and I drove home at breakneck speed, feeling like I was running away from something terrible, it wasn't terrible it was lovely and I'd been longing to be with her, but I realised the moment had gone and it was a mistake to go back. I also realised I needed a break from women so I could find myself.

That statement *"find myself"* sounds ridiculous because I knew where I was, I just seemed to have forgotten who I really was and what I really wanted, only time alone and being single would allow me to do that.

The next day we spoke, and I told Kathryn I didn't want to be back in a relationship, I needed to be single, she replied, *"That's a shame Steven, you have a lot to offer a woman."*

What a beautiful thing to say, even though I was rejecting her.

I think about her, more than I like to admit. On occasion, when my journey takes me that way and I drive past her house, I still think about our days together. Even now, as I write this the memories bring tears to my eyes and a lump in my throat, pondering on what could have been.

It's fair to say I cared more than I wanted to admit, but things ultimately went bad. I wasn't in a place where I felt I could commit, and Kathryn also moved on with her life. She's married now.

It feels like only a few years since we split up, yet I was thirty-four and it was actually twenty-three years ago. I had neglected my friends while I had been with Kathryn, but now, newly single, I realised that I needed to change my life, I'd lost contact with a lot of my friends who had already moved on. Kathryn made me realise I could make more of myself and question whether I could perhaps get a better education.

I decided I would go to university and also take some salsa dancing lessons. Surely, I would make new like-minded friends there and hopefully address the inadequacy I felt due to my poor education and lack of a degree?

The lesson learnt was major events in our lives can be the catalyst for change, they can direct us down a different path from the one we ever thought we would walk, but walk it nevertheless, and enjoy the new destination when you arrive.

Chapter 30
A Proper Education

I'd been attending night school for a number of years before splitting up with Kathryn. I'd studied electronics to help with my vintage jukebox repairs, also metalwork, woodwork, and cabinet making because I enjoyed working with my hands. I always say *"hands"*, I guess because I still feel like I have two arms and never dream of myself with one arm.

I studied computer programming, Spanish language, you name it, I studied it. I wanted to correct my lack of education from school. However interesting these night school courses were, I didn't take any exams, and I didn't think exams in these subjects would help. After all, I was still unemployable, and with or without exam results I would not get a job due to disability discrimination. That was OK, though. I knew that and I wouldn't waste my time going to job interviews. I would just enjoy learning for the sake of learning.

I loved night school, so much in fact that I even returned to the old high school that I'd hated with a vengeance. I studied history there, but although history of the industrial revolution was quite interesting, it didn't grab me enough to make me want to do two years of it to A Level standard.

I loved challenging my mind, and as a result I came up with some great projects while studying Microsoft Visual

Basic (VB), I invented a small software package that decoded the colour codes of resistors used in electronics and electrical circuits. This was in the 1990's, when no other programme of that type existed. The same decade that Microsoft launched Windows 3 and Creative Labs introduced the Soundblaster Pro soundcard.

A very large electrical company in Leeds, who, due to legal reasons I can't name, wanted to buy my software to give away as a freebie with their component catalogue. However, negotiations didn't go well, and swiftly went from bad to worse after they had played with my software for a couple of weeks. They claimed that there were other freeware packages, already in the public domain, that could do what my software could do. They still made an offer, but it was derisory, so I chose not to accept. In hindsight I should have accepted because I ended up with nothing.

Allegedly, a month later, a version of my software was being given away as a freebie by this company. A friend rang to tell me that he'd seen something that looked like my software.

It was apparently very similar, if not the same, but I didn't pursue it. This type of intellectual property theft was becoming way too common, and companies seemed to like my ideas, enough to copy them and claim them as their own, without acknowledgement. I was asked by a lecturer if he could use my resistor programme idea as a project for his students. It was nice to be acknowledged in this way, but I had to refuse because it would have breached my copyright.

By now I had learnt, at least, how to copyright my own work. Copyright belongs to you as soon as you create something new, but it counts for nothing if you cannot prove it. Creating proof is very simple really. The way I do it is to post my idea to myself, recorded delivery and when it arrives in the post, it will have been date stamped. I don't open the envelope and leave it sealed. This is a basic form of copyright proof. Keeping electronic versions of any work you create will also be date stamped with its creation date, and therefore copyright is considered to be automatic. If that helps you in the future, then I'm pleased to share it.

I had learnt a lot at night school, more than I ever had at school, but this was about to change as adult learning courses were undergoing restructuring. This meant the end of courses that people were doing for fun. If the course didn't have an accredited qualification associated with it, it was dropped from the night school's curriculum. It was a disaster for those who wanted to do all the fun, social, and interesting courses that didn't warrant a qualification.

Fortunately, I had exhausted the majority of the courses I had wanted to do, but what would I do now?

I never thought I was good or clever enough for uni, after all, the teachers and the other students always told me I was stupid. It was a sequence of events that lead me there and I didn't really have a plan from the onset to attend. In fact, I probably only thought about it because Kathryn's brother was studying computer science at Leeds University. I had tried computer studies many years earlier, and was in fact offered a computing course at Leeds College of Technology, but that was way too soon after my accident and it felt like I was being offered it because it was something a one arm man could do, it was, but I didn't want to hear that! I wanted to hear I could do the same things as a man with two arms could.

I had enquired about university a number of times, but I

was always given the same response. I needed to do an access course to gain entry into university. My acceptance to universities would be dependent on my results.

I wanted to be university educated but university wouldn't take me because I had no qualifications from school. I think that I must have hit a mental block here. I didn't want to do the access course, I just wanted to go to uni and so I applied more than once, always getting the same response, do the access course.

Eventually, I realised that if I had done the access course when it was first suggested I would have finished it most likely and would have been at university! I decided not to procrastinate any more but apply for an access course in computing at Leeds College of Technology, the same college I had studied motor engineering at sixteen years earlier, although the name of the college and the venue had changed.

I started my access course and to my surprise, I enjoyed the things I previously hated at school. The course was more academic, like school and not so hands on manual work like I had been used to. I really enjoyed mathematics and I excelled at it, and according to my maths teacher I was doing higher level mathematics. On one occasion he asked if I'd studied calculus before, because my work was verging on calculus. I didn't even know what he was talking about, I hadn't studied anything at school, how could I be doing calculus?

English was a subject I'd always hated because of my dyslexia, I hated having to read aloud in class. I had only ever read one book from cover to cover in my life, it was a book called the 'Day of the Minotaur', I enjoyed that book, but generally I hated reading. English was all about reading though. I was told as well as studying all the aspects of computing I would need a minimum level of GCSE maths and English. I had to write lots of essays, which I had previously hated but now I was introduced to similes, metaphors and alliterations. I found I liked writing essays, my words came alive and it was easy to write 2000 words. There were always lots of spelling mistakes, but I used my computer and its spell checker. One handed I was quicker at typing than I was at writing about 50 wpm.

I had a newfound appreciation of the art of writing. I had to read a book from cover to cover so I could write a book review. I must admit I didn't want to, and I told the teacher about my hatred of reading, she suggested a book by Roald Dalh, 'Matilda'. This access course was changing the way I had thought about education in the past, I really enjoyed reading Matilda, what a great book.

Maths and English had been my weakest subjects at school, but they were pleasantly surprising me the second time around, they were also a prerequisite of going on to university. Without passes in maths and English no university would accept me.

In fact, I was enjoying all the aspects of the access course, from mixing with the other students to working on complex computer algorithms, programming languages and software packages I'd never even heard of. I was getting top marks in every subject; my overall results were topping the course.

At the end of my access course my results had been better than I had thought, so good in fact, I was awarded student of the year. My grades weren't just the highest in the access course, but they were the highest in the whole college. Me, the boy who failed education miserably at school, that was the point in my life when I truly realised that I could do anything I put my mind to, it had only taken 34 years to come to that realisation!

Jimmy Cliff sang the song *"You can get it if you really want",* I hadn't realised I wanted a proper education so bad, but the lyrics of that song reminded me that persistence would get me the things I never thought I'd have.

I'd had an academic and personal awakening. I felt mentally strong and capable of reaching the goals I previously doubted I could reach. I was liberated from the abyss of stupidity and it felt like a cloud had been lifted from me.

It doesn't take much to build a child, but it takes even less to break one. Had just one teacher taken the time to encourage me or find a way to reach me, my time at school and self-belief would have been so much better.

I realise looking back that those school years were wasted on fear and frustration. No child should go through that, but maybe the bullying gave me the strength after my accident and the lack of school education gave me the determination to better myself.

It's never too late to better yourself!

The lesson I learnt was sometimes it takes more than one attempt to realise you can achieve anything you want in life. If at first you don't succeed, try, try, try again.

Chapter 31
Accidental Landlord

It was 2002, Princess Margaret died in February of that year, the Queen Mother in the month of March and I became an accidental landlord,

I had decided that I wanted to own more property and thought it might be a good idea to buy my next-door neighbour's house. She was, coincidentally, also called Margaret and like us, was a council tenant, but we had managed to get a mortgage and were in the process of buying the house where I lived with my mum.

I still refer to the house next door ,as Margaret's house because to me, it will always be that, even though I am now the owner. Although I am only really its custodian until I depart this world, then it will be for someone else to take care of and they might, one day, call it Steven's house.

I managed to buy Margaret's house, I gave her the money to purchase it and she then left it to me in her will. The first month I was the owner, Margaret came round to my house to pay me the rent she had been paying the council. I told her no, that it was her home to live there for the rest of her life rent free. It gave me great pleasure in telling her she could spend the rest of her days without worrying about paying rent. She was a lovely neighbour and I was terribly sad when she died. I inherited the house, but at the time it was scant consolation because we had lost such a kind person and great neighbour, who had known my mum since she was a young woman. She had worked with my Grandmother and was known as *"little Margaret"*. As they did in those days, she married young and her husband went off to fight in the second world war. On his way back home after surviving the horrors of war he stood on a landmine and was killed instantly, leaving behind a wife and a new-born child, a son he never got to meet. Such a sad event that affected Margaret for the rest of her life.

One of my early memories was going round to Margaret's to see if she could change some money for my mum into 50 pence pieces for our electric and gas meters. Margaret saved all her 50 pences for Mum for when we needed them.

I wasn't ready to inherit the house, but when are we ever ready? I was going to live in it, but I was busy studying at University and didn't have time for the upheaval of a move, so I decided to rent it out. To my surprise I got £600 a month for it, even though the estate agents quoted rentals of only £450, but knowing the house was in a great location, with a beautiful open aspect, views over Sugarwell Hill, Mean-wood Valley and all the way to Adel, Otley and beyond. I knew I'd get more than they said.

After the sad passing of my next-door neighbour, Margaret I'd become a landlord and I was £600 a month better off than I had ever been. It was a good wage for me, I'd never had a wage and had been unemployable and retired from the age of 18, I was now thirty-five and finally had a modest income. The fact that Margaret's house rented out quickly gave me the confidence to think about buying an-other.

I had heard that houses were affordable in the East of

Leeds and I knew of a very nice tree-lined street. I drove over and looked to see if there were any properties up for sale. There was one, it was beautiful, it was an old Victorian terrace on three floors with one of those lovely peaked roof attic dormers, the whole house had gorgeous leaded windows and I fell in love. The only problem was that it had a sold sign up. *"Oh! What a pity",* I thought, I would have to just put that down to experience and keep looking.

I drove past that house for the next couple of months, nothing seemed to be happening, there was no work being carried out, no one moving in and the sold sign was still up. Why had no one taken down the sold sign? It would have been the first thing I would have done.

There seems to be a lot of songs playing in my head, but Shaking Steven's song *"This old house"* was bouncing around and felt really appropriate as the house was built in turn of the century, around 1895.

I asked my sister Tracy to write a note for me.

"If your sale has fallen through, I'd be very interested in purchasing, please call Steven Robinson" and I added my contact details. Tracy posted the note for me.

Two weeks later I got a call from the owner to say the sale had fallen through and it was for-sale, but he wouldn't take less than £84,000. I knew I wanted it but had to go through the process of viewing and sorting out mortgages. It was in a terrible state, but I could see its potential and I loved the windows. That was house number two.

I fully intended on living in this house, I was in love with it and wanted it to be my home. It was the windows that captured my affection. I spent hours and hours restoring it with the help of my mum and sister, knocking out walls and replacing the architraves. We removed all of the carpets and sanded the floors; the final result was stunning. It had taken a while, almost a year and I had been using money from the sales of my jukeboxes to cover the costs, but when it was completely finished, I realised that I had spent £25,000 and I needed recoup costs. To be honest I was devastated when I realised that I would have to rent it out. I still own it today and I know that in my heart, it's my favourite property. Of course, it was another good lesson learnt in not giving too much of my heart to a property and to think with my wallet when it came to refurbishments!

After that I got braver and started buying more houses. It became second nature, buying houses was as easy as buying a pair of trousers. I no longer felt the pressure or stress associated with house purchasing.

Other landlords I knew would say it's not worth buying in that area, but I had learnt not to listen to others when they told me what I could or couldn't do. I did my calculations and if they worked on paper, I figured that they would work in practice.

Throughout my life I have learnt lessons. Some the very hard way, others through stubborn determination and I can say, hand on heart, that you have to go with what feels right to you. You are the one that lives with the consequences and so you must always go with your instinct.

A very important lesson I've learnt is never listen to those who tell you *"you can't"*, because you can! Only listen to those who encourage you. If someone else can do it, why can't you? If it's been made before, why can't you make it?

Chapter 32
House Of Fun

Madness sang a song in the 80's called "*Welcome to the House of Fun*" and someone, unknown to me, had turned one of my rental properties into a house of fun or to be more precise a skunk farm, a cannabis factory. Many of my properties have been a house of fun, all night disco's and parties, Hostel of Hungarian teenagers exploited by an unscrupulous employment agency, although I've yet to have a brothel or at least that's what I believe.

I had rented a five-bed property to a Chinese family that seemed really lovely, they viewed my house with their two young children and decided they wanted to rent my property there and then, on reflection they were too keen and I had a nagging doubt about them. The referencing process began, which they passed with flying colours and started their tenancy a matter of weeks later.

They always paid their rent on time and so there was no need to suspect anything untoward. Until 6 months into their tenancy when they stopped paying their rent and stopped responding to phone calls, text messages and emails. One of the tell tail signs that a tenant has gone bad, is when they go on radio silence. So, after the tenant was a month in arrears I went round to the house. There was no one in the property or so it seemed when I knocked at the door for over 30 minutes and tried looking through the windows that now had dark blackout curtains drawn and no sign of life. At this point I wasn't sure if the tenant was still resident or whether they had in fact left without informing me, which was a common occurrence when tenants got into debt. I decided to let myself into the property to make sure everything was ok. It wasn't though, because the tenants had changed the locks and that is forbidden and is against the tenancy agreement. I couldn't get into my property via the front door nor the back door. I was panic stricken at this point because I realised something was definitely wrong.

It was 2009, the US had just arrested 303 people over 2 days, all members of Mexico's most ruthless drug-trafficking organization, a cult-like group known as *"La Familia Michoacana"*, and I was desperately trying to get into my property ASAP. I rang the local locksmith to come out and change the locks. He was drilling the back-door lock to gain access when a Chinese man turned up from out of nowhere saying stop, stop. I said to the Chinese man I will stop as soon as he paid me the outstanding rent, he said he would and went away to get the rent money. At that point the locksmith stopped drilling the lock. I asked why he had stopped, he said because the Chinese man didn't want him to drill the lock. I said,

"I'm the landlord and property owner, ignore the Chinese man and get me in my property"

However, after an hour we still couldn't get into the property via the back door, it had multiple bolts and internal locks that were locked from the inside. The Chinese man never returned. We had no option but to put our efforts into the front door lock. After another hour drilling locks the front door finally opened to a waft of acrid, damp, musky wall of vapours. It was like opening the door of an oven, the heat and smell that hit me, almost knocked me over. There were plastic blackout curtains covering the foot of the staircase, the letterbox was sealed off and there were moth ball strewn all over the floor.

I walked tentatively into the ground floor rooms, there was no one there. I shouted *"hello"* but no one answered. I climbed the stairs after fighting my way through multiple blackout curtains until I emerged on the landing of the first floor. I opened yet another blackout curtain to see what could be only described as a war zone, or more precisely a production factory, a huge house of hydroponics. I felt like I was fighting my way through the jungle of cannabis plants like an intrepid explorer of old, chopping away with my machete at the undergrowth, but I didn't have a machete nor any type of protection from venomous snakes or tropical spiders that would have been in the imaginary jungle I was now trying to escape. I decided it wasn't safe to go any further, there could be something or someone lurking about inside. I went back downstairs to call the police.

I've been asked on many occasions why I didn't just sell the contents of the house, the cannabis plants and the hydroponics equipment. The money from the sale would have paid for the vast amount of damage that had been done to my property, but there was no way I could do that because that would have made me no better than the people that had been growing it. My only recourse was to call the police.

The conversation that followed with the police was somewhat bizarre. I asked the police to come out to my property as I suspected it was being used as a skunk farm. The lady officer on the other side of the phone asked if I could see cannabis, I replied,

"I don't know what cannabis looks like"
she said, *"can you smell cannabis?"*

I then explained that I don't know much about cannabis plants or about their smell to which she replied, *"In that case what makes you think it's cannabis"*

I said in a somewhat sarcastic tone, and still in shock from my discovery,

"I doubt very much that they're growing potatoes with this amount of hydroponics"

She then told me she would proceed to make the necessary calls and send someone out to come and investigate. I told her, *"that would probably be a good idea".*

They took control of the property and I left them with a set of keys. Quite a long time after, they called to say they had finished but couldn't secure the property, so had left it open. I rushed round worried that someone would be able to enter the house, they would have been able to do that because when I got there the door was wide open and the property had been completely trashed by the police. The property was ten times worse than when I had last seen it, a mere 5 hours ago. There was running water into all floors, the police hadn't bothered to turn the water supply off to the hydroponics. Soil had been trodden into all the carpets and ducting had been ripped out of walls leaving massive holes throughout the house.

I opened an upstairs door to find a bin bag full of cannabis. I didn't have a clue what to do with it. I couldn't sell it or give it away because that would have made me a drug dealer. The only course of action was to ring the police, yet again. When I explained to the lady on the other end of the phone that the police had left a full bin bag of cannabis, she refused to believe that they would do that. I assured her that they had to which she replied *"can you bring it to the police station"*

I said, *"you've got to be joking, do you think if I get pulled by the police with a full bin bag of cannabis in my car, they would believe I was taking it to the police station?"*

I then made a flippant comment saying, *"if you don't want to come out for it, I'll put it on eBay"*

To which the lady operative replied, *"I'll send an officer round now"*. She clearly wasn't amused by the situation.

Three hours later a policeman with an arsey attitude turned up and said where is this alleged bag of cannabis we were supposed to have left. I guided him through the house into a small box room on the first floor at the front of the property. I entered the box room and beckoned him in, I closed the door behind us and pointed at a full bin bag, busting at the seams that had been left behind the box room door. I said, *"there is the alleged bag of cannabis."* The police officer took a look inside, his tone now completely changed. *"How did we miss that?"* he said.

With that he took the bag with him and said he would dispose of it. To this day I have an image in my mind of that police officer and his mates smoking the dope in their man cave or even back at the police station, but that's not a reflection of the police just my imagination and sense of humour.

I had to get the commercial deep cleanse cleaners in to clean up after the skunk farmers and police. They were just finishing the deep clean when they rang to say they had found two full bin bags overflowing with cannabis in the cellar. I thought, not again. I asked if they could dispose of them, I wasn't going to ring the police yet again. The cleaners said they would sort it, I'm sure I could hear a smile in their voice.

That, and so many other events almost made me sell all of my properties and get out of the property rental game. I say game because it is. I'm constantly battling with bad tenants not paying rent or damaging property and often anti-social behaviour. Fortunately though, with time and experience, you get to recognise the bad from the good just as in life in general; we start to recognise the good and bad in all things.

The lesson I learnt and one not to be ignored is trust your intuition, it is seldom wrong.

Chapter 33
University

Whilst it was vintage jukeboxes that bought Margaret's house, I wanted to get out of the jukebox business, I needed a change of direction and a new challenge.

I had applied to a number of universities, Leeds University was high in the league tables and had a very good reputation, but also a high-grade acceptance level as did York, although York was possibly even more prestigious than Leeds with much higher entry requirements. Leeds Metropolitan University was an ex polytechnic but had some really good connections in the world of industry and had two campuses within the city. Huddersfield University was somewhat unknown to me but was added to my applications as was Bradford just in case I wasn't accepted at my preferred choices of Leeds or York. Of course, any acceptance depended on me getting a pass on my GCSE Maths and English. I waited for what seemed like an eternity, I was stuck in limbo waiting to see what my next move in education would be.

After the longest wait ever, I eventually got my results and had passed both Maths and English, in fact, I'd achieved top marks, so I waited to see which universities would accept me.

I wasn't accepted at York, that was OK, it was a long shot and I'd only applied to see if I could make their high entry requirements. I thought however, before I accepted any university place, I should visit the ones that had accepted me. I'd actually been offered a place at every application with the exception of York, I was stunned. I hadn't really known what to expect and now it seemed like all the hard work had paid off. I decided to stay within Leeds where I lived. I already had a home so why pay for student accommodation in another city or even do a long-distance commute?

I really wanted Leeds University because I could see the Parkinson building from my house. It wasn't that far away, and I lived in an elevated position overlooking the city of Leeds. Across Meanwood Valley far in the distance was Leeds University's, Parkinson building and its famous clock tower.

The building was named after a rich benefactor donated £200,000 towards its construction in 1938 (Frank Parkinson) but the outbreak of World War II halted its construction and it was finally finished in 1951. It's a grade two listed building designed by Thomas Lodge in the Greek Revival style and has to be one of the most impressive buildings in the city of Leeds.

The only two sensible options I had were Leeds University and Leeds Metropolitan University. The open day arrived, and I went to Leeds University first. I was so disappointed with the concrete jungle and the computer science buildings that were 1960's throw backs, a concrete monolithic building that transported me back to my youth and the prefab houses of Crossgates and the Arndale centre. The facilities were second to none, but could I spend 4 years of my life here?

The next day I visited Leeds Metropolitan University at

their Beckett Park Campus, it couldn't have been more different, a polar opposite to Leeds University, it was surrounded by greenery in the middle of a park, a sanctuary nestled in nature.

The area in front of the main James Graham building was a green field called the acre, because it was an entire acre in size, there were beautiful big trees with students sat beneath resting their backs against the giant trunks and reading their books. I thought immediately, this is the place for me, I could spend a lifetime in these beautiful surroundings, reading my books beneath those great oak trees. Ironically, I wasn't to know that only a year later the large oak trees would be cut down due to disease and no one told me a science degree would not afford me the time to indulge in such romantic, even whimsical pursuits as relaxing under a tree and reading! A science degree was full on.

My first day was a revelation. I had expected all the students and school leavers with multiple A Levels to be super intelligent (of superior intellect) and I would be totally out of my depth. That couldn't have been further from the truth, how wrong I was! I was amazed at the levels of stupidity and none intellectuals that were at university, I considered myself a non-intellectual, but I felt I was leaps and bounds above a lot of the students, I guess common sense and life experience really were valuable qualifications that my younger peers didn't yet have.

The first year however did feel slow and repetitious, it covered almost subject for subject what I had just spent the previous year studying. It felt a bit of a waste of time having done the access course if I was simply to be repeating it all over, but at a different academic institution. It took about 6 to 7 months before I was being pushed academically and then it really wasn't a struggle. I had been warned that my second year wouldn't be such a breeze though.

My grades were super high, but I was really disappointed with one subject because I dropped 1% on a programming assignment, I only achieved 99%. Crazy really, just how disappointed I was, but it was a subject I didn't really like, programming in C++. I know how that reads, I should have been happy with 99% but it bugged me.

I went to the head of the computer department to speak to Tim Balls, he was dealing with some students that were trying to talk their grades up. When he saw me, he dismissed the other students saying, *"Get out, I have a real student here who is disappointed he only got 99%!"*

I told him I didn't like programming and thought I would like to change my degree for something different. He urged me to be patient saying I was a good programmer and that I would really enjoy the next language, I would learn *"java"* I listened to his advice and stuck it out in the programming route and computer networking. To my surprise he was right, I really liked the Java programming language.

It was different, very trendy, a nice language to work with and much quicker than other computer languages to get results from. It was a breath of fresh air, it was my saviour and would prove to be a great money earner in the future, although I wasn't to know that when I first started to learn it.

My grades in the first year were great all well above the average, I was getting 100% on most subjects, the subjects I didn't like would never fall below 90%. All in all I enjoyed that first year, I made some great friends, many of them were Spanish and I became the unofficial Spanish - English translator because I could speak both languages, I excelled at foreign languages, I attended all the parties although many of my friends were considerably younger than I was. I even had to buy a pair of pyjamas at the age of 35 for my first ever pyjama party in the halls of residence! I've still got those pyjamas.

My second year, however, was completely different. It challenged me in ways I never expected and brought me close to abandoning my dream of a degree. It started with a bang, a rude awakening and a real shock to the system.

I would say my access course was much more advanced and interesting than the first year of Uni, but the second year was known as the shock year, pressure would be deliberately put on, deadlines imposed that were near impossible to meet. I did meet them all, but at considerable cost of burning the midnight oil and often working throughout the night without sleep.

Second year 'blues' was a term I had heard a lot and it seemed many people suffered from it, however my second year at Uni was in fact my third year of full time education, so I had managed to stave off the blues for 12 months but then it hit me like a tonne of bricks. I felt it the most when we had to do a group project.

In our classroom, one day we were told to put our names on a piece of paper and place them into a hat. We then had to take turns a picking a piece of paper from the hat, this is how we would be grouped together in groups of 3 or 4 for our group project.

I suppose like most students I'd hoped I would get the people I liked working with and also with my Spanish friend Jose, who was also paid by the disabled student support office to be my helper. He would open doors for me, carry bags and help out whenever I needed assistance.

Luck however, was certainly against me that day because I got three Asian boys who didn't really want to be at Uni, they were merely postponing the inevitability of having to get a job, I guess when you are a school leaver and don't know what you want to do with the rest of your life it might seem like a good idea to spend more time in education while you make up your mind. I didn't have the same luxury of time that they had, I was already thirty-five and this would be my one and only chance at Uni.

I had asked the lecturer to allow me to swap groups so I could be with my disabled support helper, but he'd said no. Unfortunately for me my three team members never arrived to scheduled meetings for progress reports and group work sessions and consistently failed to complete deadlines or deliver any work that had been assigned to them by the group. It was becoming a joke and yet the lecturer refused to let me work with my disabled helper and other mature students. Finally, I couldn't take the stress anymore and I developed shingles, I was so ill I just wanted to pack it all in.

I went to the disabled students support office and told them about my situation, the fact I couldn't get any work from my other group members and that the lecturer was ignoring my needs as a disabled student. I was told to put it in writing requesting a move to be with my support worker and mature student network and to send a copy to the lecturer and the disabled student support office. I heard nothing, I kept sending the message to my lecturer, who by now had issues with me and was making life quite difficult.

He would, in my opinion give me marks that didn't correspond to the amount of work I'd done. Including giving me 50% on a project that I'd correctly done 75% of the work for.

When the grade came in for the group work, I got 25% the other members of the group had made excuses and were marked up, but my only excuse was poor team effort. I was so upset, disheartened and felt victimised, I needed to do something.

If I had accepted the grades my lecturer was subjecting me to, I would have failed the group project and that would have brought my overall grade for the second year down and that would directly impact my final degree results. At this point I decided to make an official complaint against the lecturer and provided the evidence. The result was to meet with the head of the department to put in an official complaint that would be taken very seriously. The complaint was officially accepted, and my supporting evidence was upheld. The lecturer was shown to have been anti-disabled, that he had ignored my requests, I was therefore awarded an average mark based on my other subject results. I never spoke to the lecturer again and he avoided me, never actually acknowledging how he had treated me nor apologising. I realise now, this was the first time that I had actually challenged disability discrimination that had been deliberately directed at me.

I hated my second year from start to finish and the only way I could get through it was on a day by day basis. If I thought about getting through a whole week, I wouldn't have lasted. I told myself every day, just get through today Steve, don't think about tomorrow until tomorrow. It worked, but I was fighting the urge to quit. I hate quitting and even when I don't like what I'm doing, I need to see it through to the end.

I faced each and every day one at a time and finally the last day of my second year of Uni arrived. What a relief. It was a mixture of emotions, I felt like I'd been to hell and back, I had been stressed, driven to illness, but yet survived the experience.

I'd enrolled onto a sandwich course, which meant my third year would be a year spent in industry. One of my friends on the same course route as me (computer networking) was a Spanish guy called Arturo, his father was very well connected in Spain, he was the boss of Iberdrola, the power generating company of Spain who was best friends with Vincente Del Bosque, manager of Real Madrid Football Club (if you're into football, which unfortunately I'm not).

My friend Arturo said he could get us both a job in Madrid with one of the companies that subcontracted to Iberdrola. I wasn't sure whether this would be a real job or one fabricated so the subcontractors could ingratiate themselves with the big boss of Iberdrola, I guessed only time would tell.

Normally *"practicas"* as it's known in Spain (placement year), don't pay wages to the placement students, but we were different according to Arturo's father and the subcontractors, we would receive a wage. Arturo's parents would organise accommodation for us in Madrid, even though Arturo was from Salamanca a mere one and a half hours away from Madrid by train.

I had hoped we'd have our own little place, a little apartment or studio flat where we could cook, invite friends around or even share with other students. That wasn't to be, we ended up in an apartment in the centre of Madrid, on the corner of Conde Duque and Alberto Aguilera in an area

known as Arguelles, a very posh and up market area, apparently, although you really wouldn't think so by the looks of
the place. I thought it was very run down, but it had a beautiful entrance with Moorish inspired tiles and was
surrounded by the hustle and bustle of traffic, there was no
rest from the incessant rumble of the city.

Arturo's mum, in her role as a considerate and caring
mother had found an apartment owned by a Spanish lady
who rented out rooms to students. We would have to live in
someone else's home and live by their rules, something I
didn't really want to do, but I was advised that accommodation in Madrid was very expensive and this was the best
we could get for our money.

The rules of that apartment were strange, and I struggled
with them. The owners didn't want me to cook at English
hours of dining of 6pm, they didn't like that and they didn't
like it if I cooked a curry because it was a smell they weren't
used to, this frustrated me and got me down, where was the
freedom I was looking for, the fun of cooking for myself
and my friends?

I'd been really excited about cooking and being self-suf-
ficient, I'd done a cookery course, I'd taken all my
disability cooking aids, pots and pans, a mini food proces-
sor and my recipe book, made up of recipes from my mum
and sister and some other more exotic dishes. I can't tell
you how much I was looking forward to it.

The shower regime was equally strange, the shower was
in the far end of the kitchen, it was a little awkward having
to walk through the kitchen having just left a shower, I
didn't have to walk through unclothed, there was a small
area in the bathroom to change, but everyone in the kitchen

could hear you getting a shower and it didn't feel very private, the glass door didn't help either.

The water boiler and the rules of using it were in my opinion crazy and somewhat bizarre. In Spain back in 1999 they didn't have piped gas supplies all they had were Calor gas bottles that were connected to the gas supply inlet. The rules for using the shower were:

Turn on the gas bottle, which was outside on the terrace. Turn on the gas supply valve to the boiler, turn on and ignite the pilot light and then you could take a shower, if the gas ran out halfway through, tough. After finishing your shower, you had to extinguish the pilot light, turn off the boiler gas supply valve and go outside to turn off the gas bottle supply.

What a stupid set of rules! Why couldn't the gas bottle be left on, it had two valves and why could the pilot light not be left on? It was just annoying, I know why the pilot light needed to be extinguished, it was to save their gas supply, I knew that and accepted it, but it was a pain in the arse to say the least.

My bedroom joined on to the main living room and the glass door that separated my room from the lounge/TV room didn't offer me much privacy nor did it provide any noise insulation. It really wasn't ideal but at least I had a window; one that looked out onto the busy roads of Madrid, again not much in the way of noise insulation and my sleep suffered because of those two issues. The window was nice though and I enjoyed letting the daylight into my room and I would leave the wooden Persiana blinds open so I could enjoy the daylight and warmth of Madrid when I returned home from work at the end of the day. However, this was against the house rules and every time I returned home someone had closed the blinds.

I kept opening them until I was told by the lady owner, I was not to leave them open because it would create too much heat in my room. It was my room, I didn't mind but the landlady did.

I struggled with my time in Madrid I was bored. My friend wasn't any company as he never left his room and was always there by himself. There was nothing to do at work, I was told on a daily basis to play on the internet, this of course wouldn't be accepted by my lecturers and placement officer at Uni, they wanted to see my work progress of which there was none. My only saving grace was the fact I knew one Spanish girl in Madrid who was a salsa dancer, so I would go out dancing with her as much as was possible, but that wasn't often enough.

We used to go to a great salsa club called *"El Son"* close to Puerto del Sol. The entry fee included a free drink, my drink of choice was a Bacardi and coke, Spanish measures are enormous, an almost full glass of Bacardi and a tiny bottle of Coke. I've never been a big drinker so after one drink I was really tipsy, but full of bravado and confidence on the dance floor. My tipsy state gave me the confidence or lack of inhabitations to ask women to dance and to be brave enough to free style for the first time in my dancing life. I was liberated and after that I would never look back, I would dance with everyone even though my moves were somewhat limited, I'd only been doing salsa lessons for a short time.

On one occasion I asked the DJ if he knew someone who would dance with me, it was a night that my Spanish friend and moral support wasn't available to go out. The DJ said he would find me a dance partner he brought a young woman over to me and introduced us, I don't remember her name, but what I do remember was that she only had one arm! How crazy! He must have thought that because I had one arm, only another person with one arm could or would dance with me. I found that really strange, it felt wrong, I didn't want to be a book end with matching missing arms but to my surprise she was a great dancer, I bet we looked a picture, like a circus show, two one arm salsa dancers performing for the crowd that were watching with amazement, like being at a freak show! It was a funny situation, although somewhat bizarre, the DJ meant no offence and none was taken, but it was a surreal moment.

I'd been in Madrid 3 months, the only thing I had done was play on the internet, go salsa dancing, see the crazy area of Madrid known as La Casa del Campo that became a legally tolerated prostitution zone, the street of a thousand prostitutes *"La Calle de la Montera"* and the gay quarter known as Chueca. Not that I frequented them but a friend I had made, liked to show me these strange places, they were weird but also very interesting in their strangeness.

I was amazed by everything, the tapas market *"el Mercado de San Miguel"* and *"Los Mesones"* the beautiful little tapas bars that lined the western side of the Plaza Mayor, but work was killing me with boredom, and I was super depressed. My placement officer, back at Uni was asking when he could expect my first progress report. Arturo had already finished and had returned to England to finish his final year, he had never intended staying the whole year, he just wanted a summer placement.

I decided although very reluctantly, to return home. I felt gutted about the fact I would leave and not complete a whole year, but I realised that playing on the internet would be a year wasted. I returned home after Tony my friend from school and later my mum and sister had visited me in Madrid.

I was so happy to go home, I had been so depressed in Spain, so much so I would not return to the country I had previously loved for another 10 years. Madrid really put me off the country I wanted to make home, but in retrospect all capital cities are very similar, they are vast unsociable places, sprawling metropolis where making new friends is hard and one of the few places one can feel truly lonely surrounded by people.

I informed Uni that I had returned home and that I was taking a year out. I didn't want to return when all my friends were doing work placements, I wanted to finish my studies with them so I decided to take the year out and concentrate on my final year project, even though it couldn't be agreed until I was back at Uni. My project idea had to carry high enough marks for complexity and the required research worthy of a first-class honours, I wanted no less. In the back of my mind I wanted to get a better grade than my ex-girlfriend Kathryn, who had a 2-2 in French and History. I decided I would take the plunge and do the project I wanted to and make it fit the requirements.

I didn't really know what that project should be, but I knew a lot about jukeboxes, so it seemed a logical step to create software for a digital touchscreen mp3 playing jukebox, after all digital jukeboxes were in their infancy and the mp3 format was the big thing in digital media. It was also a rational choice to use the java programming language because it was a nice language that I understood well enough and enjoyed.

After many incarnations of software and hours spent re-searching media formats and available hardware technologies, I had a crude but working piece of software, I would spend the next eight months perfecting it and adding more functionality and error resolving, using well known software testing methodologies known as *"break me if you can"*, performance, load and stress testing and studying product development life cycles.

Eventually, I had working digital jukebox software, but I wanted to go one step further and actually create a working jukebox with a touchscreen, a coin mechanism, a cabinet and audio system. I drove all the way to Edinburgh to buy a CRT touchscreen monitor that cost the bargain price of £80, I bought a coin mechanism and a coin mech controller and connected it all through a used keyboard micro control-ler, everything was put into one cabinet and audio connected to a set of active pc speakers, voila! I had a work-ing jukebox.

It was a masterpiece of simplicity, and it worked incred-ibly well. I had completed all the software before returning back to Uni for my final year, the hardware side and cabinet building was done while in my final year, all that remained was to convince my tutors that my project was suitable, I had taken a massive gamble, but would it pay off?

I submitted my proposal with as much technicality as possible, outlining the problems and solutions and the re-search needed to achieve my goals. I was right to take the gamble it was accepted by both of my final year tutors. Now all that was left to do was to write up my dissertation, but I had a whole year to do so, well more like 8 months. It wasn't all I had to do, I had to get over 85% on all of my subjects if I wanted to get a first-class-honours, and that wouldn't be easy. I had to study hard, but I also wanted to enjoy my final year so had to play hard too, if I was to balance my life.

I had time-tabled my life to military precision with my days planned out hour by hour, specific hours dedicated to specific subjects and also free time when I would party the night away at the many salsa scenes in Leeds, especially now I'd found my courage to free style. I can probably say that my final year of university was my best year, I enjoyed finishing my project and my social life was great.

When final year exams arrived, I'd been given extra time due to only having one arm, I had to type everything, and whilst I was pretty quick at typing, I still wasn't as quick as I used to be at writing when I had two arms. I was also given extra time due to my dyslexia, but I had to take my exams in a different room from the other students, so I wasn't disturbed by them leaving and because my start times were different.

The room I was given was in a portacabin, when I got to the door where my exam was about to start, I found that I couldn't get in. This *"special location"* they had chosen for a disabled man with one arm, had a door with two handles. A handle that was at a high level and a lower level handle, they were both round doorknob types that couldn't be operated with one hand at the same time. José my disability support was taking his own exams in the main exam hall. I was locked out and nobody was coming or going because it was a special location for me only. I stood there for about thirty minutes waiting for someone to exit the door, but no one did. I eventually found a passer-by and asked them to help me, they did, thankfully; but the situation had delayed me forty minutes.

It was funny really and especially with a retrospective view, but at the time it was stressful and a ridiculous oversight by the disabled support team. It took a while longer to explain why I had turned up so late to my exam, but a simple demonstration proved everything, and the invigilator hadn't heard me knocking at the door.

The day arrived when we were told our results would be posted on the student notice board. I turned up, read the results of my friends, one of them told me she had got a first class. Strangely out of 350 students on the computer science degree only 5 of them were women, not the course to do if you hoped to find love.

I looked at my results and I didn't understand them, it said *"1"* my friends said things like 2:1, 2:2, but I wasn't sure what *"1"* meant until my friend Paula said

"You've got a first Steve!"

I'd done it, I was overjoyed, a bit shocked, I was like a rabbit caught in the head lights of a car, I was looking but in disbelief. It's what I had been working towards and what I'd put in all the effort for and all the trials and tribulations I had gone through to get this result was testimony to my determination.

I'd wanted to pack in university on so many occasions but the idea of not finishing something that I had started was inconceivable for me. I felt invincible, I truly could do anything I put my mind too, even academia and I certainly wasn't a natural academic, but I realised I really enjoyed learning and since losing my right arm and having to develop the right side of my brain (left handed and left footed) I had become more creative, with the positive attributes of a lefty.

I had started my university journey at the age of thirty-five, I was now forty, it had taken five years of my life, that it was finally over was a big relief, yet I also felt sad because it had become a routine and I didn't have that to return to the next day. I initially started the educational journey to make new friends as well as beat Kathryn's 2:2. I had, but to be honest that was no longer the reason. I had stopped competing with others and was merely competing with myself.

My friends went their own way and I lost contact with them, which was a great pity. Now though, I had to look for a job, I'd never had a job and wasn't keen on applying, remembering the days when I was point blank refused on the basis that I had one arm. I toyed with the idea for a while and even made a few applications, but to no avail, I didn't even get to an interview. I realised that I should stick to my original plan after losing my right arm and I would employ myself because I would not self-discriminate.

The lesson learnt was no matter what age you are, it's never too late to learn and no matter what obstacles get in your way, you can always climb over them.

Chapter 34
Salsa

I'd always wanted to be able to dance with a woman. In the past, I'd seen men dance so confidently and make their partners look great, and I wanted to be one of those men. How I wished Grandad was still alive to teach me to dance. I think about Grandad a lot, wishing all the time that he was still alive, but he isn't. It's been over 30 years since Grandad died and I still think about him every day!

I'd heard about a place called The Boston Exchange, it was in Headingley, a place more famous for its cricket and rugby grounds. Headingley stadium has been home to Leeds Rugby League and the Yorkshire Cricket Club since 1890. The grounds are celebrating their 130th anniversary this year, 2020. The Boston Exchange did salsa classes on a Tuesday. I didn't dare go by myself, so I convinced my mum and sister to come with me.

After a couple of weeks, I knew some people to say *"hello"* to, and my mum and sister stopped coming with me. When I started to learn to salsa there was an abundance of women and men were in short supply. This worked in my favour for a while because it meant male partners were in demand and the women would have to be more pro-active if they wanted to dance, so they would often have to ask men to dance. It was a wonderful feeling being needed or wanted; I loved salsa. I felt great inside, I didn't need to ask women to dance again and wouldn't be rejected anymore, or so I thought. I knew how hard it was to ask a partner to dance so I would never reject a woman who had the courage to ask me to dance. It was just a dance after all, and I was so grateful for that dance.

I was in the beginners' class for years, and they had to drag me out of beginners to intermediate.

Six months later, they dragged me into the advanced class. You had to be invited to move up a level and couldn't just make the move by yourself. I am a natural dancer; I love it and couldn't get enough of salsa dancing. I was going to the club six nights a week, even when studying for my final year at university, and I was making loads of new friends, mainly female.

My objective had been achieved, I had finally become that man that I so wanted to be, the one who could dance confidently with a woman and make her look and feel good, which in turn made me feel good.

I never looked back again. Salsa dancing was my saviour and still is today. I still go dancing around three times a week, on average. It's great exercise and the most social activity I've known. It was never something I did to find romance, although dancing did lead to romance on a couple of occasions! However, that wasn't the driving force for me. For me, it was the dancing I was passionate about. A song by the Nolan Sisters summed up that passion *"I'm In the Mood for Dancing"*, but there was never a point when I wasn't in the mood for dancing.

These days, people typically ask me, *"How long have you been dancing, Steve?"*, and I usually tell them I've been dancing all my life, but salsa dancing for around 15 years, but in fact, I started salsa in the year 2000—20 years ago!

From salsa, I swiftly moved on to learn new dance styles such as, merengue, bachata, kizomba, salsaton, boogaloo, samba, ballroom, Latin American, rock 'n' roll and swing jive. I was born to dance, and I learnt I never wanted to dance by myself again. I only ever want to dance with a partner. It's an amazing feeling, and I can only liken it to a love affair, a love affair that lasts for the length of the song. With a woman in my embrace, and me in her arms, I got my emotional fix, an emotional fix that was wonderful, without any expectations or conditions.

When I dance, I give myself completely to the dance and to my partner. I'm liberated from my Englishness and the need for my personal space. After all, I have invited my dance partner into my personal space, and once the dance has connected us, it is as though we are the only two people in the room!

I was once at a salsa dancing congress in Southport at Pontins Holiday Camp with a group of salsa dancing friends, I felt uncomfortable about doing a class because it was a big class and I was worried that I'd be dancing with people that didn't know me and would simply think I was incapable of dancing with one arm. My anxiety levels were quite high, and I was expecting that I would experience the untouchable scenario again where women simply didn't want to touch my shoulder where my arm was missing. However, I wasn't expecting what did actually happen. The class started, there must have been somewhere between 300-500 people, the room was jam packed with hardly any space to dance. We had started a move when the teacher said from the stage

"This class isn't suitable for a one-armed man; it will be too difficult for you."

I felt so small, so humiliated in public, in front of all those people. I had to do a walk of shame whilst everyone watched me. How can one keep his pride in such a situation, how was I supposed to walk tall with my head in the air and my chest pushed out? I couldn't! I also couldn't escape quietly and unnoticed. I would really like to name and shame that teacher, but I also don't want to ruin or tarnish his career just because of his ignorance. I watched the dance routine from the back of the room. It was super easy and wouldn't have presented any problems to me. The teacher had underestimated my ability as a dancer, but this wouldn't be a one-off occurrence, it would be an issue that would haunt me forever, others underestimating my abilities.

That said there were also some great teachers that were more than aware of my abilities and would teach the class for the two-armed people and the one-armed person. In effect they would teach two routines to the whole class. Inclusion is a massive thing in the workforce these days and in general life and wellbeing, but these teachers went above and beyond their duty to include me and give me the dance skills I have today. Tanya Cusan, a Colombian salsa teacher living in Leeds, taught me everything about salsa dancing and was my salsa saviour, she still teaches today, and I owe her such a debt of gratitude. Nicolai Vigneswaren and Gormack Dione would change their whole pre-planned routine to accommodate and include me in their classes. I'm now an advanced salsa dancer with twenty years of experience, thank God for those who could see beyond my disability and saw the same challenge in me as I saw in myself.

Never judge a book by its cover, you never know what someone is capable of until you give them a chance.

Chapter 35
Exposure Therapy And
The Psychotherapist

I met a few interesting people while salsa dancing, mainly women, that was because I would spend most of my time dancing with female partners. My circle of female friends was enormous; however, I was always relegated to the friend-zone, which was OK because sometimes I wasn't sure if I wanted anything else, but also at times, I wanted someone to love. I was in turmoil, an inner struggle that continues to this day. I don't want to be single but at the same time I value my freedom and my social circle.

One of the few men I knew from the salsa scene was Peter, he was of Iranian descent, but he looked like a Latino. He had long dark hair, dark skin and was a great success with all the women. Unbeknown to me, he was a psycho-therapist working for the NHS in Leeds.

We used to meet up for a drink at the Deer Park pub on Street Lane, Leeds and he would tell me of his exploits. To a guy who wasn't too comfortable with the dating scene, I thought there may have been some nuggets, pearls of wisdom I could use to better my chances of finding love. I'm not sure Peter was looking for love really, but it's what I longed for and still do to this day.

Who doesn't want to find love and find someone to

spend their life with and grow old together? However, I couldn't get past first base, asking a girl for her telephone number. Even thinking about it put me into a near state of panic, I would over analyse how to ask, what their response would be, how to handle the rejection etc... I told Peter of my fear during one of our meet ups at the Deer Park and Peter told me about a therapy used by psychotherapists, known as exposure therapy.

In the early 1920s, psychologist Mary Cover Jones, known as the *"mother of behaviour therapy",* used an early form of exposure therapy to help one of her clients conquer his fear of rabbits.

Peter went on to explain what exposure therapy was. He said, *"if someone has agoraphobia and is afraid to leave the house, we give them a set of tasks to do, task one is to open the door every day for a week, then close it and go back inside the house. Task two was to open the door walk to the garden gate or just outside their house, then turn around, walk back inside the house and close the door"* This was done for another week. The weeks after entailed walking to the shops and back, then a little further and a little further until they de-sensitised, at which point they were cured, or at least well on their way to recovery.

Peter said I should use exposure therapy to cure my fear of asking for women's telephone numbers. He explained what I should do. He said, *"every woman you meet, ask her for her telephone number. It doesn't matter whether you fancy her or not this is just about de-sensitising"*

I told him I wasn't sure I could, but I'd try.

Raffaella Carra sang a song in 1978, it was called *"Do it, Do it Again"* and that was exactly what I'd do until my fears were beaten and conquered.

The first time I asked a woman for her number I was super nervous and asked in a rather pathetic manner *"Can I have your number please?"* the answer of course was no. I kept asking though. I got lots of rejections until I realised, I was doing it all wrong.

I needed to be more of a man about it and not such a shrinking violet, so I changed my approach by saying *"give me your number"* it was more direct and surprisingly it worked. I started having success after success. I got braver and started handing my phone to women and saying, *"put your number in there."* Still a command but a bit easier than having to put their number in my phone myself. Other occasions they would just give me a missed call, so I had their number. I was so successful I had a phone full of women's telephone numbers however, I didn't go the extra mile and actually call them. I felt I'd got their numbers under false pretences by saying *"give me your number we should go dancing"* How I wish I'd said *"Give me your number, let's go for dinner"* maybe if I had I wouldn't still be single, but I thought that maybe they were just being friendly or polite.

I wish I'd had the courage to call them, but my training hadn't extended to what to say or do after getting their numbers.

I'd heard of something called the three-day rule that men use, they think they shouldn't appear too keen so leave it at least three days before contacting their potential date. Stupid really, if you like someone, isn't it best not to let the grass grow under your feet and call them straight away, why leave it any time at all? At least she would have known I was keen and what's wrong with being keen?

Some of the numbers however had been in my phone for months, I'd conquered my fear, but it hadn't actually got me anywhere! I felt liberated, strangely though I very rarely ask a woman for her number these days but when I do, I don't feel uncomfortable I do however, make sure it's for dinner or sometimes I'll mention the date word, but that word often scares women as they must think that more is expected of them, when in fact nothing is expected of them other than their company.

I would become a master of exposure therapy later in life that would see me doing the thing I never dreamt I would ever do, the fear of horses, flying and getting back on a motorbike would all be conquered. When I think back to my time in hospital, when I was a shy young man and the female nurses were doing all my personal care, I realise now that I was experiencing exposure therapy. Literally, being exposed to all that personal care at female hands had desensitised me. I'd been naked and vulnerable which put an end to my shyness.

I would never be the same again, now I had recognised the power of exposure therapy. I truly was going through a metamorphosis like the chrysalis of a caterpillar to a butterfly, still not 100% sure how I would emerge but when I did, I would be unrecognisable from my previous state.

Exposure therapy taught me a very important lesson. Without fear I could achieve anything. Most of us have a fear of something, imagine a life without them, a life where nothing will hold you back!

Chapter 36
Robinson's Jukeboxes Ltd.

After University it seemed a logical step to further develop my digital jukebox. In fact, I had to redesign the software totally so that Uni didn't own the copyright. Eventually I had redesigned everything and created a novelty digital jukebox into a full-size fibreglass astronaut statue. One thing that has stopped me from working with other university projects, is that I don't believe in handing over copyright for my inventions.

The Police sang "*Walking On The Moon*" in 1979 that went to number one in the UK charts, ten years earlier in 1969, Neil Amstrong and Buzz Aldrin had actually walked on the moon, if you believe in that or whether you subscribe to the conspiracy theory. The fibreglass astronaut statue was modelled on their iconic flight suit.

I had remodelled the statue to accommodate a touchscreen monitor into its chest and a coin entry into its stomach area, a mid-range speaker was placed in its lower abdomen, tweeters in its shoulders and a bass speaker into a custom base box on the statue's plinth. I'd created a rear opening and hollowed out the inside of the statue so that all the electronics, computer, amplifier and coin handling could be placed inside. I then made a novel coin draw that was opened from behind the statue at its lower back.

If I say so myself, it was a masterpiece, I made this juke-box to prove that I could put my versatile system into any conceivable cabinet. I decided to do yet another jukebox show and my *"Astrojuke"* as I decided to call it would be the centre piece, the jewel in my crown.

At the jukebox fair the Astrojuke got lots and lots of at-tention and was particularly admired by a Scottish chap that kept coming back and looking, eventually he said,

"Did you make this digital jukebox?"

"Yes" I said, *"do you like it?"*

"I do, but could you build one into an old NSM cabi-net?"

I asked him if there was such a cabinet at the show, there was, and he showed it to me.

I explained before seeing the NSM cabinet that my sys-tem was the only retrofit type on the market and it would fit into any conceivable cabinet and that was the whole pur-pose of my Astrojuke, it was to prove the concept. When I saw the cabinet, the Scottish guy wanted me to build my system into, it was just a plain but well-built wall mounted cabinet. I could build my system into this and it would be easy, I wouldn't need to put as much work into the refit as I did with the Astrojuke.

The Scottish guy was called Angus, he was a jukebox and slot machine operator from the highlands, he said if I could do the refit, he would guarantee that he would buy the first two from me at my price of £2200. My Astrojuke didn't sell at the jukebox show but my other vintage juke-boxes did, and I secured an order for two NSM refits, Angus would supply the cabinets free and he would have them de-livered to me.

The retrofit wasn't too difficult, the hardest thing was

finding the correct touchscreen interface to use, I found the solution after a visit to a local jukebox manufacturer, in Leeds. They were using a touchscreen technology used by estate agents that allowed customers to control their website, via touchscreen through their shop window. I won't go into details as to how I found the right manufacturer, even though I'm tempted, let's just say I had a few false starts but eventually found what I needed.

Angus arranged to pick up the two jukeboxes and paid me £2200 each, the price represented a good profit, approximately £1200 on each jukebox. Angus ordered another 4, and then some more.

The later versions were called plasma touch and incorporated a plasma disk as a feature that created blue plasma arcs on a circular plate that pulsed sound to light. Angus loved them but wanted so many I struggled with production. He wanted them at a greater frequency than I could produce; but Angus had a suggestion, he knew a company in the North East of England that would manufacture my jukeboxes under licence. He would get my jukeboxes much quicker, but it would mean I wouldn't be making the profits I had been making, I would have to agree on a royalty/license fee for each of the jukeboxes made.

The idea was, I would provide the technical know-how, the software and hardware solutions. Angus was quite sharp and said I needed some security features in place to protect my product, he suggested a hardware security dongle so I could keep a count of how many of my jukeboxes were being manufactured.

I was in talks with NSM, a German jukebox company that was now owned by a Leicester based electronics company, they had shown a great interest in my product, after all their old cd wall mounted jukeboxes were obsolete and people were throwing them away as scrap. My system would revolutionise the jukebox industry and turn previously scrap machines back into modern and popular digital jukeboxes.

I had two companies vying for my product, I was going to go with NSM but I wasn't happy with the way they negotiated, as the deal with NSM was becoming less and less desirable, the company from the North rang to say they didn't believe I could make a digital jukebox, so I said I'd call up and demonstrate it.

The date was arranged, I went up to the Northern based company and demonstrated as agreed, it wasn't just an audio jukebox, it also played videos and was a fully functioning karaoke system. I set the system up and selected a karaoke track and sang to the track. I was an ex-karaoke presenter, so I knew what I was doing.

After the karaoke, I played a video song and then an audio track. The demonstration went really well, and the company owner was convinced I could deliver what I had said. He loved my jukebox, he wanted to be a jukebox manufacturer and with my system he could. We went to his office to talk money.

The owner of the amusement machine distribution company in the North East was a really belligerent character, the type of overweight, arrogant, successful businessman type, whose body and health had been ravished by an opulent lifestyle, not many friends just employees that jumped when he said jump and didn't dare incur his wrath. He had mood swings that affected the whole office and he ran his business like a dictator. He wanted to dictate terms to me, but it was my product not his and if he wanted to manufacture my system, he would have to come up with a decent figure for each of the jukeboxes his company manufactured, that figure started at £500 but swiftly came down to £350 per jukebox. I realised I had to employ a different mentality, the mentality that the greater number of sales he could offer would mean larger overall profits for me, we shook on the deal and had a gentleman's agreement.

The following week the belligerent owner said after he had priced up all the components, he needed to renegotiate the license figure, as you can probably guess the renegotiation was not in my favour. He said the cost of the components was higher than he initially thought. He wanted the new license fee to be £250, I wasn't happy with this new deal. I had let the cat out of the bag though and my system had been thoroughly examined and no doubt examined with a fine-tooth comb. If I didn't accept this new deal where would I go from here?

I resisted and made the dealings difficult, so that he didn't think this was an acceptable thing to do, to renegotiate after we had shaken hands and already agreed on a figure. I reluctantly accepted under the condition that no matter how component pricing or labour cost fluctuated I would not accept any further renegotiations. We shook hands yet again and the deal was done.

I was in a strange mood, I was happy that a deal was agreed, but also disappointed that the license fee was so low. I also didn't have much faith or trust in him. He had apparently, a somewhat shady reputation. I always realised the threat would be from within. I thought the people that knew the most about my product would more than likely be the ones to try and copy my system and cut me out of the deal, so Angus's idea of a security device was more important than ever, before I could let anyone have any of my systems.

I researched these security devices on the internet, thanks to my time at university I knew how to thoroughly research. I found a security device called a *"Dinkey Dongle"* by a company called Microcosm, voila! That would be my solution. With security hardware dongles installed my system was only now executable with the presence of a Dinkey Dongle, I could control the number of my jukeboxes that would run. I also incorporated some other software security features that weren't apparent to the naked eye but were hidden deep in the software and could only be operated by me. You may think that this was overkill, but I'd learnt the hard way that people weren't to be trusted.

After weeks of showing the technical team at the amusement machine distribution company how to build my jukebox and make it work, we were ready to start distribution. I was amazed that I was the most technical person in their company. I hadn't realised how proficient and technically savvy I had become. It was a bit of a shock to me at first, I didn't think I would be leaps and bounds above their most technical engineers.

When we were ready to start distribution, the company needed some security dongles to allow the jukeboxes to run. The millionaire boss wasn't happy about the security devices, but I assured him it would protect us from other companies copying my system, the truth was I knew that he and his company were the biggest threat of all. He threatened to cancel the whole deal unless I removed the security, that made me very suspicious, it made no sense to remove security, surely this should be continually increased. I point blank refused to remove it and told him to do so would destabilise the software, that wasn't exactly true, there was a destabilisation issue with removing security, but the workload needed to remove security was something I didn't want and it certainly wasn't the direction I wanted my system to go in.

He mumbled and grumbled and didn't want the security, he was adamant, he wanted it removing, I merely argued back, telling him it wasn't in both our interests to remove security. This would have to be a subject we would forever disagree on.

There were other ridiculous features that some of his customers wanted including, like reduce the volume of songs that were playing in background mode, also known as background attract. This made no sense because the general pub goer wouldn't know whether the track was playing in background mode or not, in fact they could think it had been paid for but was a low volume recording so wouldn't pay to play it again. There were some good suggestions, but the majority represented so much work for little if no benefit to the system. Again, I would decide what features should be added to my system nobody else.

Things went well until one day when I went for my weekly meeting with the company owner, he owed me £12,000 and he wasn't forth coming. He had run out of security dongles and wanted more. I told him he could have more when he settled his bill for the £12,000 owed, he didn't like that! Who did I think I was, holding him to ransom? He said he hadn't used or sold that many jukeboxes, I told him that was irrelevant, I had supplied the security dongles and it was agreed that he would pay £250 per jukebox, which meant per dongle, as each jukebox needed one dongle to run. It wasn't my fault if he had lost or broken them or in fact if they had been stolen by his workforce as he claimed.

We had a big row in his office, he threatened to get another programmer to remove the security, saying he could get another programmer easily and pay them much less than he was paying me. I had to remind him, I didn't work for him and the jukebox software and hardware solution was mine not his and he wasn't allowed to remove security from my system.

The lesson learnt here was stick to your guns and do not be brow beaten to change things to suit someone else's agenda.

Chapter 37
Litigation

That was the start of the end of our agreement. It was 2006 Dan Brown had just won a litigation case upholding his claim that he hadn't plagiarised earlier material for his book *"The DaVinci Code"* and unbeknown to me I was about to go down the litigation path. I had become friends with the technical team, and they kept me informed of any illegal activity or attempts to copy my system.

The belligerent boss would inevitably try to infringe my copyright, fortunately for me I had had the foresight to take out intellectual property insurance, by Hiscox Insurers, a big name in the insurance underwriting industry. I wasn't sure I would ever have to use their services, as I believed my software was reasonably well protected by the security dongle and was sure that the team at the company were not technical enough to circumvent my software security. That had been a great idea of Angus's and I thank him for that. He obviously knew the type of character I would be dealing with.

I was friendly with the workforce because I had worked closely with them and especially their main technical person Brian. I liked Brian a lot, he was by far their most technical electronics engineer and grasped the new things I had to teach, but he was more than that, he was a friend and colleague, I had always longed for work colleagues, having been self-employed all my adult life, I always wanted work mates and this was the one thing I enjoyed about working with the technical team.

During lunch times when I had been at the amusement machine company, I had joined the technical team and not the boss as he wanted, he was arrogant and not the type of person I wanted to socialise with, plus I didn't want to be sat in an office with just the boss when I could be in the canteen talking to like-minded people.

Brian rang one day to say the software had been sent out to a third-party company who were specialists in circum-venting security systems. He would keep me updated on their progress.

At first Brian reported back that the attempts by the third-party wasn't very successful and had made very little progress, but four weeks later the software had been cracked and the company were working overtime making my jukeboxes and preparing to flood the market with cheaper inferior versions of my creation.

I was devastated! It had taken six years of hard work for someone to break in four weeks. I was desperate and didn't know what to do.

I called the police, but they were not interested at all, it was a civil matter according to them. I wasn't sure whether the information I was getting from Brian was correct or whether it was information that was being deliberately planted to mislead me. I suspected that the boss knew that Brian was keeping me updated. The only way I would know for sure would be to make a trap purchase.

This would do a number of important things for me, it would give me confidence and trust in my friend Brian and prove that the company were in fact, infringing my copyright.

I arranged to buy a jukebox through a friend of mine who lives in the New Forest, he placed an order and a week later it arrived. I paid my friend for the cost of the jukebox and said I would come down to inspect it.

A week or so later I travelled down to look at it. There were a number of checks I had to do. The first check was a visual inspection of the software, to make sure it was mine or looked the same. It looked exactly the same, I couldn't spot a single difference. The second was to remove the security dongle that was in the jukebox, replace it with my dongle which meant if it ran it was one of my original versions. That second check failed; it would not run with my dongle. That meant the security had been messed with and the security dongles had been replaced.

My initial suspicions were proving to be well justified. The third check was to input on screen a specific pattern of key presses in a non-obvious input manner to reveal a copyright message. This was the final test needed to confirm the jukebox was a direct copy.

I input the key presses one by one to put in my hidden password. I'd hoped this hadn't been circumvented too, but it was hidden deep inside the software programming and all the code had been obfuscated. Obfuscated is a technical term for a type of encryption that jumbles up language to something that is no longer readable.

As I input the password complete with my spelling mistakes, I was full of emotion, I didn't want it to be a copy because that would lead to legal action, but I needed to know…

Surprise surprise… my password worked!

The software was a direct copy. I could now prove this in a court of law using my hidden activation methods to display my copyright information. I was totally devastated and distraught that someone would do this to me, this was six years of my life and thousands of pounds of university fees, research and development costs.

I decided I would have to make a claim on my insurance. The boss of the company would not know what was going to hit him, he certainly didn't expect I had the means to fight him, he had expressed as much to Brian who in turn had told me.

The company weren't ready for my determination and the level of my knowledge. I instructed my solicitors to implicate not just the company owner but also his wife. The company owner was secretary of his company because allegedly he had been banned from being a company director for some previous business impropriety. My argument was that if his wife was director, she was ultimately responsible for any business dealings and the secretary was subordinate to the director, this way I could implicate both and made sure the management structure of their business could not be swapped around to avoid their responsibility.

I was also aware that the company boss had used his property business to pay his employee's wages at the amusement machine company, this was enough to implicate the property company into the litigation. My solicitors didn't grasp why I wanted to implicate the wife and the property company, I was amazed at the solicitors, they obviously weren't used to dealing with slippery characters or weren't aware how potentially easy it would have been to avoid responsibility if I hadn't insisted on these measures. Was I going to have to study law too? At this point in my life, I did seriously consider going back to university and doing a law conversion degree.

It was now just a matter of gathering evidence to back up the numbers of suspected sales of my copyright software, however, the only people that would truly know the scale of these sales, were the copyright infringers and they were not about to divulge those numbers. My argument was the only true measure of sales were to apply a business model based on the numbers sold during our first eight months of sales, and use a projected figure based on that number, of four hundred jukeboxes and projected over the lifespan of a new product which is recognised as six years. That was four hundred sales in eight months. If we assumed that the first three years continued at this frequency, not allowing for increased sales, which is normal in a new product life span. Sales normally start to slow down by year four eventually coming to an end by year six. The sales were therefore at a frequency of fifty per month, that was approximately 3,200 of my jukebox design and infringed software, at £2000 per jukebox that equated to £6,400,000 turn over on my product.

Yes, it's a lot of money and looking back it had far more potential had we continued development and sales together, I can't see why he went down the route he took. I won't lie, it was a terrible time in my life. I suffered continual death threats and thugs trying to kick my door down, was this the price I would have to pay for standing my ground fighting back? The legal battle was consuming all of my time which meant my jukebox business was being neglected. On top of that my jukebox system had started to get a bad reputation due to the copy machines being put out in their masses. Machines that were substandard and of very poor quality that came with insults from the infringers instead of technical support that customers so badly needed.

Intimidating calls and death threats came in on a daily basis. I was told precisely how they would kill me if I didn't drop the case. Even if I had wanted to drop it, which I certainly didn't, it was too late, the wheels had been set in motion and my legal team were in the driving seat. I contacted the police about the death threats…

They were next to useless… again! They said let us know if anything happens, but if anything did happen, I would have been dead and not able to let the police know! How did they expect me to let them know? Through a spiritualist or medium?

Other things did happen though. One day my next-door neighbour, who was a tough and hard man and well known for being so, rang our mutual friend Mark for reinforcement, as two men were trying to kick my front door down.

Mine was the only house in the area at that time with a burglar alarm fitted and it was obvious with the external alarm box. They continued to try and break the door down even when the alarm was sounding, they were intent of getting to me regardless of the commotion. The thugs had no chance against my neighbour though and by the time Mark had got there my neighbour and seen them off. That was the catalyst I needed to increase my home security and make it harder to get into my property.

A matter of days later I had security grills fitted to the doors and windows of my property. I don't know what the thugs wanted to get, maybe it was me or my software, I don't know. But that wasn't the only attempt to get to me. I was now living in what felt like a self-enforced prison.

It was a dreadful period of my life, the worst experience

I have ever had. Far worse than losing my arm. This was something I'd worked so hard to achieve, I just felt I didn't have that amount of effort in me again. The stress was getting to me, my fantastic product was being destroyed in front of my eyes and I felt powerless to stop it. How many times does someone come up with an invention worth millions of pounds? Was this my one and only chance at that level of success? It felt like it was.

My legal team kept reporting back to me with their progress. I use the word *"progress"* loosely, but in fact it was a lack of such. It was a case of solicitor ping pong. They were just exchanging letters back and forth. Many stupid claims were made by the infringers, one's that had been sworn on oath, as the truth, signed and witnessed by their legal team. This was a big deal because knowingly lying and signing a lie is perjury. One such claim was, we had a written contract that the infringers still had. So, I told my legal team to get a copy of this so-called contract. It was a handshake and a gentleman's agreement; nothing was put in writing!

When the email came through with a copy of a contract, it was ridiculous. It was an unsigned electronic document. A really complicated contract that basically gave the infringers ownership of my copyright after a certain number of sales. I insisted the solicitors requested the original computer system that contained the actual version of the contract. I researched forensic computer specialists online and found a company called 'Kroll On Track' that did exactly the forensic testing I needed. My solicitor said the infringers had told them the original pc had been replaced, they had an excuse for everything, but their excuses were ridiculous. I told my solicitors to insist on them providing the original hard drive for forensic testing by Kroll On Track. The belligerent boss must have thought that because he had dated the word document with the date, he alleged the contract was agreed upon that would be sufficient. At no point was there any signed copy produced.

After extensive analysis of the hard drive and files it was discovered the word document contract was in fact just weeks old and was a total fabrication. This came as no surprise to me, but my solicitors were surprised, this was in effect a lie to the courts which is perjury and an imprisonable offence. This happened on a number of occasions, when I proved without a shadow of doubt that he had lied under oath. To this day I don't know why my solicitor didn't take advantage of that. That would have stopped him in his tracks there and then and not allow him years more of infringing my product.

My case was finally won in an out of court settlement, my solicitors insisted I accepted a deal through mediation and had threatened to advise my insurers to no longer underwrite my legal costs should I decide not to accept a settlement. I had no choice but to accept. My final settlement would be a derisory amount, but the solicitors would get their £250,000 legal fees paid and they would have a statistical win.

That statistical win left me a broken man, the solicitors had also overlooked a major flaw in their settlement agreement, which gave the infringer a continued get out clause to keep selling my copyright. My solicitors allowed the addition of an 11th hour clause that I was unaware of, which meant the infringers were allowed to resell any second-hand jukeboxes that came back to them. This meant they could simply sell all their newly made jukeboxes relabelled as second hand. My solicitors didn't grasp the enormity of that simple clause.

The day after the mediation settlement, the infringers website had been updated and miraculously all of their new jukeboxes were now second hand. I contacted my solicitors to tell them what had happened, they didn't get it and just didn't understand and didn't appreciate the gravity of that simple contractual addition. In that single defining moment, my business was destroyed along with my entire life. All my future hopes and dreams were shattered. The whole experience almost drove me to taking my own life.

The Smith's song *"Heaven Knows I'm Miserable Now"* was pounding in my head and explained just how I was feeling.

I was so depressed and suicidal; I think I was on the brink of an emotional breakdown. It's not every day you come up with a successful idea and product that's a million-pound seller, and I realised I would probably never have the same success again in my life.

The six years had taken their toll on me, towards the end of litigation, I'd been in a disastrous and very damaging relationship, that came to an end only a few days before mediation. My mind wasn't on the task at hand, not as much as it should have been, and I missed some really important pieces of evidence. Evidence that was there right in front of me, but I couldn't see it for the shadow of sadness that was covering me, from the destructive delusion of a relationship I'd been in for 18 months with a sociopath.

The litigation has meant that despite thousands of ideas, creations and ingenious designs, in my head or in prototypes, I have never been able to trust a person or business to share them with.

I have tools and gadgets that would help other people in my situation, I have designs that would make for a better and cleaner environment. I'm just waiting for the right moment to unleash my inventions on the world.

The lesson I learnt was a very hard one that shook me to the core. Not everyone can be trusted and a 'Gentleman's agreement' is worth nothing. Always make sure you have a signed contract. Even if you have a contract and can prove copyright and patents, if you don't have the financial means to fight in a court of law, you cannot defend your rights. Insure, insure, insure.

Image Set C

1 - My first flying instructor, FSDP instructor John Griffin. Photo taken at Kemble airfield 2014.

2 - Alastair Breckon my flying instructor at Sherburn airfield presenting me with a certificate to commemorate my first ever solo flight.

3 - My first aluminium prosthetic arm that allowed me to do my solo flight.

4 - FSDP group photo with the new candidates. I was there as my role as a mentor. Helping the new candidates.

5 - Being awarded the Douglas Bader memorial trophy by Prince Faisal of Jordan on the left and Sir Stephen Dalton (Chief air marshal of the RAF)

6 - Aerobatic flight training with my instructor Peter Atkinson.

7 - Harpurry RDA national dressage qualifiers. I came 5th 2015. I was riding Ben.

8 - Harpurry RDA national dressage qualifiers. I came 3rd 2019. I was riding Lottie.

9 - Riding across the desert of Wadi Rum, Jordan 2019. FSDP fund raising.

10 - In the desert of Wadi Rum dressed in my Arab headwear.

11 - Being presented my BEM British Empire Medal at Bowcliffe Hall Bramham by the Lord Lieutenant and his aide 2018.

12 - The Royal garden party May 2018.

13 - Stock photo of BEM medal.

14 - 2017 being awarded the Yorkshire inspirational individual of the year at Elland Road, Leeds.

15 - Photo shoot with Touker Suleyman at his main offices in London. After I bought a mannequin dummies arm to make a prosthetic to ride my motorbike after 37 years out of the saddle.

16 - Taken in my workshop just last year 2020. I rebuilt this jukebox during the first lockdown. It was in a real state but now it's amazing.

17 - Rock n roll dancing with my dance partner Jane. At a 1950's event in Otley 2017.

18 - Rebuilding my Montesa motorbike in preparation to ride it on national TV 2018.

19 - Speaking in London at the PSA national conference 2019.

20 - My new 3d printed prosthetic arm, printed by Crispin Orthotics, Leeds. 2018.

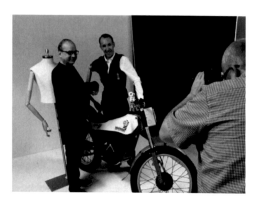

Chapter 38
The Sociopath

I'd been single for fifteen years; I'd been trying to find myself after my long relationship with Kathryn the school teacher. It took me a few years to get over Kathryn, but once I had, I threw myself into an exciting single life. I loved travelling, meeting new people, studying, salsa dancing and restoring vintage jukeboxes and building up my property portfolio. My life was full, and I really enjoyed this period of time.

One day I had a chance encounter with a friend of Kathryn's who asked how my love life was, I told her I'd been single for about 5 years since I'd split up with Kathryn, she said that was 15 years ago! I'd been so consumed with fun and adventure, I hadn't realised it had been so long since I'd dated.

I didn't date on the salsa scene, I enjoyed dancing just for the sake of dancing and not to find a partner. I guess I missed loads of opportunities, until one night, dancing at a place called Woodkirk Valley Country Club, I danced with a Japanese woman called *"Akiko"*. We seemed to get on really well, so I gave her my number. However, she didn't call me, so the next week I asked for her number and she gave it to me, I had got over my fear of asking for women's telephone numbers, thanks to my friend Peter and the exposure therapy he had introduced me to.

Someone had told me however that Akiko had a boy-friend, so when I asked her about that she told me that was why she hadn't called me, because she was in the middle of breaking up with him, but now she had, it was OK for me to call her.

A friend of mine was a Spanish flamenco guitarist and he had told me he was playing on Wednesday night at a Spanish bar in the centre of Leeds. I thought this was a great opportunity for a date. It's strange when I think about it because as a man, if I want to take someone out on a date, I think it has to be something special and not just the pub. Finding somewhere special to take a date to had always eluded me, but this felt like the perfect opportunity.

I rang Akiko and the date was arranged. I'd done a lot of reading, of sorts, with my dyslexia, about having a date plan or strategy. I didn't really have one, but I thought I'd call the restaurant, book a table and ask them to reserve a romantic table near the guitarist because he was a friend of mine.

We arranged to meet in Leeds, and we walked through the streets, not hand in hand as I had hoped but just side by side. I thought don't expect too much too soon Steve. When we arrived at the restaurant my friend, the guitarist. was just setting up. I said hello and introduced my date. The management had picked the most perfect table for us, a really romantic table right in front of the guitarist.

He serenaded us while we ate and chatted.

It was the most perfect night and yet I didn't have a clue whether she was interested or not! I walked her back to her car at the end of the night wondering if I should kiss her. You know that uncomfortable moment when you don't know if you should or shouldn't. It just didn't feel right, she got in her car and drove away, and I thought, that's it, I've blown it before it had a chance to even start. I'd enjoyed the night, but I was super disappointed with myself.

Two days later I got a call from Akiko asking if I'd like to go to her house for dinner. That would be lovely I thought, thinking all it would be was dinner, after all we hadn't even kissed. It was dinner but she had intentions of more. To be honest, I was disappointed it moved so quickly to the bedroom. She didn't like kissing which for me was a major part of any intimacy and foreplay. Sex so early in our encounter felt like a rushed relationship and after two weeks, I had a lot of doubts.

There was something not quite right about her, but I couldn't put my finger on it. I told my mum and sister that I was going to end the relationship, but they encouraged me not to be so hasty. I should have listened to my initial gut instincts. I got quite worried at one-point thinking there was something wrong with my libido, there wasn't, I just didn't enjoy any form of intimacy with her. In hind sight I should have ended the relationship at that point.

Akiko was cold and not affectionate; she had no compassion for others and wasn't affected by acts of cruelty seen on TV or in real life. I asked myself a lot, why would I want anyone like that, but I'd been single for so long and didn't want to be single anymore. I also thought maybe things had changed in the time I'd been single, and this was what the modern woman was like.

I made too many allowances for her attitude and the things she said and put them down to cultural differences and language difficulties. However, these errors were too frequent. I had a nagging doubt that she was in fact, not sane. In fact, reading this back I could say the same about a few of my recent romantic relationships. I'm really seeing similar patterns.

Akiko told me she was an expert horse woman in Japan and used to ride while shooting her bow and arrow from horseback at moving and stationary targets. One day she told me a friend of hers had offered to give her riding lessons. What? I thought, she was supposed to be an expert horsewoman already. I have to tell you when I saw her attempt at riding, she obviously wasn't an expert horse woman at all.

Sophie was a good friend of mine that I'd known for many years from the salsa dancing scene and she had been my ballroom partner for the last 5 years, Monday nights were our regular ballroom dancing night. Just because I was in a relationship, I didn't end the dance classes or my friendship with Sophie nor my other female friends.

I loved ballroom dancing. Akiko told me she shared my love of ballroom dancing and was in fact, an expert ballroom dancer and she'd done it for years, she suggested we went together to the Princess Ballroom in Birstall, reluctantly I agreed, reluctantly because I already had a ballroom partner and was comfortable and enjoyed dancing with Sophie. I'm sure you can guess what happened next!

Yes, you're right, she had no idea how to ballroom dance. We did our first and last ballroom class that day. I didn't want to ever repeat that with her again. To say I disliked it would be an understatement, I hated it. I was beginning to realise I didn't enjoy dancing with her at all even though we met salsa dancing.

I was questioning what it was I actually liked about her. I think I liked the fact she was oriental and different; she had been the first non-English woman I had dated, and I quite liked the fact I was dating someone I thought was a little exotic. She was also a pianist and violinist and I liked the idea of waking up with her playing music. That did happen and although it was quite pleasant, it was the only entertainment she had in her house, she had no TV, no radio, no record player, no books, no nothing, we couldn't even cuddle up and watch a film. I bought her a TV with a built-in video and DVD player just so we could watch TV together. Nights in with her, however, were horrendously boring, with the highlight of the night being sex. You might think that would be enough for a man but it's not! Or at least it's not for me. I want the whole romantic experience, and anything less is worthless.

Sex wasn't great but I thought maybe it would improve with time and she would become more affectionate and fun loving. Akiko was super serious in personality and I was just the opposite. I guess we weren't compatible, but I was still in denial.

We visited Japan to see her parents. If I take nothing else good from this relationship, I have the memory of this beautiful and interesting place. I'd often had to encourage Akiko to keep in contact with her family, to me it's strange that you wouldn't speak often to people you cannot easily visit; but as with me, Akiko was disconnected from her family too. I was interested to see how she would interact with them in person. To be honest, she was no better in their presence either, but maybe that's a Japanese thing. All that aside, we did visit some incredible places and a memory that will stay with me always is bathing in the Onsen Springs, in the Shiga Highlands, Nagano. Nagano was the location of the 1998 winter Olympics and saw the introduction of snowboarding as an Olympic event.

Akiko went to a lot of trouble to arranged for the two of us to bathe together (it was segregated into male & female baths) she explained to the resort that I didn't know the customs and rituals. They actually closed the baths so that we could bathe together. You have to go in naked and wash yourself in front of everyone so that they can see you are clean before you enter the springs. Without Akiko's help I would not have known and could have embarrassed myself and so I was grateful that she arranged this. It was a symbolic ritual and such a tremendous experience. I also bathed with her father on another occasion so knowing the ritual was important to me.

It's so quiet and peaceful, with a slight hint of sulphur in the air and the smell of the pine trees and forests all around. You cannot help but feel refreshed and at peace whilst there.

After we got back I thought I'd make more of an effort dancing with her, so we took up rock n roll lessons in a place called Horbury Social Club in Wakefield; it was over the road from Horbury School, where she told me she worked once a week as a peripatetic music teacher. Rock n roll classes were fun, I enjoyed them and although she lacked any natural ability I persisted, there were always others to dance with too, because according to the teacher we had to swap partners so we could get used to other people's styles and rhythms.

Akiko had wanted to move from her rented accommodation to her own property, she wanted me to buy with her, but I didn't want that, I wasn't sure I wanted to be with her, never mind living with her. I wanted to buy a public house or a unique property to turn into a nice home for myself, that I may or may not invite her to join me in.

I found a public house and took her along to view it with

me. To my shock and surprise Akiko told me she had put in an offer for the property before I did. Her offer was unsuccessful, and she didn't get it, but neither did I. I found another lovely property I fancied buying, it was a cemetery gate lodge house in Beeston, it was beautiful although not in the best part of Leeds. My girlfriend asked how I would finance it, so I told her. It wasn't really a secret, I said I would put down a deposit, the minimum required and then take out an interest only mortgage.

The next day she had a viewing of the property and subsequently bought it.

I think she thought or hoped I would move in with her, if she bought the house I wanted, but at that moment I wasn't very happy with her. I could write a whole book on how to pick the wrong woman but suffice to say things weren't going too well. I helped to make the house a home because she wasn't able, or she wasn't interested in creating a warm loving atmosphere.

Things took a turn for the worse when she was about to move into the cemetery lodge house. It was a Monday night, the night I went ballroom dancing with Sophie. I received a text from her to say she was being rushed into Pinderfields Hospital by ambulance following a 999 callout. It said not to worry about her, she would be OK, but might be out of contact for a whole day. It then went on to say she had taken her expensive violin with her. Akiko owned a violin that her parents had bought for her as a child, it was a super rare Italian-made 1860 Ceruti, worth £100,000.

I went to ballroom class as usual but when I got there, I felt so bad, I told Sophie I felt like a bad boyfriend and I needed to go and support my girlfriend and I was rushing over to Pinderfields hospital.

When I got to the hospital I explained to the receptionist my girlfriend had been rushed in via a 999 emergency call, she looked in her emergency call log, I explained she could have been picked up from either her Wakefield address where she was still legally tenanted or from the Leeds address of the property she had just bought. The receptionist asked me to confirm her name a few times, then looked at me in a strange way.

"Are you sure she said", I showed her the text message on my phone. The receptionist could see I was concerned for Akiko's well-being and so she went to check the systems again, then she rang the emergency department responsible for the dispatch of ambulances to 999 call outs in Wakefield and also from Leeds.

There had been no emergency ambulances dispatched during the time frame Akiko had claimed, either to Wakefield, nor Leeds. The receptionist said, your girlfriend isn't telling you the truth. She isn't here and she hasn't been picked up by an emergency ambulance. They didn't have her name on record as even attending as an out-patient, they simply didn't know or recognise her name. She wasn't on their system. So, where was she?

I read her message again, this time I realised what she had said about the violin. I thought what? If she had called out an ambulance on an emergency call, did she ask the ambulance person to please wait while she went to collect her violin to bring with her during a medical emergency. I realised that was just lunacy, it would never happen! If a patient was well enough to collect their violin, they wouldn't have needed an emergency call out in the first place.

I rushed to her house in Wakefield and her car wasn't there, so I rushed to the new Leeds house and her car wasn't there either. I drove backwards and forwards between the two houses at breakneck speeds for the next two hours, desperately seeking the whereabouts of my *"seriously ill"* girlfriend. That is when it dawned on me, did she also ask the ambulance driver to wait while she got her car?

Where was the car, if it wasn't with her? Who had driven it away from her home if she was in an ambulance? She didn't answer the phone when I called but she had told me she would be out of contact or may not be able to answer the phone while she was in hospital, so I knew she wouldn't answer, but I also knew she wasn't in hospital. The fact she was lying about her whereabouts meant she had to be doing something that wasn't innocent, otherwise there was no need to lie.

The next day I was at a friend's funeral, I was at the wake and all I could think of was, where was Akiko? I decided I'd call her bluff and send her a text message, it read

"Hi Akiko, I hope you are ok? I'm so worried about you I'm coming down to Pindefields Hospital to see you"

I knew she would have to respond because I knew she wasn't at Pinderfields and she would realise that if I went, her lie would be uncovered.

Two minutes later she rang with a pathetic poorly voice, saying the hospital was just letting her out. I listened to her lies for a while until I couldn't contain myself any longer and I said

"Do you want to tell me where you really are and where you've really been all night?"

She tried to act all innocent.

She went on to tell another lie and another, lie after lie trying to redeem her story. They were all variations of being taken to hospital, to not staying in, but being an out-patient to just sitting in the waiting room. All of which I could disprove. Again for the second time and in hind-sight I should have finished the relationship there and then but to my dismay and my self-respect and that of my family, I continued the relationship, so strong was my desire to not be single I was putting up with the worst girlfriend I'd ever experienced. I never felt the same about her again and totally mistrusted her because I never got a satisfactory explanation for where she had been.

I replayed conversations we'd had, arguments over cultural things such as Geisha Girls, I even suspected she may have been the UK version, an escort. I know that the west presumes Geisha's to be nothing more than prostitutes for businessmen, which of course isn't true, and she was vehement in her defence of them, but she was often missing without having a reason and would be covered in very suspect marks the following day. I'm not judging or saying there is anything wrong with Geisha girls or escorts. My problem is with lies.

Only a few months later she destroyed my family Christmas by assaulting my mum and verbally abusing my family at our Christmas Day get together. This was over a ridiculous argument. Again, hindsight is a wonderful thing and I could have handled the situation differently, she had bought a poor present for my Mum and I mentioned to Akiko that Mum was unhappy with the gift; Akiko got very angry and it quickly escalated out of control. That was the worst Christmas of my entire life. I was torn between family and a rubbish girlfriend, there should have been no choice. I would rather have been with my family, but I was thrown out of my sister's house on Christmas Day morning along with my girlfriend, who had caused all the trouble and was now happy and smiling that she had destroyed my Christmas and damaged the relationship with my family. Christmas day lunch was at Kentucky Fried Chicken and I was desperately sad.

Only a matter of weeks or possibly months later she was at it again, lying about her whereabouts, this time it was the final straw, I'd had enough, and it was time to get rid of someone who was so damaging to my mental health. So, I finished it. It was the best thing I ever did. If I could turn back time I would. I would go back in time and tell myself she was bad news and not to bother with her. In fact, if I could erase her from my life, my past, my relationship history I would do so in the blink of an eye.

The end of the relationship couldn't have been timed worse, it was the day or two days before my court hearing mediation. My mind was distracted during mediation and at the time I felt I was missing a vital piece of evidence. I was and I did miss it. It was a distraction that cost me an enormous sum of money.

I was becoming paranoid; had she been planted by the infringers of my copyright to try and de-rail the case and damage my concentration?

The boss of the company I was in legal dispute with had bragged to me in the past about his contacts owning lap dance bars in the North East of England and my ex-girlfriend had lived in Sedgefield in the North East of England. Was this just a coincidence or had she been planted?

I did an internet search on the word *"sociopath"* and it described her to a tee! I was shocked but really happy I had gotten out of that 18-month mistake. There were so many other awful things that she did, including sending covert text messages to another man telling him a pack of lies about me, the time I caught her taking a guy's number at the bar we were drinking at, and the time I suspect she had poisoned me. I'd been for a meal with her one evening which she cooked. I had been fine on the day leading up to dinner, however, within a very short time of eating I became incredibly ill, it came on too quick for it to be natural. I know that this might sound as though it could just be a bad reaction, but having eaten the same meal, she was perfectly fine. My mum and sister came to pick me up but I was too ill even to get in a taxi. It took a couple of days before I was well enough to leave, at the point where I was going Akiko, "suddenly" became ill and pretended to have the same symptoms. I went to call someone for her and found that she had been talking to other men whilst I had been ill. I know that she wanted to keep me from my family and loved to control all aspects of my life. This was just another way that she could do that.

It was a period of pure lies. I never realised a person was capable of so much dishonesty.

By the end of the relationship I could never be certain that a single word she said was true, you can't love someone like that, and you can't love yourself when you're with them.

I found a letter I wrote to her, just reading it now makes me feel stupid that I didn't take action earlier and allowed the delusion of a relationship to continue for eighteen months. I won't detail the contents here as they are raw and personal, but it was a stark reminder to me, never to sacrifice my own self-respect and heart just for the sake of a relationship.

It's been 13 years since I've read the letter, reading it brings back all the emotions, all the hurt I was feeling. I thought I'd deleted all the emails from her. I wish I could delete the painful memory of that relationship.

However, like most bad things, there is always something positive to take away, I struggled for a while to find anything good from this disastrous relationship though, until I remembered how I had told her I had always wanted to play the trumpet.

A couple of days after that conversation she borrowed one from a school she worked at. That was the first time I played a trumpet and I really enjoyed it. That was the start of my passion for learning the trumpet, I still play today although I have a lot to learn.

I listened to the song by Gotye the other day, *"Somebody That I Used to Know"*, sums it all up for me as I get on with living my life.

I have never had counselling, this is one occasion where I should have sought help. I know now, that the damage done to me psychologically has never healed and led to more relationship mistakes. This relationship destroyed what little value I had in myself.

The lessons I continue to learn are. Be careful what you tolerate, you are teaching people how to treat you! There will always be people in your life who treat you wrong. Be sure to thank them for making you strong!

Chapter 39
Unplanned Adventures

I continued running Robinson's Jukeboxes during litigation, but it was difficult, my product suffered because of the substandard copyright infringements that had flooded the marketplace. My jukeboxes, however, didn't have the problems the infringing copies had. They were well supported, and I knew them inside out and would always make sure my customers were happy with their purchase. It was 2010, David Cameron became prime minister and 33 Chilean miners were rescued from a collapsed mineshaft half a mile underground, in the San Jose mine after surviving 69 days. Me and Brian were travelling to Ireland to build some digital jukeboxes for an Irish customer.

When we arrived at the offices and workshop of the customer we were expecting to show their technical team how to build my digital jukebox system into their obsolete cabinets. It was obvious however after 20 minutes explaining the complexities of the refit that Brian and I would have to do all the refit work. A mammoth task for just the two of us and not one that we were expecting. It took us four days to refit their old jukeboxes into state of the art, modern and commercial digital jukeboxes. All that was left was for Brian and I to show the Irish customers how to install their new jukeboxes, which left us time to enjoy the local bars.

To be fair we had been enjoying the local bar most

nights, as the atmosphere was so welcoming, as were the locals who knew how to drink, enjoy themselves and party like professionals, especially on band and karaoke nights.

The bars were full even though the no smoking ban had just been introduced to the Irish bars, that didn't seem to dampen their spirits though and me and Brian had a whale of a time in our temporary new surroundings. The Irish were great dancers, I didn't expect that, don't ask me why but I didn't associate that great nation with dancers other than a Riverdance style or Irish jig.

The local bar band night however was a real eye opener, the majority of the clientele were dancing a type of rock n roll but to almost every type of music genre, they were amazing. We watched as we soaked up the atmosphere and joined in the evening's festivities. The time went too quickly and before we knew it, we were heading back to Dublin to catch our ferry home, somewhat disappointed our adventure was over. Time wasn't on our side though and nor was the traffic and the incredibly congested small narrow streets of Dublin.

Fortunately, I had an early version of a satnav. It was a PDA (Personal Digital Assistant) with a fresh installation of Tom Tom navigation software and a satellite receiver. We were directed by the dulcet tones of Tim the satnav voice who knew exactly where we were going. The time was running out though and we had mere minutes to get to the ferry port, thankfully, we arrived just as they were about to close the gates to embarkment. What a relief!

A relief that was only enjoyed for milliseconds as we were told by the official, smiling and welcoming us that we were at the wrong ferry terminal. Smiling back and assuming the correct ferry terminal would be the neighbouring jetty, I asked for directions. The official said it was a 30 minute drive across Dublin centre to the correct ferry port. We shot across Dublin at breakneck speed like Batman and Robin responding to an emergency. Not in the bat mobile but in a Volvo 740 estate that burnt more petrol than rubber. We were guided again by Tim the satnav and we raced up and down small back streets, major dual carriage ways and circumvented diversions and road works, to eventually arrive at Dublin port, to be greeted again by an official who told us the embarkation gates had closed. I could see they were still open. I said in a rather excited and hyped-up voice *"but I can see the gates still open, can't we just embark now and slot in behind the traffic that is still loading?" "No"* said the official *"the loading of cars finished half an hour ago and this is all commercial freight, we can't accommodate you now but you can catch the next ferry. Just go to the load master's office over there"* as he indicated by pointing to a blue portacabin with some port worker coming and going in their high-vis jackets.

I entered the load master's portacabin to be told we could in fact catch the next departing ferry and there would be no extra charge. What a relief, the expense of this trip was already high and I was super concerned it would now spiral out of control. *"Great"* I said. *"Thank you, when is the next ferry leaving?"* expecting to be told in a couple of hours, after all it was only 4pm. *"Tomorrow at 4pm"* said the load master. My heart sank because I knew the cost of this business trip would now outweigh the profit.

We were given tickets for the following day's ferry and off we went guided by Tim the satnav again, but this time into the centre of Dublin to try and find a budget hotel for the night. The hotel we found was just over O'Connel bridge on the South side of the river Liffey. I was hoping for a Budget hotel but €85 was the going price. It was a lovely hotel. I made the decision to make the most of what I initially thought would be a setback. The hotel was really charming, it was a mixture of Victorian class and contemporary modern style. I loved it, so did Brian. We hit the town as soon as we had settled into the hotel. We went to eat at a fabulous Indian restaurant then walked the streets of central Dublin, until we heard the sound of the Irish fiddle being played. We entered a bar at 7pm and didn't leave until well after midnight. What an amazing night out. The band was fantastic, their show stopping signature tune was *"Galway Girl"* not the Ed Sheeran version but the one by Steve Earle. The bar must have been the busiest in Dublin. The place thronged with people. The atmosphere was electric, and you could physically feel the good vibe and energy in that place. We danced chatted with the locals, drank and soaked up the surroundings until we were the last ones to leave. What an amazing night out, spent in the country of my ancestors. I never thought for a moment that the disaster of missing the ferry would turn out to be such an amazing adventure. That mistake made the whole business trip an exciting and unplanned adventure.

A similar adventure happened when I'd gone to Riga, Latvia with a couple of friends. We had gone for a salsa dancing congress. The congress was fantastic, all the women were wonderful dancers and really attractive, Me and my friends loved the time we spent there. Dancing the nights away and sight-seeing during the day. The time we spent went so quickly. It felt like I'd blinked, and we were due to return on our flight home on Sunday at eleven o'clock.

In the morning we went for breakfast, we were chilled out and relaxed when a text from home made me realise something. I said to my two travel companions *"what time is our flight home today?"* Eleven o'clock they both said in unison. Like the song by Olly Murs and Rizzle Kicks, my heart skipped a beat as I replied 11 o'clock or 23 hundred hours? That's when the realisation hit us all. It was 11 o'clock in the morning and not at night as we thought. Aviation uses the 24 hour clock.

We rushed like madmen to the airport hoping there may have been a delay in our flight, but we needed a good delay, we were already 2 hours late.

When we arrived at the airport, we had missed our flight home and the next available flight was three days later. My travel companions were in a panic they had to start work on Monday morning. I realised though that this was just another unplanned adventure and I was getting excited at what might happen next. Where would we go, what would we do, I thought.

I know, let's fly somewhere else then fly home from there. Fortunately, there was a flight leaving in an hour for Amsterdam and there was a flight from Amsterdam to Manchester airport, a couple of hours later. So, we took the plunge paid the £500 extra charge believing we would be able to claim on our travel insurance, unfortunately that wasn't to be the case. In reality things were slightly different to what we planned. When we arrived at Schipol airport in Amsterdam, we were told there had been a cancelation of an earlier flight and all the passengers from that flight had been put on the plane we were expecting to catch.

The friendly assistant said not to worry we could catch the following flight. What a relief! *"What time is the next available flight?"* I said. *"9:30 tomorrow morning"* she replied. It was only 4.30 in the afternoon or should I say 16:30 not wanting to ever forget aviation and the 24-hour clock again. *"OK can we have tickets for that flight please?"* I asked. The tickets were booked and our places secured, but my friends were concerned. What were we going to do until 09:30 in the morning? We had 17 hours to wait in the airport. I suggested that we caught a train into Amsterdam centre, we could go and eat then hit the bars and clubs. We could party all night then catch the 6am train back to the airport and relax until our flight was ready to depart. I thought it was a great idea, but my fellow travellers were worried. They both said, *"Steve, Amsterdam is a dangerous place!"* I replied with a reassuring voice, *"Don't worry guys, I'll look after you"*. Both my friends were big, husky, burly, muscular and intimidating looking men but they were afraid of the unknown. But they trusted me, even though I was really only joking with them, because I knew they didn't need any protection.

I'd been to Amsterdam many times with my mum and sister and knew it wasn't what my friends thought it was. With that we caught the train to the centre of Amsterdam. We went to a lovely restaurant in the red-light area that was buzzing with activity. Not just men perusing shop fronts selling naked flesh, rather than shiny tourist trinkets but families on a night out. We had a great meal. I'm not sure if it was the meal that was fantastic or our hunger and the vibrant atmosphere. After our meal we strolled round stopping for donuts and deserts until we walked past a massive queue of people, men, women, couples, and families. I said to my two friends, it must be that new movie Matrix playing at the cinema. As we walked past the front of the queue, the headline said in flashing neon lights *"Live sex show"* I was amazed, as were my friends. It was just normal to everyone, just an average night out. It was a surreal experience, but I loved the liberal attitude of the Dutch. We hit the bars and night clubs until we were drunk and exhausted. Before we knew it, it was 6am and we had to catch the train back to Schipol airport and our flight home.

That holiday was one of the best holidays I'd had with my two friends. They loved our adventure and if people ask me about it, I tell them with a laugh in my voice and a cheeky smile *"What happened in Amsterdam stays in Amsterdam"*

The lesson learnt was sometimes when you think it's all gone wrong, it goes better than you could ever expect. Embrace the unplanned adventure.

Chapter 40
The Medium And The
Spiritualist Church

My sister Tracy and me were always interested in all things spiritual, spooky and the mysteries of the afterlife. Tracy had heard of a lady in Leeds called Marylyn who was a medium, so we decided to go along and see her. What an interesting experience that was. I had become more open-minded since my experiences in hospital with the third man. I was definitely still sceptical, but I was prepared to give anyone and any idea a chance, no matter how far-fetched they may seem. I had an open mind; it was no longer closed like it previously had been.

Marylyn said some really interesting stuff that my sister wrote down during the reading. She mentioned I would visit Japan. Why she said that I had no idea, I didn't know any Japanese people and I didn't speak Japanese, I spoke Spanish. She also said something that made no sense at all. She said Shaggy would get his sight back. I didn't know anyone called Shaggy. She then said I would buy a small silver car. I wasn't even thinking about changing my beautiful big Volvo estate car. My Volvo was like a car and van combined, an antique dealer's dream or in my case, a vintage jukebox dealers dream.

She also told me I had spiritualist abilities. Is that why

I'd seen the third man? A lot of what Marylyn told me made no sense, but it would later in life.

I would in fact go to Japan, even though at that time, it wasn't on my list of things to do. I did in fact go with Akiko to visit her mum and dad in Nagano.

By the time I had become a proficient salsa dancer, I had met a lot of interesting likeminded people that were doers more than watchers, as I was. Surprisingly or maybe I should say not surprisingly I knew mainly women, but I knew a handful of men most of which were called Steve. You can probably imagine how difficult that was, we all had to be referred to by some additional name.

I was one-arm Steve, for obvious reasons, another was called tall Steve, there was a big Steve and a salsa Steve, although that referred to all of us really! Just to make things more interesting we decided we would call ourselves shaggy, just for a laugh. When people asked why we called each other Shaggy, we would say it's so that we don't all have to be called Steve, but now we were all called Shaggy. However, it was always good for a laugh.

I thought nothing about this and had forgotten about what Marylyn had said. Shaggy wasn't my suggestion, but I went along with it anyway. We'd keep singing *"Mr Lover Man"* at each other, after the Shabba Ranks hit song from 1988. That was also the year of the Bill Clinton and Monika Lewinsky scandal and that Europe agreed on a single currency. There was a friend called Dave who wanted to be a member of the Shaggy gang too, so we gave him the title of honorary Shaggy.

Tall Steve *"Shaggy"* was about 6'5" and super popular with women, he was good-looking and a good cook to boot. He had the choice of any woman, they swooned over him because of his height and looks, he had everything, and more than other guys could hope to have, he was Mr Smooth and charming with it.

He had the opportunity to go and work abroad in the Dominican Republic as a scuba diving instructor, so Shaggy left to live a new exciting life.

Then came the news, Shaggy had had a major road traffic accident in the Dominican Republic. While riding his motorbike home after a day's work, Shaggy had ridden down a dark unlit road. Unbeknown to him there was an articulated lorry around a corner that had broken down and had no light on, not even the hazard warning lights. That and the remote location with no streetlights or other source of lighting meant Shaggy didn't see the broken-down truck and he went headfirst into the back of it while not wearing a crash helmet.

He was so badly injured, his plight saddened me immensely, he lost the sight in one eye and his remaining eye was so badly damaged it was unlikely he would gain his sight back in that one. After multiple facial reconstructive surgery Shaggy was left with a slim chance that surgery on his only remaining eye might be a success. Shaggy took the gamble and to everyone's surprise his sight was partially restored.

At the time when all this was happening, I'd forgotten the words of Marylyn and only recently I found the notes my sister had taken during the reading, and there it was in black and white *"Shaggy would regain his sight."*

There is so much more to this world than we realise, is chance really chance, are the accidents we have just freak accidents, or are they preordained by a higher power? There must be some preordination if Mr McGill and Marylyn knew things before they would happen.

I did change my car for a smaller silver Toyota Corolla. I hadn't intended to. but my lovely Volvo had some major issues, so it was time to trade it in. Again, this was foreseen by Marylyn and not by me.

I enjoy anything spooky that challenges my beliefs, so it was a natural progression that I would attend a spiritualist church where many of the congregation were mediums. Often, they'd tell me things I didn't understand some of the stuff they said was very accurate. Strangely the venue of the spiritualist church was at the old dispensary on North Street in Leeds. The same dispensary I'd attended as a young boy to get stitches in my head after running headfirst into Dads car headlight. Everything seemed interconnected somehow.

I had some strange experiences at the spiritualist church. We've all heard of a clairvoyant, someone who can see things but there are also clairaudients, those who hear things and clairsentients, those who feel things.

The first experience I had was when a man walked past me and I had a sudden pain in my right leg so I approached him and told him my right leg really hurt as he walked past me. He went on to tell me he had a problem with his right leg. He didn't limp but he was awaiting surgery. How could I have felt his pain? It made no sense but according to him I was clairsentient - the ability to feel the past, the present, and the future emotional state of other people.

On another occasion, there was a young woman with her friend, her friend was stroking the young woman's leg and for some reason I was infuriated, I had a strong desire to stand up and say *"for pity's sake leave her alone",* but I didn't know who I wanted to say it too, it wasn't her friend. Then all of a sudden, the girl burst into tears screaming *"they're crowding me, I can't move for them"* she was referring to spirits that were crowding her, suddenly my reaction made sense, I had wanted to say *"BACK OFF"* to the spirits that were crowding her and that was why I didn't know who to direct my frustrations at.

I'm still not convinced about the time the hall was super busy, so busy we had to create two circles of chairs. One circle had their chair backs towards the walls and then there was an inner circle with the chair back towards the outer circle. I was sat in the inner circle in quiet contemplation, when I heard two ladies whispering to each other behind me. How rude, I thought. This was a quiet contemplation time and no talking or whispering was allowed. I couldn't help but look around to see who was talking. There were two women behind me, but they didn't appear to be speaking.

When I turned back to face the centre of the inner circle the whispering started again, again I looked round. This went on 4 or 5 times before my sister and a friend who was sat at the side of me said *"What's up Steve?"*

I replied, *"Those bloody women whispering behind me are annoying me."*

To which my sister and friend replied, *"They aren't whispering Steve!"*

To this day I'm convinced it was the women behind me because they were female voices I heard, but my sister and friend insisted they heard nothing. Was Marylyn correct, did I have spiritual abilities, was I hearing spirits and had that ability come from my near-death experiences?

I would maintain an open mind and would never write-off other beliefs, nor the possibility of something more than the here and now. My ability to look beyond what we think is possible, what had led me to the firm belief that *"anything really is possible"*

I didn't realise just how useful a lesson that way of thinking would be and how it would help me achieve more than I ever thought I could.

Life is a lesson; we just don't realise we are continually learning and the whole world is your classroom. Also, don't be quick to dismiss things just because you don't understand them.

Chapter 41
The Teacher

I was so down and depressed after the litigation and the relationship with Akiko that I found myself thinking about the unthinkable, suicide!

My life was spiralling out of control, my character was changing in a way I didn't like. I found I would dismiss people of any status with verbal abuse and I couldn't stand fools nor authority. I came to believe there was no such thing as justice and the law was only a concept that the lower classes and poor people had to abide by. I experienced first-hand that if you had vast amounts of money you could do anything you wanted.

My faith in people and the judicial system was gone. All the values I had, felt worthless as did my miserable existence. I wanted out and found myself thinking of ways to end my life. I was in a perpetual haze, a fog that I just couldn't escape, I kept walking forwards, but I felt like I was walking backwards, and the end of the fog could never be reached.

In an effort to distract me from my own negative feelings, I decided I would take an intensive CELTA course (Certificate in Teaching English to Speakers of Other Languages). I would throw myself completely into something new, and hopefully, it would consume all my waking thoughts. I was told that it was an incredibly rigorous four-week course and it would be so stressful and intense that I wouldn't have the capacity to cope with or think about anything else. To me it sounded exactly what I was looking for. Queen sang *"Under Pressure"* and that's exactly what I was deliberately putting myself under, in an attempt to block out my negative thoughts. It was as though I was beating myself with an educational stick and new knowledge, like a monk or holy man committing self-flagellation. The educational and informational overload was just what I needed, although it wasn't as intensive as what I'd just been through and in some ways felt like a walk in the park!

The school that offered the training provided opportunities for newly qualified teachers to get experience working voluntarily, in a classroom environment, twice a week. I really enjoyed this and after a few weeks I started looking at job opportunities in the papers they had in the library. There were a lot of jobs in Thailand and I thought that this might be an opportunity to have a fresh start and a clean break. It was 2010, Prince William and Kate Middleton announced their engagement, Apple launched the iPad and I was a qualified English language teacher with classroom experience. My father was living in Thailand at the time and I'd recently started talking to a lady that lived over there. I decided to bite the bullet and go over for a visit to see if I liked it. I went away for three weeks and whilst there the relationship developed with the Thai woman, so much so that when I came home, I thought that my initial instinct had been right, and a move there would be good for me. I arranged to go back for a further three weeks, this time with an agenda. I'd apply for work as an English language teacher. All of the initial feedback was good, they liked my degree and qualifications and so it seemed perfect.

On my return visit the first interview I had went very well, until they realised that I only had one arm and then I was told *"no we don't want you, you will frighten the children."* I approached a teaching agency to see if they could find me work. They told me that no-one would want me or it would be very difficult to find me a teaching job, the only way they may be able to do so would be to offer me at a much lower rate than other able bodied teachers and I would most likely be placed in a village school.

I was so upset and demoralised, even more so that I began to feel that the lady I'd started a relationship with was looking at me as a financial opportunity, not a boyfriend and of course I'd been spending time with my father; which I found both emotionally and financially draining.

I spoke to a contact I had in the UK who said he could get me a job teaching in China, but again they were very blunt about not wanting a disabled teacher. I didn't have it in me to continue along that path and so I put it to one side and went home.

It's only now that the words of one of the early doctors come back to me, he suggested that I wear a prosthetic arm to make other people feel comfortable and to accept me, I realised that in saying this, he was doing it for my wellbeing. If I wore the prosthetic no one would know I had one arm, there would be no stares, no cruel comments and most likely more opportunities.

I've also realised over the years that disabled people have so much more to prove, they have to show that they're a worthwhile member of society. It's as though losing an arm meant that my worth as a human being had somehow been diminished.

I'm still contemplating a new arm; I'd prefer to live in a

world where we're accepted for how we are now, but I do understand the benefits it could have.

Yet, it wasn't all negative, one of the other volunteers I worked with at the training school told me about the Refugee Council at Leeds Central Library, where they had a space from which they offered English lessons. I jumped at the chance to be involved. I worked there for about two to three years, teaching refugees and giving them the opportunity to communicate in this country. It was only after the government cut funding that it stopped, which seemed such a shame to me as our class was really self-funding, all we needed were pens and paper which I would have happily supplied and a free space in the library.

After the funding was cut, I worked with a homeless charity for a few months that helped refugees get free English lessons.

I met some amazing people there and they really were inspirational, having struggled to try and make better lives for themselves. These people helped me in ways that they didn't even realise, we had some fun and I was able to see the good in others at a time when my belief in people was so badly damaged.

The lesson I learnt was that healing works best when you throw yourself into something new and let the new learning consume your thoughts, it gives you the respite you need from your negativity and makes room for positivity.

Chapter 42
Flying Scholarship

The CELTA course had helped in some small way to get me back on the right track, but the disabled discrimination I experienced had undone all the good work the CELTA course had done. I was right back in the fog of depression again, struggling to find my way out.

I was wasting time one day looking at Facebook, I wasn't really an avid user of the site and I'd lost interest in everything else. I didn't want to create things anymore because I felt they would just be stolen by more unscrupulous people and the law would not protect, nor help me. I had lost all my dreams and ambitions. I was an empty shell without desire for anything, I always need to be chasing a dream. Without dreams and desires to chase, what is the point of life?

I was scrolling through the vast feeds on Facebook when I saw something that caught my eye. It was an ad for a charity called Flying Scholarship for Disabled People (FSDP). I was super afraid of flying; I was the guy who would spend all his time praying while flying to Spain on a summer holiday with my friends. *"Please God, don't let the aircraft crash, Please God, don't let the aircraft crash, please please"* it was like a mantra I would repeat during almost the whole of the flight. My friends thought there was something wrong with me because I would cancel holidays just before we were due to fly. There was something wrong with me! It was called extreme fear of flying. The amount of money I've lost on cancelled flights is scary. But here was an opportunity to either cure my fear of flying or die trying, it was a win/win situation.

I told a close friend I was going to apply, and his immediate reaction was, *"Steve its really dangerous flying in a light aircraft."*

I replied to him, *"What's the worst that could happen?"*

He said, *"you could crash and die."*

I was OK with that; I'd been contemplating suicide for months anyway. I'd made up my mind, and when I make up my mind, that's it, there is no stopping me, I would apply for the scholarship and see what happened.

I'm dyslexic and hate filling in forms. The majority of the form was just personal information, but there was a section where I had to write an essay explaining why I deserved or wanted a flying scholarship. This is what I wrote:

I lost my right arm at the age of 18 on a motor bike. I am now 48 and I'm still looking for something to take the place of my motor bike.

Ever since losing my arm I've experienced negative attitudes towards my disability. I have never had a job, I found it too demoralising to be confronted with continual rejection. Despite all of this I tried working for myself, I went to Uni at the age of 35 and most recently studied and got a CELTA certificate to teach English as a foreign language. I even got into debt to go to Thailand for a job interview, only to be told when I was face to face with the employer, that they didn't want me because I had one arm. This happened on three occasions in Thailand, this experience has been the worst of my life.

I had a job offer in China to teach English. They liked my qualifications. Again, I was rejected on the basis that it was because I had one arm. The Chinese and the Thai make no excuses for why they don't want you.

Basically, I need a goal in my life. At the moment my life is meaningless. I'm tired of negative perceptions of disabled people. I feel I have no prospects, no hopes and no dreams. As soon as I let myself hope and dream, they are dashed every time because I have one arm, yet I am unable to resolve that.

I am sorry my letter is so negative; it's just that bad experiences have got me down. I am the same as everyone else, I need a cause, a dream and something to aim for. I would put everything into a flying scholarship because I have nothing else.

When I graduated from Uni my mum bought me a flying lesson experience, I loved it, it was the same sense of freedom that my motor bike used to give me.

I don't know what else to say, I don't expect I'll get anywhere with my application, but at least I can say I tried.

I sent in this letter as part of my application to FSDP not expecting I would ever hear anything from them. I had given up on people and lost all my faith, so I went about my life, just trying to survive day by day and desperately seeking a new direction, desire or anything to take my mind off the depression and suicidal tendencies.

The fact that I would even consider learning to fly, something I was terrified of, shows just how close to a nervous breakdown I must have been—such was my lack of interest in living, my life seemed to be on hold while I was waiting to see if I'd been accepted by FSDP for a flying scholarship.

It was a Monday afternoon in January 2012, the same month and year that the Scottish Government announced its plan to hold the referendum on Scottish independence and the European Union agreed to impose an oil embargo on Iran. While greater world events were taking place, my phone was ringing. I answered with my normal greeting

"Hello, Steven Robinson speaking"

A voice on the other end of the phone said

"Hello Steven, my name is Sue Whitby I'm the General Manager of Flying Scholarships for Disabled People (FSDP) I am very pleased to tell you, you have made it through to the selection process at RAF Cranwell" she went on to explain that I hadn't been awarded a scholarship but I was one step closer.

I had been selected out of 250 applicants to the final selection process, which would take place in April, at RAF Cranwell, the famous RAF College, where Prince William and Prince Harry were trained to be pilots. Sue asked if I wanted to accept and attend the selection process. I of course replied with *"Yes!"*

I was so excited and in that split second something happened to me that hadn't happened for over 6 years... I smiled!

I tried to prepare for the selection process, but how does one prepare for the unknown? How should I behave or act? We were all assigned a mentor, someone who had gone through the selection process before. My mentor was a guy called Mark.

In all honesty I only heard from him a few times. The advice he gave me was, just be yourself, but I was lost and didn't know who I was anymore.

The day finally arrived when I had to drive to Cranwell.

The selection process started on a Sunday and ran for three days.

Wow…! It was such an imposing and impressive place, steeped in history, it made me feel so insignificant, but I enjoyed that feeling of being humbled.

I'd been humbled before, it's almost like looking up at the stars without any light pollution, you feel so small in space, a place we can just not comprehend the size of, the feeling was very similar in such an overwhelming place.

I had to register at the guardhouse before I was allowed beyond the armed guard security, but behind the guards in the grounds of Cranwell, it felt so safe, a haven of peace and tranquillity, there was no fear of people making cruel disability jokes, or even people staring, that behaviour would not be tolerated by those in command. This after all was an RAF college for officers in training and there is much more expected of officers in the RAF, they are expected to conduct themselves impeccably at all times. I can't tell you how reassuring the temporary inner peace was that I felt in those surroundings.

When I had settled into my accommodation, I made my way to the candidates mess to meet my mentor Mark. He talked me through what would happen then left me by myself. Although the surroundings at Cranwell calmed me, my mental health was in a bad way and I was struggling with everything, socialising, trying to fight my demons and worrying about what lay ahead. I don't imagine I was particularly good company nor easy to be with.

There were 22 people at the final selection but only 18 scholarships were available, 4 of us wouldn't make it and would be going home unsuccessful.

I'd been told we would have an initial interview, almost

like a mini version before our big selection board interview in front of 20 or so people. I wasn't looking forward to that either.

We'd been asked to study a book on the principles of flight in preparation for a small exam I'd studied really hard for it, like with everything else, I wanted to be well prepared. The timetable of events while I was at Cranwell included full physical medicals, eyesight testing and I had to climb inside an aircraft, sit down, put my seat belt on and then get back out all unaided.

I was super worried about my interview, still not really knowing how to respond to what might be very difficult questions. Two other mentors there were great with me and asked me to tell them my story. It was a story of death threats, litigation, loss of faith in humanity and the court system and a total destruction of my business, wealth and my spirit. It was a story that was difficult to tell, I hadn't told anyone before and just admitting my feelings was almost like opening the flood gates of emotion.

Sean Allerton and Debbie Grice were my surrogate mentors, they told me to just tell my story during the final interview and if I was given a chance to speak, that was my opportunity to tell all.

My first preliminary interview was a nightmare, it was with a trustee of the charity and a flying instructor. The interview started bad when the instructor said, *"I've read your application letter and you seem very negative."*

I told him he'd be negative if he'd been through what I had, obviously he didn't know I was referring to recent events and not to losing my arm. He then asked why I thought there was a negative perception of disabled people.

I told him I was fed up of people staring and making negative comments to which he replied

"Why don't you laugh them off and make a joke out of it?"

I wasn't in a joking mood and couldn't do that, I'd had enough of people and I'd had enough of the interview. I ended the interview early and was ready to go home, I hated that preliminary interview. Looking back now I can see that this just wasn't me. Throughout my life I've rarely been negative about the accident, I've always tried to be a problem solver first and foremost, this morose, angry man in my shoes was someone I just didn't know and didn't like.

I told Sean I was going home but he and Debbie persuaded me not to leave and to stick it out, Sean said the preliminary interview was the hardest.

The day of the medicals arrived, and it was a full medical if you get my drift. The doctor was a pretty young woman and she had another female colleague with her. My chest was checked for any signs of breathing problems, my heart, blood pressure and my hearing were all tested. My medical history was looked over including any medication I was on, fortunately I wasn't on anything.

The traumatic amputation I had suffered and other non-visible damage was scrutinised. My eyesight was tested, and colour blindness tested using the Ishihara test, the test we all had at school, little coloured dots on a circle of other coloured dots and you had to pick out the number in the centre, I failed that continually. Apparently, I have red/green colour blindness along with 9% of the male population. It's very rare in women according to the lady doctor who had just finished testing my limb reflexes and now wanted me to drop my trousers and underwear so she could do a cough and drop test, to see if there were any other health problems... There was a problem though, and I wasn't too sure how to explain before dropping my trousers...

It had been my birthday in December and then shortly after Christmas. My sister had asked me what I wanted as a gift, to which I replied,

"Buy me an experience, don't buy me any more items, I've got too much stuff already."

So, Tracy my sister had bought me an experience I would never forget, but what was it...?

Tracy had bought me a back, sack and crack wax, that's the same as a Brazilian for women, sometimes called a *"Manzilian",* but basically it involves waxing the whole pubic area, testicles and crack of your bum. When I tell my friends they say you didn't go through with it did you?

Of course I did, I'd asked for an experience and I certainly was going to get one, one I wouldn't forget. It was of course a young pretty woman doing the waxing, better that than a man though. People ask was it really painful. Yes, it was painful but not unbearable, it was more of a momentary sting that went away just as quick as it arrived plus the paracetamol I'd taken before the wax were doing their job. However, how was I going to tell the doctor that only two weeks prior to her examination I'd had a back, sack and crack wax?

She said *"Drop your trouser Steven..."*

"Uummm I'm a little embarrassed", I said,

"No need" the doctor said, *"Would you prefer my female colleague leaves the room?"*

"No," I said, *"I'm not embarrassed about that."*

I explained the gift of an experience my sister had

bought me, their eyes lit up and they had big smiles on their faces.

"We're not bothered about that Steve."

So off came my trousers and the cupping and coughing took place. When I left the examination room the doctor said to me, *"You're my favourite Steve."*

I liked that. During the rest of the selection process she and her colleague would smile at me with a knowing smile and wink at me as if to say, we know your secret!

The day I had been dreading was finally here, the day of the selection committee's final selection interview, in front of twenty people. My interview was at 1pm. Sean said to me,

"Tell them your story when they give you the opportunity don't waste the chance of a lifetime."

Sir Robert Wright controller of the RAF Benevolent Fund and one of the trustees came out to get me. I was sat down on a chair at the front of a large room with 5 people immediately in front of me with about 6 feet between us and 15 other people that were involved with the charity, including Edwin Brenickmeyer, who's family own C&A and the rock legend Bruce Dickinson of Iron Maiden, there were incredibly successful and wealthy people in that room as well as highly decorated military men and women. I was by far the least educated and successful person there, I was surrounded by the best of the best.

Then the questions started. I'd answered a few simple questions like my name, address and how I'd lost my right arm. Then came the big question, *"Why are you here"* I thought

"This is the opportunity Sean told me about."

I'd only just started to tell my story when I could feel the emotion building up inside me, a torrent of feelings I had managed to hold back while telling Sean and Debbie, but this wave was too big to hold back, my voice started wobbling as I told my story, I had a lump in my throat and my eyes were filling with tears. I could feel the deluge of emotion welling up inside me, it was just too much to contain and I broke down in floods of uncontrollable tears and sorrow. I just couldn't continue the interview.

Sir Rob came to my help, he took me outside of the room and sat me down while I tried to recover. It took me ten minutes to collect my thoughts. Sir Rob said

"Can you tell me what happened to you to make you so sad Steven? Can you tell me, and I'll go back in and explain to the group of trustees?"

I told him of the six years of litigation, the death threats and the metal bars I had fitted at my doors and windows to protect me from the frequent visits from the thugs, I told him of the shadow of darkness that was shrouding me like a veil and the suicidal thoughts. The systematic destruction of my product's reputation that ultimately cost me the business I'd been working so hard to keep afloat, the loss of my wealth and the near loss of my family. Sir Rob went back into the room to explain, he was gone five minutes.

When he returned, he asked me if I could go back into the interview and continue. I said I'd try but I couldn't guarantee my emotional stability. I'd let my emotional beast out of its cage and there was no putting it back in.

The interview started again with less probing questions to start with but eventually the questions started to affect me again and I had to just say I can't answer that, not because I didn't want to, but because it was emotionally too difficult to answer.

Finally, the interview process was over. I was a wreck, but it was done, I'd survived, and it felt good to have finally told my story and to have let the emotion out. I needed that release; it had been building up for years and my male conditioning would not allow me to cry; but crying is something we have to do sometimes in order to be able to heal. Maybe my healing process had just started. I said my farewells and drove home.

As I left, Sue Whitby told me she would call in a couple of days, to let me know how I had done through the scholarship process and whether I had been successful or not. I returned home feeling a little different inside, the emotional release had helped but now a long two-day wait was ahead of me.

I was in a bit of a daze; I didn't think the selection process had gone well for me and I was convinced I hadn't been selected. I felt like nothing was going right for me and depression seemed to be my only friend.

I was walking through the centre of Leeds, across millennium square to be precise when my mobile phone rang

"Hello, Steven Robinson speaking" I answered.

"Hi Steve, it's Sue Whitby from FSDP, how are you after the selection process at Cranwell?"

I said, *"I'm OK thank you."* I didn't really want to know that I'd been rejected, so I just wanted to talk before the inevitable *"sorry you haven't been successful on this occasion".*

Sue said, *"Would you like to know how you did?"*

"No not really, I'd just like to chat!" I said, nervously.

"You've been successful" she said, *"we'd like to offer you a scholarship, would you like to accept?"*

I went numb from head to toe, my mind couldn't take it

in, I totally wasn't expecting that.

I said, *"Yes please I want to accept!"*

"I thought you'd say that, you were one of our easier decisions, we all feel you really need this opportunity" replied Sue.

I walked through the centre of Leeds with tears streaming down my face. I couldn't contain my emotions. I'd been on an emotional rollercoaster and I just couldn't seem to get off. I felt really strange inside, not a sickly feeling but more like something had changed in me. I felt relief, my faith in people restored. No one had ever given me anything, people just took from me, my ideas, inventions, kindness and willingness to help were all taken for granted and abused. Yet here was a group of people, well educated, professionals, well connected, millionaires, even billionaires and celebrities offering me this precious gift, the gift of flight. A gift that had a hefty price tag, all paid for by the generosity of good and kind people, the kind of people I had not been lucky enough to meet before.

Their generosity and willingness to help me recover from my ordeal restored my faith in people because at that moment when Sue said the *"scholarship is yours"* was the turning point in my life. There were still good people in the world, and I had been lucky enough to meet them. Not only that but the date of the call from FSDP was the 19th of April 2012, a date you might recognise. I certainly recognised it because it was the very same date, I'd lost my right arm, 30 years ago to the day. I thought it must be an omen, a sign that everything would be ok, that everything would work out for the best.

It soon became apparent that the whole ethos of FSDP was to help people recover from their despair and dark place they had found themselves in, due to their disability or in my case the dreadful experiences I had gone through.

However, I knew from the very beginning what I wanted to get out of my flying scholarship, and that was my PPL (private pilot's licence).

I had been liberated from the desperate doldrums of despair, what a difference one phone call can make, and the massive impact generosity would have on my life.

I can't thank FSDP enough for their gift and belief in me. Abba sang *"I Have A Dream"* and now, so did I. I had a goal in my life a new dream and something to occupy my thoughts. I was going to be a pilot... or was I?

The lesson I've learnt is there is nothing wrong with dreaming, be a dreamer and chase your goals.

Chapter 43
Flight Training

The years previous to my flying scholarship people had been given forty hours flying time and generally went overseas to take flight training; normally to South Africa or the USA, due to their better and more stable weather conditions. However, mine was the first year of the new scholarship programme that consisted of twenty hours only and all flight training would be carried out in the UK, due to the global banking crisis and reduction in donations.

Forty-five hours was the minimum requirement for a Private Pilot's License (PPL). Before my scholarship had even started it seemed that getting my PPL would be almost impossible without financial help. Forty-five hours, however, was a long way away, I hadn't even flown for one hour, other than the graduation gift my mum had bought me. I might not even like it. I was afraid of flying after-all, so maybe twenty hours might be too many hours if I couldn't handle it. I'd needed hypnotherapy just to fly to Spain on holiday with my mates!

Where would I take my flight training? We were told it would be a three-week residential course and we would be put up in a local hotel or guest house for the duration. I was told I would be learning to fly with two other scholars. They would be my flying buddies. The idea was to match us with other people on the programme, so we could bond in our little group and help each other when things got tough.

My flying buddies would be Mary and Sylvia, we were told we would be flying from a Southern airfield called Blackbush and I would be flying an aircraft called a Bulldog, made by Scottish Aviation.

It was a wonderful looking aircraft, that was flown with a stick rather than a yoke, the yoke being more like a car steering wheel. I was super excited that I would be flying this aircraft it was truly beautiful.

We were all sent a flight bag containing seven flight manuals covering all aspects of flight training, along with a manual flight computer, rulers and plotting pens all courtesy of Pooley's flight equipment.

We were told that the minimum requirement to be able to do a solo flight, was to have passed the aviation law exam, there were seven exams in total covering: flying training, aviation law, meteorology, human factors, human performance, air navigation, radiotelephony, aeroplane technical and radio navigation and instrument flying. It was suggested that we started reading aviation law as soon as possible so we would be more prepared for our flight training and in order to be able to do a solo flight if we were ready.

I got stuck into reading aviation law with gusto and I was determined to be ready for the start of my flight training. I was getting more and more nervous day by day.

I passed my aviation law exam before the start of my training. I wanted to make the most of my flying experience, so I took my exam locally, in Leeds at my own expense. The whole ethos of FSDP wasn't to create pilots but to provide a life changing experience, to turn people's lives around via the medium of flight but I wanted to be a pilot.

Three days before my flight training was due to start, I got a phone call from Aerobility, the organisation that would be giving me my flight training. The phone call was to tell me that the Bulldog aircraft I would be flying had been sold. I would be flying a PA28 instead.

A PA28 however wasn't stick flown, the controls were a yoke type.

I was told I would need to bring my prosthetic arm with me to fly the PA28 because that would be the only way I could control it. *"Which prosthetic arm would that be?"* I said.

"Don't you have a prosthetic arm you can bring with you Steve?"

"No, I don't have a prosthetic arm, I can probably get one made by the NHS but not in 3 days!"

Things were postponed for me before I'd even got off the ground, excuse the pun. My scholarship would have to be put back until a new arm could be made. Mary and Sylvia my flying buddies would have to start without me. Perhaps naively, I hoped that I would be able to join them, and the NHS would pull out all the stops for me and I would have a new arm within a week, however, I realised that was an unrealistic expectation. I was really upset and whilst I knew deep down it wasn't anyone's fault, I didn't expect I would be placed in this position so near to the start of my flight training.

When I approached the NHS to have an arm created, I talked with the prosthetist about what I needed the new arm to do. We looked at a catalogue of joints and locking mechanisms. It was like looking through a Meccano kit or a tool store brochure. It took around an hour to find the components that me and the prosthetist were happy with and another thirty minutes to take a plaster cast mould of my shoulder. The shoulder cast would be turned into a carbon fibre shoulder cap where the prosthetic arm would be connected, that cap would be held in place by a single 1 1/2" elasticated Velcro strap. It was quite a basic ecsosketal design. Finally, after 12 months in the making I was ready to start flight training, but where?

I was still going to be doing my flight training at Blackbush with Aerobility but their main instructor Mike was away for quite a long time, their other instructor was only part-time because he was the main child minder in his relationship. Things just weren't going my way.

I was losing confidence in Aerobilty, I'd heard great things about them, but in the end, after some serious thinking, following a few other issues, I decided to approach FSDP to see if I could train elsewhere.

FSDP started looking for an alternative flight school which was very tricky, the only other one that would take me was Bristol Aero's, not actually based in Bristol but at Kemble airfield near Cirencester in the Cotswolds.

Their CFI (Chief Flying Instructor) was John Griffin, the flight instructor I'd had a bad preliminary interview with at the first interview at Cranwell, during the final selection process for FSDP.

I had my reservations, but despite what had been said previously and my own experience of John, I decided I had to give him a chance, maybe it was me and I'd been in a bad place when I first met John, I know I was!

The day eventually came, although a year late when I had to travel down to Cirencester to settle into my three-week accommodation and prepare to start flight training. Ironically the number 19 came up again, as did a name from my past. It was the 19th of May 2013, the same year Jimmy Savile was named as the UK's most prolific sex offender.

The following morning, I was up at 6am so I could get ready and be at Kemble airfield for 8am, the time John was expecting me. What a pleasant surprise John was, he was normal, he wasn't part of the PC brigade and would call every situation as he found it. I really liked that attitude and it suited me. I couldn't understand why Mark had tried to discourage me from flying with him. John was a breath of fresh air. He was the saving grace of my time spent at Kemble.

I stayed in a beautiful public house and B&B called The Elliot Inn in a lovely sleepy village called South Cerney. Wow, what a fantastic quintessential English village buried and almost hidden in the Cotswolds, almost like a place time had forgotten.

I fell in love with that picturesque haven of peace and tranquillity and I thoroughly enjoyed my stay at The Elliot. Now that I was settled in my accommodation, I could concentrate on my flight training.

This, however, wasn't going that well, I was continually afraid of flying, although I didn't let anyone know of my fear. I wanted to want to fly but the truth was I didn't want to fly, I was just too nervous about the unknown, but I didn't let that stop me.

The weather wasn't very good during my flight training and during the first two weeks the only thing I learnt was how to drink and make tea. I knew how to make tea but suffice to say I got more practice than I needed. Although I really enjoyed my time sat around bonding with John, who by this time had become my best friend.

The day came when the weather was fine and John said,

"Great let's try this arm of yours." He said, *"How good are you with it and how long have you been using a pros- thetic arm Steve?"*

"I've never used it John, it's been made specifically to learn to fly this aircraft" I said,

"But you've used a prosthetic arm before, haven't you?"

I replied, *"No I've never used a prosthetic arm before"*
"In that case let's go try it!"

John thought the best way to try out the new arm was a test flight at an altitude of 3500ft. I put my complete faith and trust in John and went with the plan.

My first ever flight training experience would be one I'd never forget. John explained that I needed to repeat every- thing he said, so he knew I had understood and then to do the things he said. We were at 3500ft in straight and level flight, which sounds easier than it actually is. John said

"You have control Steve"

I replied with *"I have control."*

Oh wow, how exhilarating! At the time all I could feel was intense concentration, but I was up there, doing it! De- spite the nerves and the fear, I was flying.

John then went on to give me instructions that I needed to carry out. He told me to let go with my left arm and fly the aircraft with my prosthetic arm only.

"Bank left 15 degrees" said John, I replied *"bank left 15 degrees"* then turned the yoke to the left until we were at an angel of 15 degrees. My prosthetic arm seemed to handle that ok, the next instruction was bank right 15 degrees, I

repeated the instruction back to John then started the manoeuvre, the next instruction was to put the aircraft into a dive followed by the final instruction of this sequence which was to pull up into a climb, but something went wrong!

I said to John *"You have control John"* my voice pitched far higher than normal with fear.

John said *"No, no Steve, you have control, you have to learn to fly the aircraft with your prosthetic arm only"*

I'm not sure he was aware of what was really going on with my arm, but I said with a little more urgency as we went into a spiral dive and dropped through a cloud

"No John you have control, my bloody arm's fallen off!"

It was on the floor of the aircraft. John took immediate control and when we stopped laughing, John said *"Sort yourself out Steve"*

I picked my prosthetic arm up off of the floor strapped myself back in and said *"Right, I'm sorted John"*

John said something to me at that moment that I'll never forget, he said,

"It doesn't matter if it all goes wrong Steve, there's 3500 feet below us, there's loads of time to correct" he went on to say *"the most useless bit of sky is that bit above you and the most useless bit of runway is that bit behind you"*

That made a lot of sense to me but the more I thought about it, the more I realised, that was a great metaphor for life because it doesn't matter what's behind you and in your past, the only thing that is important is what's in front of you and in your future. With that in mind John said,

"Let's try again."

We tried it another 5 times and every time my prosthetic arm fell off. But, if at first you don't succeed, try, try, try again. It was obvious by the fifth attempt and subsequent failures that my newly made NHS prosthetic arm wasn't up to the task and wouldn't be the solution I hoped it would be. We needed a quick fix, something that would stop my arm from falling off. After a few cups of tea back at the portacabin, otherwise known as Bristol Aero Club HQ and some pacing up and down, we came up with a super-duper technical wiz bang solution.

A bungee cord!

Yes, the technical bungee cord. What we planned to do was hook one end of the cord to my prosthetic arm, pull it tightly, wrap it a couple of times around the seat then hook the free end to a secure mounting point under my seat.

We rushed out to the aircraft, all excited like young children wanting to play for the first time, with a new toy and I was singing *"Come Fly With Me"* by Frank Sinatra. As soon as we were airborne, we went for the bungee cord test. I felt a bit like Luke Skywalker from Star Wars, the force was strong with me, only problem was, it was elasticated force and not that of a Jedi Warrior. I wasn't a warrior although the aircraft was, it was called a Piper Warrior also known as a PA28.

We started with straight and level flight, as I said before that's not as easy as it sounds especially when all that's stopping your arm from falling off is an elasticated piece of rope. During straight and level flight John asked *"is the aircraft in trim?"* When flying sometimes you experience excessive load (force) on the yoke, it's tiring to hold that load for any length of time. We use something called a trim wheel that removes that load, I replied to John *"I'm not sure if I'm trimmed"* to which John said, *"why don't you know?"*

I could feel something pulling on my prosthetic arm, but

I wasn't sure what it was, if it was control yoke loading or the elasticated force of the bungee cord. The only way to know was to let go with my left arm. I told John of my intention, to which he replied, *"get on with it then."* I liked his straightforward talking it made me laugh.

"Letting go with my left arm" I said. The aircraft maintained straight and level flight. *"Yeh hay"* I said, *"we're ok."* I expected something to go dreadfully wrong, but it hadn't.

John said, *"so are you trimmed?"* I still wasn't sure because I could still feel something pulling on my prosthetic arm. I told John, to which he replied, *"what are you going to do then?"* I thought about my next move for what felt like an eternity, probably only a few seconds but it felt a lot longer.

"I know what I'll do! I'll unlock my elbow and see what happens." The elbow joint of my prosthetic arm had the capability of locking in position or unlocking in a free movement position. I prepared to unlock the elbow joint and said to John *"are you ready?"*

"Get on with it then!" said John. I unlocked the elbow joint…

Wooooh! The whole aircraft went into a nosedive, my stomach felt like it was in my mouth. I was in a state of temporary shock, but I was in control and had to remedy the situation immediately. I grabbed the controls with my left hand pulled back on the control yoke. John said, *"you're not trimmed then!"*

Of-course he was right I wasn't in trim and now I couldn't let go of the yoke to trim the aircraft via the trim wheel or even re-lock my elbow. It was obvious, with or without the bungee cord my newly acquired prosthetic arm wasn't up to the task and wouldn't be the solution to flight training I hoped it would be.

Eight hours were remaining of my 20-hour scholarship. I could just burn up the hours knowing I couldn't achieve my objective of going solo or I could hold the remaining hours in reserve, return back home to Leeds and wait for the NHS to make mk2 prosthetic arm. I chose the latter. At least I had a better idea of what was needed of a flying arm.

On my return home I returned to Seacroft hospital where the Leeds prosthetic department was located and started the process again. I thought this time it wouldn't take as long, maybe a month maximum two. I was wrong, it took so long I almost gave up hope. Not wanting the grass to grow under my feet I decided I would tackle the seven aviation exams. I studied and studied and memorised answers not really fully understanding the why's behind the answers, I would only ever really understand fully with flying experience.

I'd finished all my exams with flying colours. I wasn't a natural academic, but I'd learnt how to channel efforts through my university years.

I was still waiting for the replacement prosthetic and the end seemed nowhere in sight. What was I going to do? I didn't want to waste my time, but couldn't go any further with my flight training until mk2 arm was completed.

I decided I would deal with my fear of horses while I waited.

I learnt one of my most valuable lessons during my time with John. It doesn't matter what's behind you and in your past, it's what's in front of you and in your future that's important…

Chapter 44
Summer Camp

I'd given up on the idea of being an English language teacher to foreign students, because of the previous bad experiences and disability discrimination I'd experienced in Thailand. However, a friend I had made while training at action English language in Leeds, told me about an opportunity to work for a company called LSC. They ran an annual summer camp for visiting foreign teenagers at Leeds Metropolitan University; the university I graduated from in 2002. It felt more like fate that this opportunity had fallen into my lap, like I was destined to work as an English teacher, the first job I would have ever had, if my application was successful. I wasn't overly confident about even getting to the interview stage because in the back of my mind were all the other rejections I'd had, but I wanted to give it one more try, before I threw in the towel and walked away from teaching forever. I had a lot of time on my hands while I was waiting for mk2 prosthetic arm to be made, so I bit the bullet and sent in my application making sure they knew from the very beginning that I only had one arm. To my surprise I was offered the job and started that summer full of enthusiasm and optimism. I wasn't sure if I would be as enthusiastic once classes had started, but I wouldn't have to wait long to find out, because the summer camp started four weeks after my acceptance. It was now

2012, the same year as the London Olympics were staged and Britain won a record 65 medals, 29 gold, 17 silver and 19 bronze.

It was called summer camp and not summer school, so I was unsure what the students were expecting. The first day arrived, there were some difficult students that simply didn't want to work, they thought they were going on an English holiday. Cliff Richard sang *"We're all going on a summer holiday"* and that's what the students thought they were doing. I sympathised because I never wanted to work as a student at high school either and certainly wouldn't have wanted to return to school during my summer break. With that in mind it gave me a unique perspective of how a lot of the students were feeling. They wanted to be on holiday and not to be back at school, merely learning a language in a different place. I interrupted a group of students that were speaking in Spanish about how they didn't want to work. I said to them in Spanish *"you don't have to work if you don't want, you can just sit there and relax."* I would not force them to work it was totally their choice. They were shocked I understood them and that I spoke their language. I then told the other students the same in English.

One of the Spanish boys said he didn't want to work. *"That's okay, just relax, I can't let you go outside unsupervised unfortunately."* A little time after, perhaps 10 minutes later, he was messing around, his girlfriend hit him on the head and told him to stop talking and being disruptive, *"the teacher understands you,"* she said.

"What's wrong?" I asked the boy. He said he was bored. *"I know you are, so why not do the work? It's better than being bored,"* I said. That was the first and last time the

students complained about working during my class. I wasn't strict, I always gave them the option of working if they wanted and if not just sit quietly until the class was over, but I also pointed out to them that that would be a wasted opportunity.

I wanted school to be fun, it wasn't for me, so I was determined to make my classes enjoyable because fun never feels like work. We did Karaoke and a type of speed learning (a bit like speed dating) all in English, where everyone had five minutes to speak to each other before rotating tables. At the end of the speed learning the students would have to tell the other people in the class the things they had found out about each other. We would deal with the English language issues as the arose.

The other teachers were furious that my classes were having fun. They saw my students leave my classes singing the songs we had just learnt while doing Karaoke and telling their friends about things they'd learnt about their fellow students.

One of the other teachers complained to the course coordinator and I was asked to explain myself, in front of all the other teachers, during a teacher briefing. I explained that the Karaoke was more than just singing. My Karaoke class was designed to show how song and language were in fact the same. That the spoken language also had rhythm, rhyme and intonation and that song demonstrated that. Songs also introduced new vocabulary and double meanings, similes, metaphors and alterations. The next day the other teachers were doing Karaoke and speed learning classes.

My classes were so popular that one of the visiting Russian teachers asked if she could sit in on one of my lessons to observe. I said I was OK with that. Something strange happened during that class, as I was being observed. Some Russian girls were doing well at a quiz we were doing but the Italian boys weren't doing so well. One Italian boy kept asking one of the Russian girls for the answers. The Russian girl was getting annoyed when I said, *"Don't be annoyed, he's paying you a compliment."*

"But I don't know all the answers!" she said.

I replied, *"But he thinks you know all the answers and he thinks you know more than he does, and that's the compliment."*

My classes were full of optimism and positivity, they were fun and the students looked forward to my classes. The summer passed so quickly. On the final day the Russian observer came to my class to give me a gift. A gift they wanted to present me with, something for their favourite teacher. It was a beautiful Matryoshka doll.

It was a wonderful experience during the height of summer, back in my old university campus. I hoped that I could take part the following year, this would depend though on whether my arm had been made and I could re-start my flying lessons.

In the meantime, I decided I would continue teaching English as a foreign language and started working for a company called Communicaid, that were based in the South of England, but employed freelance teacher/trainers around the UK to teach business English to visiting business people. I taught so many nationalities and made friends from all around the world while getting paid. That was an added bonus. My life was busy, just as I liked it, but there was still room for something new while I continued my wait.

I learnt another valuable lesson during this period of my life. There is always room for something new - knowledge, experiences or achievements. Don't be held back by your fears or doubts.

Chapter 45
Horse Riding

Over the road from me are the beautiful fields that I loved so much as a young boy, I love them just as much today and that's why I still live in the same house 40 years later. While playing on the fields as a ten-year-old, I was attacked by a gypsy cart horse. Gypsies always left their horses there to graze.

The horse pushed me with its nose, I went flying backwards and landed on the spike that was hammered into the ground to secure the horse. My back was cut and bruised, the pain was so bad I couldn't contain my tears, the horse then proceeded to try and jump on me, it was a very unfriendly and particularly angry horse, but that was enough to put me off horses for life.

Now I found myself with some spare time, I thought I would try and deal with my fear. I'd already conquered my fear of bullies after the six years of litigation and I was dealing with my fear of flying, even though that was temporarily postponed.

However, how does one deal with a fear of horses? I'd heard about a riding school not too far from me. I lived in the North of Leeds and in the South of Leeds there was a Riding School for the Disabled Association (RDA) centre.

I took myself along to the place, it was called Middleton Park Equestrian Centre. I had phoned ahead and told the staff about my fear and asked if taking riding lessons would help. They were very encouraging and told me it would certainly help. I booked my first lesson there and then.

I sat in my car in the car park, with a dry mouth and my stomach turning over. It was even harder than flying, at least there I had someone with me to take over the controls if things went wrong. Playing on my car radio was *"Shakin All Over"* by Johnny Kid and The Pirates as I forced myself to climb out of the car, my legs and body felt like they were being instructed by the song and I was literally shaking all over, and feeling sick.

As I walked over, I could smell the horses and the stables, it was nearly enough to make me walk back to the car, but I'm not a quitter. I kept having flashbacks of teeth and hooves.

If I'm honest, my first lesson wasn't great, I was so nervous. The people there were lovely and went out of their way to make me feel relaxed and safe. My second lesson was no better. I can look back now and say that returning the second time was even harder than the first! Horses can be very unforgiving and they're strongminded when they want to be!

However, on my third lesson I was given a horse called Maddy. She was lovely and I bonded with her immediately. It's a strange feeling when you bond with a horse, it's almost like a physic link, a strange connection where you feel at one with your horse. It's so comfortable, you feel like you are with a best friend you've known for ages and someone you look forward to spending your time with.

In an unexpected twist that was the start of my love affair with horses and I would improve each time I rode. I started going at least twice a week. Isn't it funny, once your mind changes how you can overcome your fears?

Then Ben came along, he was a beautiful 16.3 hands pie-bald gelding and he knew dressage. By now you've probably realised how determined I am, and it won't come as a surprise to you that I'd not only learn to ride but I'd do something above and beyond!

I had another new goal I would become be a dressage rider and I would ride Ben; he could teach me and we would grow together in ability. However, his ability far out shone mine, for a little while at least.

To my surprise I found I wasn't that bad at dressage and horse riding in general. I guess my motorbike days had served me well. I had great balance and good weight distribution. But, because of my accident, my right hip had been damaged, and I didn't have a great deal of strength in my right leg. In fact, not much strength in my left leg either! This meant that I struggled with some moves especially canter. Some horses wouldn't move into canter and others, including Ben would often drop out. This was due to the amount of pressure I could apply with my legs.

I persevered, worked hard with Ben, strengthened our bond, and my legs and it was only a matter of time before I entered the regional dressage qualifiers.

We practiced the routine over and over and I even walked around the garden memorising how it would go. The day of the regional qualifiers arrived, I was very nervous, what was a one-armed, Yorkshire man with only a few months horse riding experience doing entering a competition? I must have been daft! Still, I went to Middleton Park Equestrian Centre to get the horse ready, warm him up and prepare myself for the dressage routine, it would be done in front of three official judges. The routine went really well, better than I had expected. Ben seemed like a different horse, he liked being on show and enjoyed performing. He had a spring in his step and he held his head in a perfect outline. He was clearly a show-off!

My performance had been at 1pm, but I wouldn't get to know how I'd done until all the other riders had finished. I'd have to wait until 3:30pm to get my results. It was going to be a long wait and I honestly wasn't sure how I'd match up to the other riders.

Three cups of tea and copious amounts of biscuits later, my results were in. I'd come first! That meant I would be attending the national qualifiers at Hartpury College in the Cotswolds, not far from Kemble Airfield where I'd been taking my flight training. I couldn't believe it. How far I'd come from that morning in the carpark scared about sitting on a horse.

The national qualifiers were another league all together, people from all over the country were competing, there were three hundred and fifty people in my classification.

Again, I had practiced and practiced. I knew what my weak areas were, but just hoped that I could pull it off on the day.

We were on at 10am and Ben was hyper during warm up, he was bucking like a bronco. He was so excited to be there. He'd been many times before, although this was the first time for me. To be honest I knew how he felt, there was an air of excitement and a buzz of support from everyone that had come to watch.

There is a different atmosphere at disabled sporting events. People are super friendly and supportive. Everyone there wants you to do well.

Once Ben had calmed down, we were led into the holding area. A bell rang which indicated I was to enter the test zone and start my routine. Ben was great except for a couple of minor issues in the corners nearest the judges-box. I thought *"that's going to cost me dearly"*, apart from that Ben performed wonderfully.

It would be a long wait before I knew my score as we had to stay until 5pm when the scores came in.

Despite it only being my second ever competition, and despite not having been riding that long, I was disappointed with my results; I'd scored 76 points, the first place went to a rider with 78.5 and I came fifth.

Fifth out of 350 riders was fantastic but, I'm a perfectionist and so I was disappointed that I hadn't come first. That might read as though I'm full of myself and expect to come first in everything. That's really not the case. I just set my own bar so high, I truly feel that if you're taking on something in life, you should always aim to be the best you can.

What was once a fear had become a love and not only that, but I was good at it. Getting over my fear had given me a new passion.

In 2019 I came 3rd in the national dressage qualifiers. It was to become a world changing year. Covid-19 was discovered in the epicentre of Wuhan, China and Britain was suffering Brexit fever.

The lesson I learnt was with practice we continually improve, even the things we think we can't do or are afraid of doing we can master. We are after all masters of our own destiny.

Chapter 46
The Support Actor

It was 2013, the same year that Mark Cahill, a 51-year-old former pub landlord from my home county of West Yorkshire, became the first person in the UK to receive a hand transplant, I was thinking maybe I could get a full arm transplant. Not really certain I would want one even if it was offered. As my mind pondered the possibilities of arm transplantation, the telephone rang. It was my friend Diana, to tell me she had been asked to be a support actor on a BBC drama called *"By Any Means"*. Diana is a Colombian woman and the role was to be a salsa dancer on a Colombian Embassy set, and would I like to be her dance partner? I said, *"Yes I'd love to"*.

We were both salsa dancers and were used to dancing together. It was the perfect role for us. The embassy scene would be shot at Spring Grove House in Bewdley, Worcestershire. It was a long drive from Leeds, so we would have to stay overnight and the money received for the job would only just cover our travel and accommodation costs, but at least we could say we had been support actors.

We danced to a song by the Cuban singer and famous Latin artists of the 20th century, Celia Cruz, called *"La Vida Es Un Carnaval"*. The title translates as Life is a Carnival, and it certainly was. I was living my life like a perpetual carnival of new experiences.

It was a long day of filming but what an adventure it was. It was so exciting to be on a filmset, I thought, I wonder whether a one arm man might be needed on set more than I initially thought. I met some great people there who introduced me to the world of support acting and their agents, they convinced me that, in fact, all types of disabilities were in demand on set, especially if a broad spectrum of society was to be portrayed. That was it, I was hooked. I would become a support actor at least in the short term while I kept looking for other opportunities.

You might have seen me on a few different TV programmes. I've been on Emmerdale a few times, sat in the Rovers Return, drinking a Rum and Coke, yes it was a real drink, and free. Well better than free because I was being paid to be there. I was on the feature film *"The Limehouse Gollem"* starring Bill Nighy and me as a beggar. I was in *"Houdini and Doyle"* an ITV drama. I've been in so many TV programmes and films that I stopped counting. I even took acting classes in Leeds for a while at a place called *"Act for TV"*. I loved it. Nothing was holding me back and I was filling my life and creating some wonderful new and exciting memories. At the same time, I was making some new friends and extending my network of contacts.

I learnt a valuable lesson, one that people often say but think is a cliché but it's not. It's not what you know, although that most definitely helps but it's who you know that's important, because they are the ones who will open doors for you.

Chapter 47
To fly or not to fly

It was 2014 Scotland had just voted *"No"* in their independence referendum and I had been waiting twelve months to get the MK2 prosthetic arm. I went to the limb fitting department at Seacroft Hospital to pick it up, only to be told that the technician had altered the fitting method at the last moment. My heart sank because previous experience had taught me that when well-intentioned people made alterations, that they thought would help, invariably the whole thing would be useless.

My fears were right. The prosthetic arm and mounting system wouldn't even fit me. I was so down hearted, not knowing where to turn next or what to do. I didn't want to ask the limb fitting centre to make another arm. I felt so ungrateful and was concerned about the amount of NHS money that was being spent on prosthetics that wouldn't work. I realised I had to do something but what?

I always enjoyed engineering and making things with my hands, strange that I still say the plural, when I talk about my one arm and I always dream with two arms.

After a little soul searching and problem solving, it became obvious. I would make my own prosthetic arm. My workshop wasn't set up for this type of metal work engineering though, so the task of fitting out my workshop with the right machinery began. I bought a milling machine from eBay; it didn't work but I fixed it. I now needed a metal turning lathe, again I found one that wasn't working on eBay.

I'd purchased the lathe at a bargain price of £343. The photos of the machine I was expecting to be delivered by courier looked great. The day the lathe was delivered I was horrified. Appalled to see they had dropped it in transport and broke and smashed many of the controls and bent major pieces of its structure. I had no option but to claim on the courier's insurance.

After many hours of toing and froing, exchanging of photographic evidence their insurance paid out in full. However, forever the optimist I thought, although technically it's now just scrap, surely, I can rebuild it.

The hard process of restoring the lathe began. First, I had to sort out the electrics which I knew were faulty from the start. Then came the hard bit, getting the broken parts welded, re-bending bits back into alignment and making parts that had simply been lost.

After a few weeks it was running, and it had only cost me the delivery price and I could now start the process of making a prosthetic arm. What started as a negative, yet again gave me the chance to solve a problem and, being a Yorkshire man, get a bargain!

All I needed was some aluminium to start machining. The aluminium came courtesy of Immediate Engineering Services and my now, good friend Kevin, the owner based in Armley, in Leeds.

I now had everything I needed except, I didn't have a design, but I had an idea. I needed to make a semi rigid jacket that I could wear like a waist coat. I planned then to attach my prosthetic arm to that waist coat; the body jacket as I called it, was needed because of the level of my amputation. I have no stump to connect a prosthetic to, I have a partial shoulder though and the body jacket would encase my shoulder and the rest of my torso and be held in place by one 50mm wide canvas belt that I attached Velcro to.

Making the body jacket was fun. It took three people to make. Me as the model, my mum dipping plaster of Paris bandages into warm water and my sister, Tracy applying the bandages to my body. I remember the song by Kraftwerk *"The Model"* that I used to do my robotic dancing too, this time I was the model, but covered in plaster of Paris, as was the patio.

When it had dried Tracy cut it up the front and back. I had two halves that fitted me like a glove although I felt more like an Easter egg, two halves pressed together with me in the middle! I then covered the inside and outside of each half with fibreglass matting and resin, coloured it black and waited for it to cure. It worked phenomenally well and was held together with an old canvas belt. All I needed now was an arm to connect to it.

I had an idea of what I wanted the arm to do, so I started machining the aluminium until my invention started looking like an arm, well sort of an arm, it was very robotic, even terminator style. I machined, invented, tested ideas. Some failed, some worked great. It was all trial and error really but three months after starting, what seemed like an impossible task, I had a fully functioning prosthetic arm that took into consideration the necessity for quick release, should I need to exit the aircraft quickly in an emergency situation.

The lesson learnt here is a well-known one, but one I was just starting to truly appreciate because of my need.

Necessity is the mother of invention.

Chapter 48
The Inventor

I've had an interest in inventors and inventions all my life, Thomas Edison was one of the inventors that was of particular interest to me, because in 1882 he discovered the principles of the electronic vacuum tube used in early radios and jukeboxes, while working on the longevity of his electric light bulb invention. As a child I knew all the dates of the most important inventions and inventors, I was fascinated by their achievements.

I've always been an inventor; I just didn't realise it. Challenges are what keep me going they are the reason for my success and the catalyst for change, they drive me in a way I never expected they would. When I had two arms there were normal everyday challenges experienced by any able-bodied teenager and in the blink of an eye those challenges were multiplied tenfold when I lost my right arm. I struggled with everything and I found myself competing with my friends to be as good or as successful as they were or at least seemed to be to me. I struggled to keep up with them and felt I was losing the battle, so I made the conscious decision to stop competing against others and compete against myself only. In this way I could never lose because I could always put in a bit more effort. Effort would never be easy though, I had so many emotional ups and downs I felt like I was on a perpetual roller coaster and I really don't like roller coasters, emotional ones even less!

My mental health took a real beating, but I was determined to have some type of success in my life. I felt my life had been spared by God so I could go on and do better things. I 100% believed there was something better for me than a life of disability and under achievement.

I was constantly battling my demons and they often got the better of me, but I wouldn't be defeated, no matter how physically painful, emotionally draining or physiologically damaging it would be. Despite my physically damaged shell of a body, I would still fight on, not knowing if I could ever win the enormous battle that lay ahead.

S Club 7's song *"Don't Stop Never Give Up"* sums it all up for me!

I'm often asked how I came to be an inventor. My mind works differently to others, I think. I can only make that assumption because I don't really know how other people think, it's just I approach things differently. I started thinking more on solutions for everyday tasks at first. Those tasks would eventually become more complex which meant I had to become much more creative and start thinking outside of what was normal. Finding things off the shelf wasn't an option for me. The adaptions and tools I needed just didn't exist or if they did, they still weren't perfect for me. The only option I had was to put my analytical mind to work on a solution and then actually fabricate the items I needed.

I made so many things, adaptions, tools and machinery. First my inventions were crude although very effective, but as time went by my inventions started to become more complex and professional. My first big project was a cnc router (a robotic wood routing machine) that was controlled by a PC. I initially did some research to understand the basic principle of cnc machinery. The research phase was quite rapid but intense. I approached the task of building the cnc router with a bit of an ad-hoc methodology. I'd just start with one piece of metal and build on to that with a design that existed solely in my mind with the odd paper drawing of some of the more complex workings. Because I was a problem solver, I would just keep building and as I encountered issues my brain would come up with solutions. The machine was taking on its own shape and didn't conform to any written plan or design, a Frankenstein's monster, it was a beautiful beast when it was finished. This machine and the skills learnt gave me so much confidence in R&D (research and development) that I would tackle the biggest job of all.

Over the years, I have solved problems on how to create cabinets, how to find ways to hold screws or even solder (this involved me holding the solder tube in my mouth – not something I recommend as you're breathing in fumes and it's not safe!), I have sold my machines, many are still working well today and are one of a kind.

I know that with two arms I took so much for granted, that's not something I ever do now. Do I get frustrated? Yes, of course, I'm human after all, but equally, I am logical and a problem solver at heart, this is what has gotten me through, has saved my sanity and given me a way to live my life, my way.

One of the biggest lessons I've ever learnt and that has helped me succeed more than anything is *"stop competing with others!"* Compete with yourself only and you will achieve more than you ever thought you could and if it doesn't exist, make it yourself!

Chapter 49
Robo Pilot

All I had to do now was continue flight training.

I never actually stopped flight training. I had however, lost the remaining eight hours of my scholarship due to the delays waiting for the NHS, but I had continued flight training at Sherburn Airfield, on the outskirts of Leeds.

I was now having to pay for my own flight training, and I can tell you, it's not cheap £175 per hour, I was spending money like it was going out of fashion, but I was also getting it done. I wasn't allowed to do my solo flight though. I'd been passed around from pillar to post, different schools saying they could train me, then passing me on to someone else. Every time I changed flight instructor or schools; I would have to demonstrate all over again how I could fly the aircraft I was training in.

I was now training in an aircraft called a Robin 2160. It's a fabulous aircraft and I still fly it today. It was totally by chance I was introduced to the aircraft. I was measuring lengths for my prosthetic arm and doing some geometry and mathematics, trying to work out how my homemade arm would control things on a PA28, when a man walked up to me and said

"Do you mind if I put my two penneth in and give you some advice?"

I said yes please I'd appreciate it. The man was the

owner of a flying school at Sherburn, called Advanced Flight Training, he told me a PA28 or Piper Warrior wasn't a good fit for me as I would struggle to close the door and control a yoke. He suggested I should try jumping into the Robin and he was spot on. He knew his aircraft inside out. It was obvious from the moment I sat in the aircraft that this was ideal for me and I would be able to fly from the left-hand seat which is the captain's seat. I adjusted my design and measurements to accommodate the Robin and I started flight training in that aircraft.

I flew so many hours in the Robin my bank balance was looking really poorly, I was up to 90 hours and still not allowed to go solo. The Chief Flying Instructor (CFI) at the time was a difficult guy who thought he knew everything, including what it was like to be a one arm man. Of course, he had no idea. He couldn't understand how I could control the aircraft with one arm so wouldn't allow me to go solo.

The CFI kept putting obstacles in my way, I could have fought his decisions but realised that would be a waste of my time and effort, the only way he would accept what I said was to show him and prove my techniques would work. I therefore decided I would jump over all the hurdles he set and through all of the hoops. If I could prove him wrong on all the areas, he thought I would fail, then he couldn't argue anymore and would have to accept what he saw and experienced.

The CFI told me one day I couldn't go solo until I'd had a medical and I couldn't have a medical until I'd proven to him that my prosthetic arm was up to the task and that I could control the flight stick, (the Robin was stick control), and the throttle at the same time.

I said *"OK, can we go for a flight and I'll show you?"*

The flight took place there and then. I'd been quite creative with the prosthetic arm, it was locked at the shoulder with a quick release mechanism, a universal joint for an elbow, a telescopic forearm that could be locked and unlocked and a cup device that enclosed the throttle knob on my right-hand side.

The CFI put me through my paces, more I thought than an able-bodied person.

He kept saying *"You won't be able to operate the throttle and the control stick at the same time."* I demonstrated how I could. He was shocked, *"Yes, but you can't put the flaps down while throttling back"*, I demonstrated again.

The flight lasted an hour, he made me demonstrate things time after time until he had no more tests to give me. I had completed everything he'd asked of me.

When we landed, he said *"I really didn't think you could do all those things. Your arm does work, and it works really well. I'll recommend you get your medical."*

The next day I had my medical, which I passed. I could finally do my solo flight, when Alastair, my flying instructor said I was ready. I'd been passed around from instructor to instructor, until I eventually ended up with Alastair, that's when I really started to progress and I enjoyed flying with him.

It was approximately two weeks after my prosthetic arm had been given the all clear that I finally did my first solo flight. Alastair and I were doing circuits and touch and goes. We were basically flying round in a specific circuit pattern, every time we would do a landing, we'd let the aircraft role on the runway for around 100 meters, put full power back on and take off again without stopping, a touch and go. I did five circuits and five perfect landings.

On the fifth landing Alastair said *"Stop the aircraft Steve"* I pulled off the runway and gave my usual radio call *"Golf-Zulu Golf, runway vacated"* My aircraft had the callsign G-BWZG or golf-bravo-whiskey-zulu-golf in the phonetic alphabet and shortened to G-ZG.

Alastair said, *"Stop here Steve, on the taxiway, I'm getting out."*

"What do you mean, you're getting out Alastair?" I said

He looked at me and replied *"You're ready for your solo. I now want you to do what you've done five times earlier today."*

He waved me goodbye and I proceeded to enter the runway for a take off

"Golf-Zulu Golf lining up runway 28 left hand circuit" I said over the radio.

I was on the runway feeling strange. My emotions were overwhelming, I wasn't afraid, I wasn't excited I was numb. It was like an out of body experience, I was there but not there. I was so focused on the task at hand that nothing else could register with me. In my 'out of body state' I watched myself from above and I just did what I had to do.

I sat on the runway telling myself *"you can do it Steve, anything is possible, anything is possible, anything is possible Steve"*, with increasing volume as if I was giving myself a pep talk. The third time I repeated my mantra I pushed full power on with my DIY prosthetic arm, I watched all the dials in the aircraft move into a green coloured section on the dial faces. All systems were good, I watched the airspeed indicator, that's like a speedometer in a car. When the airspeed hit 60 knots that was my take-off speed. I pulled back on the control stick and the aircraft took off.

Wow! I was doing it, as the aircraft climbed out, I heard a voice over the radio, it said

"Attention all traffic, first time student pilot is in the circuit doing his first solo flight, no landings, or touch and goes until he has landed, stay away from him, keep clear!"

I thought oh no that's me! I was under pressure to get my landing perfect the first time because all the other pilots were stuck waiting for me to land. It's been known for students doing their first solo to get stuck in the circuit and have to be talked down after an hour. I didn't want that to happen to me, but my first approach to landing was too fast and too high. I thought I'd do a go around, power up and fly around the circuit and try the landing a second time. I talked myself out of that though, I said to myself *"don't do a go around yet, get a bit closer see how it feels"*

I gave myself that talk three times, on those three occasions I was going to do a *"go around"* but decided to play out the scene. I was five feet above the runway, my airspeeds looked good, so I pulled off all power and gently and progressively pulled back on the stick. I did a perfect, textbook landing the first-time round.

When I called "*runway vacated*" there were rapturous applause over the radio. I guess Alastair my instructor had never sent out a man with one arm before to do a solo flight. Finally, I felt I was getting somewhere, after all the trials and tribulations my determination seemed to be paying off. I would now forge forwards and get my PPL (Private Pilots License).

Two weeks after that I had to do my qualifying cross-country exercise (QXC). I had to fly from Sherburn in Elmet General Aviation (GA) airfield to Durham Tees International Airport and navigate through Leeming's military air traffic control zone (ATZ). I had to land at Durham Tees, get my logbook stamped and have a cup of tea of course, because I'm a Yorkshire man. Then I had to fly from Durham Tees over the North Yorkshire Moors to Humberside International Airport, while missing the Bilsdale Mast that stands at 1,030ft on high ground, overall altitude is 2262ft and I was flying just below cloud at 2200ft. I could see the mast to my right-hand side about 2 miles from my position as I hit an air pocket and dropped 30-40 ft. It scared the life out of me, I wasn't expecting it and I was still a nervous flyer and I had no one with me to comfort or reassure me. I made it to Humberside in one piece though, I got my logbook stamped, had another cup of tea and headed back to Sherburn with the evidence of my landings and before I needed the toilet!

It was a mere three weeks later that I did my skills test, that's like your driving test but in the sky and it lasts two hours. My skills test had to be broken into two parts because the examiner was a difficult CFI, he wasted so much time talking about nothing and on my skills test day he spoke for too long which meant we didn't have sufficient time to fulfil the two hours at once. I did eventually fulfil my two hours in two parts and finally got my pilot's license in 2015, the same year that NASA's interplanetary space probe *"New Horizon"* became the first spacecraft to do a close flypast of Pluto.

There were times when I didn't think I'd ever get there; with so many obstacles in my way and I'd had such a difficult time with some instructors.

But I'd done it, I'd achieved what I set out to do. Not only that, I had fallen back in love with inventing and creating.

I was awarded my scholarship in 2012, it had taken three years to get my license and at a cost of £17,000 but I'd done it, I'd proved all the doubting Thomas's wrong, I'd overcome a multitude of emotional and physical problems including having to make my own arm which was subsequently patented.

I had not only overcome my fear of flying, but I was inventing again and I was doing what very few people ever do, pilot an aircraft, single handed.

Alastair believed in me as did John Griffin and I thank them both for their encouragement and wonderful support.

I'll get by *"With a Little Help From My Friends"* as Joe Cocker sang and I was living the lyrics of that song.

With determination anything is possible. The important lesson I learnt was never listen to people who tell you with such confidence that you can't do something, only listen to those that encourage you to succeed in your dreams and goals.

Chapter 50
In The Limelight

The first time I was in the Limelight, was when I was featured on BBC Look North, as the one arm canoeist. It was 2008, NASA's unmanned spacecraft The <u>Phoenix</u> becomes the first to land on the northern polar region of Mars, the Hadron Collider at CERN was powered up and I had taken up canoeing as a new hobby at the White Rose canoe club based at Roundhay Park in Leeds.

I'd started learning to canoe, but I needed an oar for a one arm man but there was no such oar available to buy, without one I would go round in circles! I think the media came to film me doing just that, which I would have done if I had not designed, invented and made an oar myself. It was a masterpiece of simplicity. It was a double ended kayak paddle, but I had bolted a handle to it, at a right angle to the shaft of the paddle. That was the first part of my design. The second part was a hoop big enough for my forearm to pass through, that hoop was also bolted to the paddle shaft at a right angle and about 18 inches from the handle. It was a simple yet very effective design similar in appearance to an elbow crutch which is where the initial idea came from.

I put my forearm through the hoop and grabbed the handle. The hoop gave me the ability to do a backwards sweep on my left-hand side or portside if you are more nautically inclined. The handle allowed me to do a normal forearm movement to starboard or right-hand side. It meant I had full control of the paddle and the canoe.

The TV crew watched in amazement as I circumvented an obstacle course on the lake, unknown to the crew the real obstacles had already been overcome. They were the design and fabrication challenges I'd faced in making an oar for a one-armed man and long before the day of filming and the interview that followed.

By now, I had become a bit of an expert at making adaptions to tools and aids to allow me to take on the most challenging of tasks.

When the press heard about me making my own prosthetic arm, I was all over the national media,

"Disabled man takes flight training with DIY prosthetic arm"

"Robo pilot or was that Robbo pilot?" I am dyslexic after all!

Opportunities were coming in from all angles. I was invited to do the TV shows, A Place In the Sun, and Posh Pawnbrokers, (where I was selling my Astronaut jukebox, that didn't sell by the way, but the TV show made it look like it had). I was on the ITN National News, BBC Look North and I was invited on The One Show.

When I was asked if I'd like to be on The One Show as a guest, I said yes without even thinking about the implications. I didn't think about how it would be filmed, what was going to be filmed, if I would be on camera or if it would be a voice-over narrated story about me making my own prosthetic arm and taking flying lessons.

It became clearer after a chat with the production team how things would progress. Initially Carol Vorderman was going to interview me on camera, talk about my flying and the challenges I had faced, to make my own prosthetic arm and gain my pilots licence. I'd met her on a number of occasions because she was doing her flight training in the same place and at the same time as me and she was very friendly.

However, the week before filming was due to start, I received a call from the production team to say Carol had become unexpectedly unavailable and that they were looking for an alternative presenter.

I was told the presenter would be Rory Reed, one of the new presenters of Top Gear. 'OK' I said, but secretly I didn't like Top Gear and had never watched it; I had no idea who Rory Reed was! However, him being a new presenter I thought would be quite good as he would most likely be very upbeat and willing to put a lot of energy into it.

My assumption was correct and Rory did a fantastic job. He was fun to be with and I enjoyed filming with him. Filming took all day, we had to do the whole back story at my home, filming the jukeboxes I'd restored and then filmed in my workshop where I had made my prosthetic arm, we did some action close-ups of me operating my lathe and milling machine and a bit of re-enactment of me assembling the prosthetic arm.

It was great fun, I forgot there was even a camera or two there and just concentrated on talking to Rory and not the camera. The trick is, apparently, to talk to the presenter and avoid looking at the camera unless you want to talk directly to the viewers like in a news report but that's not what I was doing. It got to mid-day and we'd been filming since 8am, when we had to go to the airfield to continue with the aviation element of my story.

Everyone at the airfield was very interested in what was going on and the camera crew were drawing quite a crowd. I was enjoying being the centre of attention and especially doing the filming which didn't seem hard for me, nor was I nervous or embarrassed. When it came to the flying part of the filming though Rory did seem nervous, no surprise really, imagine going flying and finding out the pilot only has one arm!

I told Rory not to be nervous I would look after him. I said to him as we were lined up on the runway, take-off imminent, *"Are you ready Rory?"* He said he was and with that I pushed on full power with my prosthetic arm and we started rolling down the runway. In no time at all we were at 60 knots, take off speed, I pulled back on the control stick and we took off. We chatted as we did a full circuit of the airfield and came in for our landing. Rory looked visibly relieved as we touched down. We did a high five and rolled to a standstill. Filming was finally over. It had taken all day but my part was now over, Rory would do a final piece to camera and that was a wrap.

I was told I would be notified when it was going to be shown on TV. The day before screening I was asked if I'd like to appear on the sofa, live on The One Show at the BBC studios. I jumped at the chance. My rail journey was arranged and a limousine was waiting for me at London's Kings Cross station. Wow! What an experience! I was greeted by the production team and taken to the green room. Strange why they call it the green room, there is nothing green about it.

I had to get my makeup done, so my skin didn't shine under the intense studio lighting and was then taken to a waiting area to the side of where the studio audience was. I felt a bit nervous but not too much really, it was more excitement of what was to come and how I would present myself to the viewers. I was more worried about how I would be perceived rather than my ability to hold a conversation live on camera.

I didn't want to be thought of as arrogant just because I was confident; I've never really doubted myself, but sometimes pressure and anxiety can cloud those abilities and not allow others to see them clearly. There is a very fine line between confidence and arrogance, and I didn't want to step over it.

I just wanted to have fun and enjoy my time on the show. There was no need for concern, the interview went better than I could have hoped for, we laughed, joked and I told my story in a humorous way and even Mitchell and Webb sitting to my right seemed surprised and amused by this unknown one arm pilot.

I wasn't too sure how I had come across on camera. However, I soon found out after a torrent of emails, text messages and social media posts saying, *"give the one arm pilot his own TV show"*, apparently the public loved my interview as much as I had enjoyed taking part.

I was taken back to Kings Cross by limo for my journey home. I was on cloud nine, I had just experienced a life changing moment in front of 4,000,000 viewers. Opportunities like these don't come one's way very often, yet was it fate or destiny that they were coming my way; or was it just the efforts I was putting in to get noticed were actually working and I was getting seen?

I wasn't expecting things to happen quickly in the media world, but I received an email asking for my contact details. It was ITV they wanted to talk to me about appearing on the Davina McCall show This Time Next Year. I sent my contact details and the production team rang me.

They asked if I'd do a challenge for the program. I said I would, I could fly to 10 airports and land in 10 hours or ride my horse in some type of horse-riding challenge, stupidly I mentioned aerobatics, something I was really scared of. To this day I don't know why I mentioned it. I think I was trying to find something I thought they'd be interested in because I really wanted to take part but secretly, I hoped they hadn't heard the aerobatics bit.

They said they would think about it and get back to me in a few days. I thought no more about it. A few days passed and I receive a call from the production team.

"Hi Steve, we've decided we'd like to go ahead and film with you and we'd like you to do the aerobatics challenge."

Oh no! Was I stupid? Why did I mention aerobatics? I tried talking them out of that challenge and convince them that the other challenges were just as good if not better. No, they wanted the aerobatics challenge.

My fate was sealed, I would have to do the challenge, after all I work as a motivational speaker, talking about how anything is possible and how we can all overcome our fears using a simple yet very effective psychotherapy methodology, known as exposure therapy. How could I not take on the challenge! My speaking career would be a fraud if I couldn't back up my words or advice with action!

It was May when I did the first part of the TV show, the part where I made the pledge to become an aerobatics pilot by this time next year and perform a one arm aerobatics routine.

I arrived at Boreham Wood's Elstree Studios and was accommodated at a hotel, about twenty minutes' walk away. I used that walk to think and relax myself.

When I got to the studios, I had a wardrobe call and then waited in their version of a green room. An hour or so later and I had a makeup call. Then back to the green room. Eventually, at almost 9pm, one of the production team arrived.

"You're up Steven let's go."

He took me behind the film set where there was a big door closed to the audience. I was told what to say, but some of it was out of my normal speech, and it didn't fit well with my Yorkshire accent. That made me feel nervous, more than I usually would be.

I was trying to remember the script I had just been given. I had seconds to remember it, but I didn't like it, so decided instead to just wing it. A voice whispered, "Get ready," all the lights in the doorway will go bright, wait for the door to fully open, wait there for a couple of seconds, then exit the door to be greeted by Davina McCall.

Boom! The floodlights hit me, the door opened, and I stood there for what seemed like a long time, but was just enough for me to count to two in my head. Then I walked out onto the stage with 300 people in the audience and Davina McCall with her hand out to greet me. I can't remember if we did a double kiss or not. It's a bit of a blur to me now when I think back. I guess I was running on instinct and adrenaline. It went so quickly that I didn't know whether it went well or not. That was it my first part of filming. I was taken back to the green room and told I could wash my makeup off. *"I'll keep it on,"* I said realising it looked quite good. Who knew?

I was asked if I wanted a taxi to take me back to the hotel, as it was almost 10 pm, but I figured another walk would do me no harm. The following morning, I returned home to Leeds and then it hit me. I would really have to do aerobatics flight training. I hadn't fancied it that much before the show, but now I had promised Davina McCall, 300 live audience members and everyone who had seen me on the TV that, yes, I would indeed fly aerobatics.

I couldn't let them, or myself, down.

The ball was set in motion, I was told I needed to make a video diary on my smart phone of the processes, whether they be simple thought processes or actual flight training.

I started receiving phone calls from the production team on a weekly basis chasing up progress reports and video blogs, but I had no progress to report, I hadn't even started. I was afraid to start aerobatics flight training. I put it off for as long as I possibly could, until the time came when I knew, I could put it off no longer. Finally, in October, I realised if I didn't start, I wouldn't fulfil my pledge.

Even the thought of the training made every sinew in my body tense. My mind was playing tricks on me and I was stuck in what seemed like an eternal circle, knowing I had to start, but at the same time not wanting to start. The first day of training arrived and I felt physically sick. Classic symptoms, a knot in my stomach and a strange foreboding sensation that this could be my final day on earth. It was a fact; this extreme sport could kill me and only when I fully accepted the possibility of death would I be ready to move on.

I figured, now I was ready, but in the bright blue sky of

a clear and crisp autumnal day, about to do our first ma-noeuvre, I bottled out and asked, Peter, the instructor to land without doing any aerobatics. On the way back to the air-field I said, *"I've got to do it haven't I Peter?"*

His answer was concise. *"You do if you want to fulfil your pledge."*

And that was it. Another catalyst for change.

Change in my thought processes. *"Let's do it"* I said.

You can still find the video on YouTube, you can see just how difficult I found it and the horror is clear in my voice when I start the manoeuvres.

A year later I was invited back to Elstree and the TV set, the process of green room, wardrobe, makeup etc, was ex-actly the same, so was the waiting behind the big door for the bright lights to hit me before I ventured onto stage.

This time it was a double kiss with Davina, we knew each other by now. The show went well and when I was asked what my next challenge would be, I told them about writing this book. I said to Davina you're going to love the title… *"No Arm In Trying"* the whole audience erupted in laughter, that was it, another wrap! And I walked out of the studio singing "Those Magnificent Men in Their Flying Machines"

It was almost two years from the start of the process until showing the episode on TV, but I guess this time in two years' time doesn't have the same ring to it. Six million peo-ple watched me on the program and added to the four million on *"The One Show"* gave me ten million people who at least know my name and that I'm the one arm pilot.

Would I do that again? Yes, in a heartbeat, I loved it, the exhilaration despite my initial terror and the sense of achievement were awesome, amazing, liberating and a thousand other adjectives I can think of. Would I take on other challenges? Yes, you bet I would.

Following the TV slot, I featured in The Times, The Daily Mail, The Sun, and a raft of other newspapers, so many in fact that I can't remember them all.

I was invited by Made In Leeds TV to do some present-ing work for their show *"The Book-it List"*, I presented an episode at a local salsa club, where I took part in a salsa class. I co-presented at numerous equestrian events and I even presented flying 2000 feet above Leeds, I loved every minute of it.

A really important lesson I learnt was if you don't take opportunities when they are presented, you'll never know what might be and those opportunities will be lost forever.

Chapter 51
The Challenge

I wanted to do some fund raising for the charity FSDP (Flying Scholarship for Disabled People), I owe this charity so much because they restored my faith in people and in myself; so it seemed only fitting that I tried to repay their generosity and at the same time help another disabled person on their journey of recovery, whether that be physical or emotional like mine.

My scholarship had been presented to me at RAF Fairford, at the Royal International Air Tattoo by HRH Prince Faisal of Jordan. Following the death of Group Captain Sir Douglas Bader, the role of Air Tattoo Patron passed to His Majesty King Hussein of Jordan, who in turn, became the patron of the Flying Scholarships for the Disabled People. This had been set up by the RIAT team in memory of Sir Douglas. Following the King's death, the FSDP patronage passed to his wife Queen Noor and then onto his son HRH Prince Faisal.

My scholarship presentation was a grand affair in front of my proud family, my mum, Pauline, sister Tracy and 200 guests and officials from all walks of life. There were celebrities present and even a rock star (Bruce Dickinson of Iron Maiden) as well as royalty. It had been such a hot day that we'd been told we could remove our jackets, which was normally against protocol in the presence of royalty.

I had met Prince Faisal on a number of occasions and so, when I was thinking of a befitting challenge, I wanted it to be a task that would be in the country of the FSDP Royal Patron; but what sort of challenge could I do, I wasn't sure? A flight in a light aircraft to Jordan would have been great, but very costly and even dangerous due to the escalating military action in Turkey and Syria, so that was out. However, having conquered my fear of horses at the same time as learning to fly I thought this alternative might work as an option.

My mind was made up, I would do a horse-riding challenge in Jordan. But, what exactly would that challenge be? I didn't really have a clue, but I knew there were lots of companies doing horse riding holidays, so I started to look at their catalogues and after a little browsing, I found just the thing I was looking for. A six-day horse riding adventure crossing the desert of Wadi Rum, the Valley of the Moon. Wadi Rum might be best known for its connection with British officer T. E. Lawrence (Lawrence of Arabia), who passed through several times during the Arab Revolt of 1917–18, he was famous for his Middle East Exploits and the writing of his adventures and experiences.

I would test myself, my emotional strength as well as my physical stamina and my horse-riding abilities, which I believed were very good and follow in the steps of Laurence of Arabia.

The challenge was set, I paid for the holiday of a lifetime and prepared at my local riding school for gallop and high-speed riding. After all, the holiday had been labelled for intermediate to advanced riders and had been described as a fast ride.

On the day of departure, I flew to Turkey from Manchester at about the same time as Syria was being attacked on their Northern border by a Turkish missile airstrike. There was heightened tension in the area and me and a friend were flying into an area on high alert. We landed in Turkey and had a two-hour stopover before connecting with a Turkish Air-Lines flight to Amman. It was a worrying flight for me because we were close to very unstable areas in the Middle East. We flew directly south from Istanbul over the Mediterranean and Cyprus, then over the Gaza Strip and into Amman, all at the low altitude of 10,000 feet, an altitude that could have been easily reached by air to ground missiles. A bit of a tense flight! Jordan, however, is considered one of the safest of the middle eastern countries, so at least I could look forward to feeling safe there.

What a completely different experience. Nothing could have prepared me for the difference in culture, the smells and the sounds. It was so bright and wonderful.

Something I did notice, that reminded me of home and the groups of men I had seen in the UK, was how men would gather together outside of shops or in the streets. I realised that this was a cultural thing and made me appreciate that if I saw this happening at home, I had no need to be concerned. It was interesting to be able to see how some of the behaviours had been brought over and to appreciate them in context.

The night before we departed for our desert adventure, I received a phone call in my room from Salem, the owner of Jordan Tracks, regarding my horse for the trip. I asked Salem if he was aware that I only had one arm, he said yes and he had prepared a special, steady and calm horse, I was worried and told him I didn't want a slow or lazy horse. I think that he was concerned about my safety as he continued to assure me it would be safe. I should have realised there and then what I was going to get, but I was still optimistic.

The following morning, we were taken to the stables to meet our horses. When I saw mine, I was disappointed, it wasn't a lovely Arabian as I had expected. Also, the equipment was a little tired I'd brought my own special reins; they are called bar reigns, as the name suggests it's a bar that connects to either side of the reigns. The twisting of the bar allows me to control the horse's bit. It was different to what the organisers were used to but I explained that this was the only way I could control a horse.

Not that controlling my steed was going to be a problem, he was a plodder and I'm afraid that there was not much galloping to be had!

However, I'm not one to allow disappointments to keep me down for long and on the plus side, the scenery was beautiful. I was a little sad to be riding at the back of the group but this gave me time to notice the little things, like the fact that we were riding across what had once been an ocean floor. When I looked down, I could see fossils and the remains of prehistorical fish. Many people forget that deserts are in fact old oceans; there is so much beauty to be found and so much history under our feet.

I had thought that being out in the desert, the sky would've been clear at night and I would have had the opportunity to see the stars in a different way. However, because of the dust, it was far easier to see the stars in Leeds than it was in Jordan. That's not to say that the sky wasn't interesting. The colours were beautiful and the haze that covered the horizon gave the distant scenery a magical misty veil.

During my travels I documented my trip with mini video blogs. I wanted the people that had sponsored me to be able to see what I was doing and where I was. I uploaded them to Facebook whenever I had internet connection. The videos are still there, and they remind me of some of the amazing sights. If you get the chance take a look. In one video I'm stood in front of Petra and the famous carvings in the rock face known as the Treasury; it's even more incredible up close, knowing that it was carved into the rock face in the 1st century BC (Before Christ) by the Nabateans, a nomadic tribe who roamed and traded in the Arabian desert. It has an almost overwhelming presence and such a depth of antiquity.

I can't really describe the presence but what saddened me was the commercialisation. The gated turnstiles entrance ruined the moment and there were just so many people there. I would have loved to have been there either at dawn or sunset when it may have been quieter. There were a lot of pedlars too, but I know that everyone has to make a living.

There's also a video of me where I'm talking about a sore arse on day 5! We did a minimum of six hours riding each day for six days. I was disappointed it wasn't all at a standing gallop which would have been far easier on my poorly bottom; It wasn't the holiday I'd expected, and I was disappointed that it hadn't been ridden at the faster, more challenging pace I was hoping for. Nevertheless, I know I'm very fortunate to have experienced things that many disabled and able-bodied people simply can't or don't have the opportunity to do. It's not something I'd do for six days again, but I would certainly go back.

Our final excursion took us to a mountain top where Moses is reported to have stood when he told his followers that they were headed for the promised land. I realised that I was standing on Mount Nebo, looking out, knowing that as an old man, Moses was unlikely to ever reach his destination. I wondered how he felt at that moment and whether he was sad about the burden that had been placed on him.

I remember well the wonderful bible stories from attending Sunday school as a young boy and the songs we sang:

"Sunshine Corner's Always very fine, It's for children under ninety-nine, All are welcome, seats are given free, Come to Sunshine Corner it's the place for me.
Deep and wide, Deep and wide
There's a fountain flowing deep and wide
Hallelujah for it's
Deep and wide, Deep and wide
There's a fountain flowing deep and wide"

It was an incredible opportunity to see those Bible stories almost brought to life. I count myself very lucky to have had the opportunity to stand in that place, a place where Moses was reported to be buried.

Although the visit to mount Nebo was intensely spiritual, I think that the highlight of the whole holiday was to float in the dead sea and to apply an all-over dead sea mud pack. I loved that moment. The intense salt started to sting my skin after twenty minutes and the mud pack after another twenty started to intensify the stinging. It took five of my travel companions to help me wash all that mud off, and we helped each other in turn. That stinging eased all my aching muscles and bones and soothed my sore bum after the skin had been taken off the base of my spine from the constant six days rubbing on the horses' saddle.

I completed my challenge and raised funds for FSDP for a disabled person to take flight training, I felt that I had given back, at least in some small way to the charity that had given so much to me.

During that journey I was constantly singing, but two songs in particular, one was by the band America *"Horse With No Name"* and the other as I rode down what looked like a well-trodden route was a song by The Eagles *"Hotel California"*, not because the desert resembled California, but the lyrics sang *"on a dark desert highway"* and I seemed to be on one.

That holiday did make me realise what I was missing at home and how good the UK really is. I feel privileged, the privilege of birth to have been born in this great country and I count my blessings for the things I have, friends, family my health and not worry for the things I don't have.

The lesson I learnt is that challenges bring out the best of us and help us realise what we are truly capable of doing.

Chapter 52
Sir Douglas Bader

Douglas Bader is a name that has gone down in history as one of Britain's most successful second world war RAF fighter pilots. He won a scholarship to Cranwell Airforce Academy in 1928 and graduated in 1930. A year later he crashed his aircraft while doing an unauthorised low-level aerobatics stunt that went wrong and resulted in the amputation of both his legs below the knees. He was retired from the RAF due to his disability, but the outbreak of the second world war made him determined to re-join the air force and by the summer of 1941 he had shot down 23 enemy aircraft. In the same year he collided with a German aircraft over Le Tourquet, France and spent the rest of the war imprisoned in Colditz Castle until his release. He was Knighted by the Queen in 1976 and died just 6 years later in 1982, the same year I lost my right arm!

In 1983, just a year later the charity FSDP was founded by Tim Prince and Paul Bowen of the Royal International Air Tattoo in memory of Group Captain Sir Douglas Bader.

I had been doing a lot of media appearances and promoting FSDP as much as possible. It was my way of giving something back and to show my appreciation for the life changing experience they had given me.

Each year, I am invited to attend the presentation ceremony of the new scholars held at the Royal International

Air Tattoo (RIAT) at Fairford. 2016 was just another year attending the annual event, or so I thought but when I arrived, I was told I would be attending a special luncheon in the VIP tent. I was already attending as a VIP, but this special luncheon was even higher up on the VIP scale. I had no idea why I had been selected as it was a very rare occasion that scholars were invited. I sat in a really posh marquee with crystal chandeliers. I sang the words of a song I'd played many times on my jukebox *"The Crystal Chandelier"* by Charlie Pride, there were approximately 50 round tables of 8 people, all were dressed with red under cloths and topped with white table cloths and matching serviettes. The expensive champagne was flowing and there were red carpets welcoming us into the venue, I was surrounded by celebrities and millionaires, Bruce Dickinson of Iron Maiden was there, David Jason of *"Only Fools and Horses"* fame and Carol Vodermann of Countdown.

Polly Vacher MBE was also there, she is well known in the aviation world for her solo circumnavigation flight around the world via both Poles in a single engined aircraft. She later went on to write her book titled *"Wings Around The World"*.

What a wonderful experience that was, being surrounded by all those impressive names, it was over way too quickly though and I returned to the presentation marquee to watch my new friends and scholars, officially receive their scholarships. Presented by HRH Prince Faisal of Jordan and the then current RAF Chief of the Air Staff Sir Stephen Hillier.

After the scholarship presentations there were some special awards, bestowed to people for different reasons. There was an award called Wings Around the World that was presented to a female scholar who had benefited the most from their scholarship, presented by Polly Vacher MBE. The final award was the most prestigious *"The Douglas Bader Memorial Trophy"*.

I was in the audience when the name for the Douglas Bader Memorial Trophy was called out. The MC said, *"The next award to be presented is the Douglas Bader Memorial Trophy, it is awarded to this person for his outstanding contribution to disabled pilots, please put your hands together in appreciation and please step forward to receive your award, Steven Robinson"*

I was totally blindsided by that one, I just wasn't expecting it. I looked at my mum and sister who were there with me, in disbelief. They said you've been awarded it Steven. Have I told you before I'm an emotional man? I make no excuse for it, but the tears were streaming down my face at a time I had to be composed to receive my presentation from Prince Faisal and Sir Stephen Hillier. I managed to dry my tears in time to receive my prize, but I struggled to talk due to the lump in my throat, that felt the size of a tennis ball.

To be recognised with this trophy was humbling, I was no stranger to being humbled but I was truly honoured to receive this award and to be associated with the legendary Sir Douglas Bader. If you get the chance, I'd highly recommend watching the film *"Reach For The Skies"* starring Sir Kenneth Moore, it's a really atmospheric black and white movie that tells the story of a disabled second world war Spitfire ace.

The lesson learnt was do things because you want to do them and because it's the right thing to do. Recognition and rewards will come when you least expect it.

Chapter 53
Yorkshire Choice Awards

It was 2017. The same year that Prince Harry and Megan Markle were engaged and scientists invented a spray gun that shoots stem cells onto burn victims to regrow their skin without scars. I was attending a big, glitzy event held every year at Elland Road Football Ground's purpose built banqueting suite. The event was well known in Leeds. It is run and founded by Joanne Maltby and Melanie Malcom. The event is called the Yorkshire Choice Awards, people from all over Yorkshire are nominated for a particular award, like Business Person of the Year, Media Personality of the Year, Inspirational Individual of the Year, plus many more.

I'd never been to the event before, but I'd heard a lot about it. I was sat at home one morning reading my emails, when one stood out in particular, it was from The Yorkshire Choice awards team, to say I had been nominated for Inspirational Individual of the Year. The winner would be decided by number of votes cast for that person and it advised me to tell all my contacts about the nomination, and to ask them to vote and share the post, to try and get as many votes as possible. I never really thought that many people would vote for me and so, I wasn't at all convinced I even had a chance of being in the top four, but if you don't try, you'll never know what could have been. I shared and shared the post as did many of my friends.

The day came when the actual event took place and if I wanted to know how I'd done, I would have to attend. I took my friend Jodie with me for moral support and so we could enjoy a night out, having a few rum and cokes and a bit of a dance at the after party. I arrived early; I don't like being late for important events, but I was really way too early. When I entered the room, it reminded me of the VIP marquee at RIAT, there were beautifully dressed circular tables for 8 people, there were tiny spotlights everywhere, they were more like fairly lights from a Christmas tree, they were white in colour with the rest of the mood lighting a charming shade of purple. We all had reserved places and as soon as Jodie and I had our first drink ordered and in hand, we started to mingle with the crowds that were now arriving. It wasn't long before we took our seats for a lovely three course meal followed by the start of the presentations.

The presentations took a while, as there were a lot of categories to get through, eventually, they got to the one I had been nominated for and the one all my friends had been voting for. The MC read out the first name, one of four finalists, then the second and the third, none of those names were mine. However, there was still one more finalist name to be read out, maybe I was still in with a chance? *"Our fourth and last finalist for the category of Inspiration Individual of the Year is Steven Robinson"* I looked at Jodie in disbelief and the MC said almost immediately after reading out my name *"and the winner is, Steven Robinson"* there was no drum roll or build up to the winners name, it felt like BOOM! And this is the winner. I was still in shock from hearing my name read out as a finalist!

Jodie shoved me and said, *"You've won it Steve, go get*

your award."

I stood to the whole room applauding me as I walked forwards to receive The Yorkshire Inspirational Individual of the year award. (I was so shocked It almost knocked me over, but *"I'm still standing"* as Elton John sang in 1985 played along in my mind). My award had been sponsored by Frank's Accountants of Wetherby and was presented to me by one of their senior staff members.

I have to mention here that The Yorkshire Choice Special Recognition Award, deservedly went to my friend Chris Pointon for continuing the campaign *"HelloMy-NameIs"* in memory of his wife Dr Kate Granger who lost her battle with cancer in 2016.

I was still stunned from *"The Douglas Bader Memorial Trophy"* and now I was in shock all over again. Thanks to all the people who know me and believe in me and voted, I walked back to my table the proudest man I could have ever wished to have been. I was representing my County of Yorkshire after all; it is the largest County in England and they had voted me the most inspirational person they knew.

I don't feel that I am special or inspirational; I feel like I've always felt, just a normal guy struggling to achieve the things I want to achieve. Yet in my struggle, I'm helping others realise they can also overcome their struggles and what a worthy struggle that is indeed.

The lesson learnt was never be afraid of the struggles that may lie ahead, they are what shape you into the person you will ultimately become.

Chapter 54
The British Empire Medal

I was on cloud nine about my previous awards, I was on TV almost every week, I was speaking at events all over the world. I was enjoying my life at last and I'd fought off all my previous demons thanks to the lessons I had learnt or been taught at considerable cost, emotionally and financially. I was counting my blessings when a strange letter came through the door. The letter was in black print and it said, on Her Majesty's Service and the address was from the home office. My initial instinct was, *"oh no what have I done wrong?"*

I opened the letter with a little trepidation but not too much worry, I knew deep down I'd done nothing wrong, but the suspense was killing me. The letter said I had been nominated for an award in The Queens New Year's Honour List. It went on to say that the letter wasn't confirmation that I had received an award but just to inform me I had been nominated and I would hear again from them before Christmas.

That's not a letter you receive every day, I couldn't imagine being honoured by the Queen.

The week before Christmas, I received a phone call from the Home Office, telling me I had been awarded the British Empire Medal, in the Queens New Year's Honours List. I was told there was a media embargo and that I could not tell any media organisation about it, if they intended to report on the award.

I wasn't sure what I was hearing. Did they just say I'd been given an award by the Queen? It took a while to sink in, but when it did, I realised I'd been awarded the British Empire Medal (BEM).

It was December 2017, 100 years since the original inception of the *"British Empire Medal"* and 100 years since the Royal Family changed its name to the house of Windsor.

Unbeknownst to me, my friend Anna had applied to the Cabinet Office for a UK honours for me and had contacted my friends to ask them to write citation letters in support of the application. I can't thank Anna enough or my friends for such lovely letters of support.

I was later sent copies of those citation letters my friends had written. I have kept them, they are a beautiful tribute and if I ever doubt myself, they remind me of the kindness and generosity of others.

I was told I would be presented my award by the Lord Lieutenant, the Queen's representative based at Bowcliffe Hall at Bramham, Leeds.

The day of the presentation eventually arrived. It was a really grand and posh event held in the beautiful Bowcliffe Hall. I'd never been there before, what an impressive place, steeped in history. I was surrounded by the Queen's representatives and by some impressive individuals who were also receiving their awards at the same time as me.

It was the most perfect day and my mum and sister were there with me to enjoy the occasion. When the Lord Lieutenant read out a list of achievements of one of the people receiving an award, it sounded really impressive, this person seemed to have done so much, I started to think, well I've done that too. At the end of the list of achievements the Lord Lieutenant read out my name. I'd never heard someone else talk about me in such an articulate and respectful manner before. I was really blown away by his description and by now my emotions were getting the better of me yet again. I did manage to compose myself and took my place at the front of the room to shake hands with the Lord Lieutenant and receive my British Empire Medal, followed by the official photos and afternoon tea. I am so proud of this award. I like to tell people the Queen knows my name! Or at least I know hers.

However, that wasn't the end of the event, it was over for now at Bowcliffe Hall but there was the Royal garden party to attend. The privileges bestowed upon me just seemed to keep coming and I was being honoured all over again.

I was given a choice of three dates to attend one of the Royal Garden Parties. I chose the May date because the long-term weather forecast was good for that month. Normally, only the person given an honour and one guest were allowed. I rang Bowcliffe hall to ask if a third person could come with me. They said it was highly irregular for three to attend, but they would ask the Palace and let me know the next day. True to their word they called the next day and said that everything had been arranged and we would be able to attend as a party of three. We were super happy that we could all go, we do everything together in our little family unit, it's always been like that since Mum left dad in 1967.

The day arrived when we would travel to London, it was a lovely day, but the forecast had slightly changed to *"possibility of showers"*. Our train was already booked so we went with our umbrellas just in case there was rain. We booked our train journey from York, surprisingly the journey from York to London's King Cross was a quicker route with less stops and an earlier departure than it was from Leeds city station. Our journey started early in the morning with a drive to York, I parked the car up and we got on the train.

I was going to book us on first class, but I'd been told when buying the tickets that there would be no hot meals served on this train and first-class meals would be cold sandwiches only, that and the fact the price increased by over £100 made the decision easier to book second class. Well, I am a Yorkshire Man after all is said and done! We took our own cold sandwiches and had a picnic during the journey to London.

Arriving in London we walked across Saint James park with people looking at us, we were well dressed and looked like we were attending the 'Royal Garden Party', but there were a lot of other equally well-dressed people heading in the same direction. The walk was lovely, the weather was perfect, and the atmosphere was electric. There was a busker playing in the park, he was playing and singing *"They're Changing The Guard At Buckingham Palace"* by Max Bygraves and that's where we were heading. We arrived at the Palace gates to be told where to wait so we could enter the palace grounds. The queue was larger than I thought it would be and in fact, there are approximately 8000 people that attend each Royal Garden Party, having said that we were admitted really quickly once we had gone through the security procedures, metal detectors, body pat down and bag searches.

The red carpet was out for all the attendees and we were welcomed into the palace and then into the magnificent gardens, where super luxurious marquees had been erected and the poshest toilet tents I've ever seen! People milled around waiting for the Royal Party to arrive. As I was looking around, I spotted snipers on the rooftops of the Palace. Wow! The security was strong indeed, but not at all noticeable nor intimidating which was reassuring.

All the people had started gathering and creating a natural corridor for the Royal party to walk down. All of a sudden, the national anthem played, and everyone stood up and sang *"God Save The Queen"* as a mark of respect and the Queen emerged onto the patio of Buckingham Palace!

The same patio we had just entered the gardens by. She walked down the naturally created corridor of people, stopping along the way to speak to some people that the Equerries had randomly selected from the crowd. It was a wonderful experience to be so close to the Royal Family. The walk from the Royal Patio to the Royal Reception Marquee took about an hour, as it swept through the crowds of people like a regal serpent, winding its way through long grass.

When the Royal Party arrived at their marquee, the banqueting tents started serving food and the many bands, quartets, quintets and duos started their sessions of music, ranging in style from old world traditional, brass bands, to jazz and modern contemporary. There was the marching of the guards and all the pomp and ceremony expected from a royal occasion. It was an assault on the senses but a really pleasant assault.

The champagne was flowing, and the food was far better than I thought it would be, everyone knows about the famous cucumber sandwiches, but I didn't expect them to taste so nice, cucumber sprinkled with mint, they were really tasty and refreshing. In fact, there was a whole host of sandwiches and food available, the dessert that followed was equally special.

After the food and desserts there were small stalls giving everyone an ice cream. The day was truly memorable, and it passed far too quickly. We were amongst the last to leave at the end of the garden party. As we were leaving, all the royal household staff lined up on the impeccably mowed and well-presented lawn of the gardens. A voice shouted loudly, *"move forwards and pick up everything!"* A line of people moved forwards in unison like a military manoeuvre, each picking up even the smallest amount of litter. What an impressive sight that was to see. At the end of the Garden Party you wouldn't have known anyone had been there, let alone 8000 people.

I learnt another lesson I wasn't really expecting, that was be proud of yourself and your achievements and enjoy the moment.

Chapter 55
The Arms Dealer

I was going to meet my new accountant who is based in Sheffield, *"Mind Your Assets Accountants"* I'd heard really good things about them and had met the owner, Bev on a number of occasions, at some speaking events where I had been the keynote speaker. Not wanting to miss an opportunity for a day out, I took my mum and sister with me so they could shop at Sheffield Meadow Hall while I spoke to my new accountant.

After I finished my meeting with Bev, I went to meet my family for lunch, we were going to eat in an area of Sheffield Meadow Hall, known as 'The Oasis', as it was still early I met them first for coffee in a lovely little independent cafe. I'd just sat down with my cup of tea when they told me they had seen a really lovely shirt in a gentlemen's outfitter store and I simply had to see it. We went there as soon as we had finished our drinks. It was only about 200 yards from where we had been sitting. Wow, what a beautiful shirt it was, it was vibrant shades of blue and of a paisley design, it really stood out and shouted, 'buy me!' But then, something caught my eye, something that totally distracted me from the shirt, something so interesting and aesthetically pleasing, I struggled to see anything else in the shop. I was totally consumed, by thoughts and ideas that had been provoked by the mannequin dummy the shirt was on. To be more precise, I was consumed by the technical beauty and amazing craftmanship of the solid dark wood, fully articulated and jointed arms.

The assistant Sean asked if he could help me. I said, *"I love the beautiful shirt, but could I buy the arms off of the mannequin dummy?"* He replied *"We're not arms dealers, we sell shirts"* he was super friendly though and took my contact details. He said he would see what could be done. A little while later my phone rang. It was Sean, he asked if I was still in the Meadow Hall complex, I said I was. He had found a solution and if I could call back to the shop, we could discuss it further.

When I returned to the shop, Sean said he had spoken to head office and they had agreed to supply two mannequin arms at cost. I paid £69 and was told Sean would call me when they arrived from the supplier. It was less than two weeks later when I received that call and returned to collect them. We did a photo shoot in the store, called Hawes and Curtis, the owner was Touker Suleyman of Dragon's Den fame, although I didn't know that at the time. Touker Suleyman had asked why I wanted the arms. I told Sean, I was going to make a new prosthetic arm so I could ride a motorbike again after 37 years of being out of the saddle.

Little did I know, that would capture everyone's imagination and the BBC wanted to film me riding my motorbike a week after I had told Sean about my personal challenge. The date for filming was set. The only problem was that my newly purchased motorbike, a Montesa Cota 349 from 1981, needed fully rebuilding and the mannequin arm needed remodelling and making into a prosthetic. I was under pressure again, but I loved the pace I needed to work at, and it challenged me in ways I didn't think it would. I had to not only rebuild the motorbike, but first had to get it running, which took me almost a week (some skills you just don't forget, even though it had been years since I'd worked on a bike).

I also had to invent a special hand attachment that would let go if I lost control of the motorbike.

Back to the bike though. Prior to my accident I used to ride my motorbike on an area of the fields over the road from my house that we called the plateaux. Every day after 5pm there was a man who rode home from work on his motorbike, a sparkling brand new Montesa cota 349. He had to get up a shallow hill to reach the plateaux and would then continue up some other hills to emerge onto the Prince Philips playing fields.

Wow! It was a beautiful motorbike, it was all white except for the frame and the mudguards, they were red. It was one on the most beautiful bikes I'd ever seen. How I wished it was mine or even to have a go would have been a dream come true. However, that was never going to happen, why would an adult let a teenager have a go on his pride and joy? I never knew who the man was, he always wore his crash helmet and never acknowledged me.

His motorbike was amazing, but he was a novice trials rider and he failed every day to get up the first shallow hill, he fell off every day without fail, he kept trying none the less. He didn't know the technique to get up that shallow hill. I really wanted to help him and show him how easy it was, it was all about managing the power of the motorbike and selecting the right gear so that traction could be maintained and never try and change gear on a hill climb, never! I wanted to show him how to do it.

The only thing I was ever any good at as a teenager was

motorbikes and I could get up and down the steepest of hills, over any obstacles and pull the best wheelies, although I enjoyed hill climbing the most because of the challenges and sense of achievement I felt when I made it to the top without falling off.

He wouldn't have wanted to take advice from a teenager, so the opportunity never arose to even speak to him.

I loved his Montesa cota 349, but I never had the money as a teenager to buy one and at 18, I was now missing an arm, so I accepted I would never own or ride that beautiful Spanish motorbike.

One day when I was browsing eBay and there it was! A Montesa Cota 349, a white one with a red frame and mudguards, just like one I'd fallen in love with all those years ago. It didn't work and was in a sorry state. I was now 55 years old. It had taken almost 40 years for this opportunity and I wasn't going to miss it. I sat and watched the auction all night watching the bids and the price increase. In the morning, I was the proud new owner of a Montesa Cota 349, admittedly a motorbike that didn't work and needed a lot of love and attention, but I would give that and I would ride it on national TV, with my homemade motorbike prosthetic arm and quick release invention.

I attached the new mannequin arm to my flying arm body jacket and bolted it in place so the shoulder joint was permanently locked in position, that meant I would be able to push and pull with that arm without my efforts being simply turned into uncontrolled rotation.

The day of filming arrived; I was told the film crew would be at my house for 12 noon. It was 8am in the morning and I was frantically trying to finish off the final piece of the jigsaw. The prosthetic arm.

It still wasn't working correctly, it needed adjusting, setting up with the correct amount of tension and positioning. The quick release mechanism needed testing and fine tuning. I also needed to get dressed into my motorbike gear and make sure everything looked spick and span. I'd only just finished everything to my satisfaction when the film crew arrived.

The film crew arrived in a transit van, they transported my bike to Squires cafe, a well-known biker cafe in the village of Sherburn in Elmett.

Sherburn In Elmett is in the doomsday book of 1086 as one of the region's largest settlements valued at that time at £34 when Leeds was only valued at £7. There is evidence of a settlement dating back to the 1st century AD.

I followed the film crew in my car. It was in the car park area of Squires café, that I rode, for the first time, the bike I had always wanted to ride since the age of 17, when it was a new bike to the market. I was incredibly nervous; I hadn't even had time to test ride it prior to the filming, so it was a case of do or die. Whitesnake sang *"Here I Go Again"* in 1982 the year of my accident and I was thinking just that as I set off on my motorbike for the first time in 37 years.

Wow! It was amazing.

It was like reconnecting with a long-lost friend, one I hadn't seen since I was 18. Having given up on my one true passion and never expecting to feel that freedom and joy again. Like all memories, the reality was never going to be the same and I couldn't re-capture the excitement of my youth.

At first I was a little slow. I had to get used to all the controls on the left-hand side. I put the throttle on the left and reversed its action, so it operated as a normal throttle would by twisting backwards and not forwards, the clutch was on the left but that was standard and the front brake was on the left too. It was a little awkward to say the least, having to throttle and operate the clutch at the same time.

If I needed to use the front brake, that also added to the complexity and dexterity required with my one hand to control the bike. As I gained confidence, I went faster and faster around a circuit we had marked out in the carpark. It was another wrap, I'd done it. I'd ridden the bike I always wanted to ride, and I'd conquered yet another fear or at least a demon that had overshadowed me for 37 years and all captured live on national TV.

I was happy that I had taken on the challenge but sometimes you can't go backwards and you have to look to the future, which may or may not include motorbikes, having said that I now own eight!

The following week I had a photoshoot with Touker Suleyman at his head office, in London, and this was an incredible experience, he was a genuinely nice man and interested in my inventions. In the end, the irony of all this was I'd forgotten about the shirt that originally took me to the store owned by Touker, but after the photo shoot, I received that shirt plus two other quality silk shirts compliments of Hawes and Curtis.

The lesson learnt, and I know I keep saying this, but opportunities are everywhere, they are in places you never expect to find them and they present themselves at the most unexpected times. Grasp them with both hands if you have two hands and never look back!

Chapter 56
Inspirational/Motivational Speaker

My journey to becoming an Inspirational/Motivational Speaker started in 1998, although I didn't know I was embarking on that journey at the time. 1998 was the year of the Monika Lewinski scandal, Google was founded, and the Winter Olympics were held in Nagano Japan, the city my Japanese girlfriend came from and a place I would visit. It was also the year I started taking salsa dancing classes.

One of the people I met while taking the classes was Richard McCann, the son of Wilma McCann, the first victim of Peter Sutcliffe, the Yorkshire Ripper.

Richard is a great guy and we just clicked, I think, because we were from similar backgrounds. It later transpired, that he lived on the Scott Hall Estate as a young boy, the same estate I still live on today and where his Mum's body was found; in fact, on the very same field where I lost my right arm. I didn't know all that back then though; Richard was just a fellow salsa dancing friend. He went on to write a book called 'Just A Boy' which propelled him into the world of professional speaking.

It was a few years later when Richard said something to me that would change my life.

He said, *"Steve you have a great story to tell, your life is extraordinary, and people don't do the things you do, they don't succeed in the same ways you do, despite you only having one arm."*

He went on to tell me that he was amazed at my dancing ability and my life story should be shared with others to help them realise what is truly possible for them too. He was introducing me to the concept of being an Inspirational/Motivational Speaker.

He said, *"You're sat on a great opportunity Steve, you need to be out there on stage sharing your unique insight to life."*

I hadn't even considered being a speaker up until that point. I wasn't even sure how to start but Richard knew and with his help, his mentoring, guidance and friendship; he coached me on how to deliver a talk. We worked on my talk for hours, until Richard said,

"I think you're ready for your first talk Steve. Are you nervous?"

"I am a little" I said, *"but being a DJ and karaoke compare I think will help me."*

I'm confident with a microphone, so I wasn't worried about that, I'd been in front of large audiences before and had been the centre of attention with everyone's eyes on me; plus, I'd had loads of people look at me on a daily basis due to only having one arm.

"How difficult can it be?" I asked.

"OK" said Richard *"I'll arrange for you to talk at the Professional Speakers Association in Leeds."*

The PSA are an organisation that helps people launch their speaking career by sharing their professional knowledge of the industry. They are a global organisation that help create opportunities and open doors. Their ethos is to help professional speakers speak more and speak better.

They were having one of their monthly meetings and I would speak on stage. I would only have 20 minutes and I would be talking for something called the Checkout Zone. This was an opportunity for new speakers to give their talk and get feedback from the professional speakers in the room.

My opening lines were the part I was most worried about because I wanted to get it perfect; they would set the scene for my talk and lead me into the main story, I also had to remember that, although it was a story about my life, that it also had to have some meaning to the audience and give them some insight on how they could deal with the stuff that was going on in their lives.

Those key points weren't really my story, so I simply had to remember them, however, when you feel under pressure the first thing to go is short term memory.

Thanks to all the practice that I'd done however, I didn't forget the really important bits. I really enjoyed giving that talk. The whole room listened in silence and after I finished, I got a fantastic round of applause. I'd done it.

The early advice I was given was get out there, speak as much as I possibly could. That advice was right and allowed me to hone my talk and try out any new material. These early talks also gave me more confidence and taught me how to handle things when they went totally wrong. Of course, there is no wrong really, it's just a matter of how you deal with problems, errors and technical issues when under pressure and in front of an audience expecting, to be inspired and motivated to do more with their lives.

Over the past few years, I've been incredibly lucky to speak at events all over the world. I've spoken for hundreds of companies, including Shell Aviation in Rotterdam, Colegio de San Jose (Villafranca de los Barros) Spain, delivering my keynote talk in Spanish, Executive Secretary live in London, The NHS Trust, the list is endless, too long really to mention them all. Although by far the biggest event was at EAA AirVenture Oshkosh.

EAA AirVenture Oshkosh is an annual gathering of aviation enthusiasts, held each summer at Wittman Regional Airport in Oshkosh, Wisconsin, United States. Their very first event was held in 1953, the same year that Edmund Hillary and Sherpa Tensing became the first people to scale the summit of Mount Everest. The Oshkosh airshow is attended by over 800,000 people and over 10,000 aircraft fly in for the event. For one week in the year, it is the busiest airport and the largest aviation event in the whole world, and I was booked to speak there.

Oshkosh was a great adventure. I flew into Chicago O'Hare international airport singing *"Chicago Chicago Is My Kinda Town"* by Frank Sinatra. I hired a car for the 200-mile drive to Oshkosh. I'd never hired a car before, because car hire companies would never hire to a disabled driver. But the US branch of Hertz didn't discriminate against me.

It was an adventure of firsts for everything. The first time I'd hired a car, the first time I'd driven a left-hand drive and the first time I used a travel planner to organise everything.

The customer service from Hertz was first class. I'd never experienced anything like it before. I had a car reserved, with a steering ball fitted, especially for a one arm driver and a satnav booked. However, when I arrived at the Hertz office, they had no satnavs, so I was upgraded to the deluxe range of cars with built in satnavs, a free upgrade.

Even the American voice that shouted at me *"Learn how to drive"* when I'd just got onto the freeway and missed my exit couldn't dampen my spirits.

The 400-mile drive there and back was amazing, it passed so quickly. It felt like I'd only driven 50 miles, I just didn't want the experience to end. The weather was wonderful, it was like the best British summer I'd ever experienced. If you ever find yourself in the area, I'd highly recommend the Wisconsin fried cheese curds, they were really tasty.

I was booked for 2020 to speak at events in New Zealand and Australia, although, at the time of writing this book, the COVID-19 pandemic is still ongoing and so the tour has been postponed. So, it's a case of watch this space.

I work as an International Inspirational/Motivational Speaker, a route I never planned to go down but a route I took, nevertheless. I love speaking and I constantly meet fantastic people, it's work, but it feels more like my social life. How can you call it work when it's so enjoyable and rewarding? To know I have inspired and motivated people to achieve more in their lives is invaluable and is what keeps me going and striving to be a better person.

Even with day to day ups and downs, we should always remember that just one more day on this earth is a blessing and I feel blessed to have survived my motorbike accident and to have had the opportunities I've had, and to share my story with others. That's part of the message I try to leave the audience with. We should take nothing for granted and should embrace every opportunity that comes our way.

I always put 100% effort into everything I do which generally means I succeed; but I've practiced so much to make sure I am comfortable and confident in my abilities, the result is, that others just see the polished finished article and they see me as the successful motivational speaker I have become; but nobody sees the blood sweat and tears behind it. Of course, on looking back through my life, that's been the case for everything I have ever achieved. People see a one-armed man who copes very well, is creative and has found innovative ways to overcome challenge. They never see the moments of self-doubt, the frustration and daily fight to do what abled bodied people take for granted.

I know that my accident, in some ways gave me more than it took away. I have learnt perseverance and how to solve problems that most people wouldn't even be aware of. I have a video on Facebook of me tying a shoelace one handed, if you want to challenge yourself, have a go and see how long it takes for you to learn, or will you simply give in?

When I walk out on stage it's like the magicians of old, the curtain goes up and the performance begins, but there is a lot of energy given and you need to be able to read your audience, to make sure that you're using the right tone and that you're bringing them along with you. It can be in equal parts both exhilarating and exhausting, but I know that this is what I want to do and how I see my future.

I just hope that people continue to believe in me and the inspiration I can give.

The lesson learnt is, sometimes all we need is a little inspiration to help us realise we can achieve anything in life.

Chapter 57
The Future

I've had so many setbacks in life! I've dealt with massive highs and incredible lows, that have led me to almost paying the ultimate price, taking my own life.

I have learnt some valuable lessons throughout my life, and I continue to learn them to this day. Some have cost me a lot of money others have cost me dearly in my mental health. The attitude that has kept me alive and brought me the successes I've had, have been down to my no defeat, no surrender, way of thinking.

I will not be beaten; I will never be defeated, and surrender is not in my vocabulary. I will persist in my dreams and goals until I get them and if I never get them, I will spend my life trying to get them.

After a recent break-up I was left feeling that I needed to speak to someone and I reached out to Menkind who deal with abuse of men. This is the first time I've spoken about a damaging relationship and I urge anyone in the same place to do the same thing. There is no shame in asking for help when you need it.

I'm yet to find love, I hope that it will happen one day, I know I have a lot to give the right person.

I would also love to share my ideas, inventions and help those in a similar position to me on a practical level. This will require a leap of faith and a strong legal backing but if

I can find someone to fight my corner and help protect my IP, then who knows what I'll unleash on the world!

What lies ahead? I don't know!

But maybe it will present itself to me on the 19th of April, because that is a date that keeps repeating in my life. It was the date of my life changing accident, the date I was awarded my flying scholarship and the date I finished my final edit of this book.

Or maybe the number 228 might be involved because that is a number that repeats a lot in my life as well. Are these numbers just coincidence or is there a higher power at work? I'd like to believe the latter.

I now travel and speak around the world, sharing my message that *"anything is possible".* A song by Sia is the tune that plays me on and off of stage and it sums me up in one word *"Unstoppable".*

I have my own TV show looming, Come Fly With Steve, where I'll be taking a celebrity or interesting guest flying.

I've had interest in making my book into a film, and a musical theatrical production, and it has been suggested that I take part in Strictly Come Dancing—all of which excite me immensely.

I have never had a plan of my life or a direction I will travel, and I've never known what I wanted to do when I grow up. I'm not good at knowing the future, but what I am good at is seizing the moment. Any opportunity that comes my way, I will take. I will enjoy the journey and see where that opportunity takes me.

One of the most important lessons I've learnt throughout my life is opportunities are everywhere. What will happen if you don't take them? Nothing! So, take them, and enjoy the new path you travel.

This is not the end of the journey, just the beginning of another adventure.

Steve

For more information about Steven Robinson go to:
www.steven-robinson.com

on Facebook @stevewithonearm

on Twitter @ stevewithonearm

For more information about FSDP go to:
www.fsdp.co.uk

Chronos Publishing
Life Stories

We sincerely hope you enjoyed this book.

If you'd like to know more about our forthcoming titles, authors and special events, or to be notified of early releases then follow us:

on Facebook @ChronosPublishing

on Twitter @ChronosPublish

or come find us on the web at:

www.chronospublishing.com

We love what we do and we'd like you to be part of a thriving community of people who enjoy books and the very best reading experiences.

Taryn Johnston
Owner
The FCM Group